TONI MORRISON

Critical Companions to Popular Contemporary Writers
Kathleen Gregory Klein, Series Editor

TONI MORRISON

A Critical Companion

Missy Dehn Kubitschek

CRITICAL COMPANIONS TO POPULAR CONTEMPORARY WRITERS
Kathleen Gregory Klein, Series Editor

Greenwood Press
Westport, Connecticut • London

Library of Congress Cataloging-in-Publication Data

Kubitschek, Missy Dehn.
    Toni Morrison : a critical companion / Missy Dehn Kubitschek.
      p.   cm.—(Critical companions to popular contemporary
writers, ISSN 1082–4979)
   Includes bibliographical references and index.
   ISBN 0–313–30265–0 (alk. paper)
   1. Morrison, Toni—Criticism and interpretation. 2. Women and
literature—United States—History—20th century. 3. Afro-American
women in literature. 4. Afro-Americans in literature. I. Title.
II. Series.
PS3563.08749Z75   1998
813'.54—dc21   98–12142

British Library Cataloguing in Publication Data is available.

Library of Congress Catalog Card Number: 98–12142
ISBN: 0–313–30265–0
ISSN: 1082–4979

First published in 1998

Greenwood Press, 88 Post Road West, Westport, CT 06881
An imprint of Greenwood Publishing Group, Inc.

Printed in the United States of America

The paper used in this book complies with the
Permanent Paper Standard issued by the National
Information Standards Organization (Z39.48–1984).

10 9 8 7 6 5 4 3 2 1

For Owen Jenkins,
teacher extraordinaire

Contents

Series Foreword

The authors who appear in the series Critical Companions to Popular Contemporary Writers are all best-selling writers. They do not simply have one successful novel, but a string of them. Fans, critics, and specialist readers eagerly anticipate their next book. For some, high cash advances and breakthrough sales figures are automatic; movie deals often follow. Some writers become household names, recognized by almost everyone.

But their novels are read one by one. Each reader chooses to start and, more importantly, to finish a book because of what she or he finds there. The real test of a novel is in the satisfaction its readers experience. This series acknowledges the extraordinary involvement of readers and writers in creating a best-seller.

The authors included in this series were chosen by an Advisory Board composed of high school English teachers and high school and public librarians. They ranked a list of best-selling writers according to their popularity among different groups of readers. For the first series, writers in the top-ranked group who had received no book-length, academic, literary analysis (or none in at least the past ten years) were chosen. Because of this selection method, Critical Companions to Popular Contemporary Writers meets a need that is being addressed nowhere else. The success of these volumes as reported by reviewers, librarians, and teachers led to an expansion of the series mandate to include some writers with wide critical attention—Toni Morrison, John Irving, and Maya Angelou, for example—to extend the usefulness of the series.

The volumes in the series are written by scholars with particular expertise in analyzing popular fiction. These specialists add an academic focus to the popular success that these writers already enjoy.

The series is designed to appeal to a wide range of readers. The general reading public will find explanations for the appeal of these well-known writers. Fans will find biographical and fictional questions answered. Students will find literary analysis, discussions of fictional genres, carefully organized introductions to new ways of reading the novels, and bibliographies for additional research. Whether browsing through the book for pleasure or using it for an assignment, readers will find that the most recent novels of the authors are included.

Each volume begins with a biographical chapter drawing on published information, autobiographies or memoirs, prior interviews, and, in some cases, interviews given especially for this series. A chapter on literary history and genres describes how the author's work fits into a larger literary context. The following chapters analyze the writer's most important, most popular, and most recent novels in detail. Each chapter focuses on one or more novels. This approach, suggested by the Advisory Board as the most useful to student research, allows for an in-depth analysis of the writer's fiction. Close and careful readings with numerous examples show readers exactly how the novels work. These chapters are organized around three central elements: plot development (how the story line moves forward), character development (what the reader knows of the important figures), and theme (the significant ideas of the novel). Chapters may also include sections on generic conventions (how the novel is similar to or different from others in its same category of science fiction, fantasy, thriller, etc.), narrative point of view (who tells the story and how), symbols and literary language, and historical or social context. Each chapter ends with an "alternative reading" of the novel. The volume concludes with a primary and secondary bibliography, including reviews.

The alternative readings are a unique feature of this series. By demonstrating a particular way of reading each novel, they provide a clear example of how a specific perspective can reveal important aspects of the book. In the alternative reading sections, one contemporary literary theory—way of reading, such as feminist criticism, Marxism, new historicism, deconstruction, or Jungian psychological critique—is defined in brief, easily comprehensible language. That definition is then applied to the novel to highlight specific features that might go unnoticed or be understood differently in a more general reading. Each volume defines two or three specific theories, making them part of the reader's understanding of how diverse meanings may be constructed from a single novel.

Taken collectively, the volumes in the Critical Companions to Popular Contemporary Writers series provide a wide-ranging investigation of the complexities of current best-selling fiction. By treating these novels seriously as both literary works and publishing successes, the series demonstrates the potential of popular literature in contemporary culture.

Kathleen Gregory Klein
Southern Connecticut State University

The Life of Toni Morrison

Readers all over the world have recognized Toni Morrison's genius. In addition to honorary degrees from Ivy League colleges (Harvard, Yale, Columbia), Toni Morrison has won many honors, including a National Book Critics' Circle Award and the Pulitzer Prize. In 1993, she received the world's most prestigious literary award, the Nobel Prize. Morrison's works appeal not only to scholars but to the general public. Her last four novels have made the *New York Times* best-seller list, for instance, and *Song of Solomon* was a Book-of-the-Month Club selection in 1977—the first book by a black writer to be selected in more than forty years, and the first ever by a black woman writer.

What personality has created this brilliant record? What does Toni Morrison mean when she insists on being known as a "black woman novelist" (Caldwell in Taylor-Guthrie 243)? What happens in the books that her diverse readers admire and learn from? In her novels, trees sometimes talk, ghosts haunt houses, and people create holidays like National Suicide Day. This companion volume will explore how her books' unusual events connect to her self-characterization as a "black woman novelist."

This phrase refers to Toni Morrison's ethnicity, of course: she is African American. But Morrison also says that, unlike in her childhood when a person was born black, an individual now has to choose an identity, decide to be black (Washington in Taylor-Guthrie 236). In this sense, her phrase goes beyond skin color to refer to a way of seeing the world and a set of values. This combination of a particular world view and traditional values constitutes African American culture. It is important to realize that not every black person in the United States agrees with every traditional value. The black community has many different ideas about how to apply these values too. Nevertheless, it is possible to identify ideas about spirituality, the nature of time, and the nature of the self that have historically been central to African American culture.

Toni Morrison notes that she wasn't aware that these ideas are true of African American culture until she started her first teaching job at Texas Southern University. Earlier she'd thought that these ideas were just how her family operated. So, before examining African American concepts of spirituality, time, and the self in Chapter 2, let's look at where Morrison first learned about them—in her family.

When Toni Morrison was born in 1931, her parents named her Chloe Anthony Wofford. She acquired her nickname, Toni, while attending Howard University. "Morrison" came later, when she married a Jamaican architect, Harold Morrison, in 1958. She was born and grew up in Lorain, Ohio. The family was relatively new to the area. Early in the century, both her mother's and her father's families had come to Ohio from the South looking for physical safety and increased economic opportunities. They were part of the Great Migration, a large-scale movement of blacks from the rural, agricultural South to the industrial cities of the North from about 1880 to 1920.

African Americans had almost no legal protections when Morrison's grandparents moved north. In the South, a system of segregation called "Jim Crow" ordered separate public facilities for blacks and whites. Blacks could not attend a white school, or eat in a white restaurant, or even use a water fountain designated "for whites." Whites always had better facilities; often no facilities were available for black people.

African Americans were not permitted to vote in most of the South until the Civil Rights Act of 1965. Without legal protection, Morrison's mother's family was cheated out of their land in Alabama. They became sharecroppers, which meant that they farmed someone else's land and received a portion of any profits. Though the system sounds fair, it was usually rigged so that sharecroppers had to buy seed, food, and other supplies at a high price from the landowners, so that sharecroppers went into debt and stayed there.

Morrison's maternal grandmother was afraid of more than poverty, however. She feared that, because Southern courts rarely punished whites who harmed blacks, white men would feel free to sexually abuse her daughters. In 1912, she traveled north with thirty dollars and seven children. One of these children was Toni Morrison's mother, Rahmah Willis Wofford. Morrison's father, George Wofford, came from Georgia, where conditions were similar to those in Alabama. Not surprisingly, George hated and distrusted whites all his life. His parents had died before he and Rahmah met, so Morrison grew up with only one set of grandparents.

The North did bring increased economic opportunities. George worked at first as a welder in a shipyard on Lake Erie. Later he worked in the steel mills of Ohio. George and Rahmah's second child, Morrison has an older sister and two younger brothers. When Morrison graduated from high school in 1949, her parents' many sacrifices allowed her to become the first woman in her family to attend college. Her father had worked two or three jobs at a time for many years, and Morrison remembers that while she was at Howard University, her mother sent her money by taking "humiliating" work (McKay in Taylor-Guthrie 138). (At this time, almost all the jobs open to African American women were "domestic" work—cleaning houses, cooking, doing laundry, or being a maid.) Morrison graduated from high school in 1949 and received a B.A. from Howard University, where she majored in English and minored in Classics (Greek and Roman culture and literature). After completing an M.A. at Cornell University, she went to Texas Southern University to teach. Morrison thus enjoyed a formal education not available to her grandparents or parents.

Morrison maintains that another, equally important education was provided in her childhood home. There, music and storytelling were everyday parts of life. Her grandfather played violin. Her mother, who had played piano accompaniment in theaters before movies had their own sound tracks, sang everything from gospel to opera. Her grandfather told stories about his boyhood. He remembered that when he first heard about "emancipation," at about age five, he didn't understand that it meant freedom for slaves and was afraid of it. Morrison remembers her father as the best storyteller of a talented family, terrifying and delighting them every night with ghost stories. In this way, the Wofford home typifies the centrality of storytelling to African culture.

Family continues to be crucial to Morrison's sense of who she is. When she won the Nobel Prize in 1993, one of her first acts was to publically thank God that her mother was still alive to see that historic day. One of Morrison's early memories illustrates the centrality of family heritage to her sense of identity. Her mother, her grandmother, and Morrison herself were in the same room with her great-grandmother—four generations of women in a direct family line. She remembers the powerful personality of her great-grandmother, who could not read but was famous as a skilled midwife. Morrison was impressed that in her great-grandmother's presence, her grandmother became youthful, with a young girl's ways of sitting and moving. Morrison has suggested that this memory might be connected to two themes in several of her novels: the relationships between three generations of women in a family, and the many portraits of strong women.

Morrison began her own family in 1958 when she married Harold Morrison. When the marriage ended in 1964, Morrison had two sons, one a baby and the other a pre-schooler. Morrison guards her privacy in many areas, including the reasons for her divorce. She has said only that she and her Jamaican husband had different ideas of the roles for men and women and that she would not be subservient to him. (There is no reason to make her life public, she says, because her creative work is not autobiographical but imaginative.) To support herself and her children, Morrison took a job as a textbook editor for a publishing company, Random House.

Morrison's work as an editor contributed to African American literature in two ways. First, she was influential in publishing many other black writers. In addition to editing text books, she edited novels by Gayl Jones, Toni Cade Bambara, and John McCluskey; and autobiographies by the boxer Muhammad Ali and the politician Andrew Young. Her editing work has thus helped to shape the tradition of African American literature.

Second, her editing work brought her into contact with materials that she later used as imaginative starting points for her novels. Morrison contributed to a project eventually published in the early 1970s as *The Black Book*. At that time, history textbooks concentrated almost exclusively on great white men and military battles. *The Black Book* contains some of the materials—and people—left out of such texts. It chronicles the everyday lives of ordinary African Americans. *The Black Book* is unusual in another way because it presents quite diverse primary sources of information; it's like an old attic trunk full of a hundred years' memorabilia—naturally, because many of its contents came from just such trunks. Its contents range from public documents (bills of sale for slave auctions, newspapers) to the very personal (pictures, family announcements) with everything in between, such as musical compositions (Denard 323). Many of the materials in *The Black Book* suggested stories to Morrison, stories of African Americans that had not been told in either literature or history. For example, this project first drew Morrison's attention to Margaret Garner, a fugitive slave who killed one of her children rather than let a slavemaster recapture them both. More than a decade after *The Black Book*, Morrison reimagined this story in *Beloved*.

For her entire career, Toni Morrison has been a single parent. Often she earned a living with editing and teaching jobs during the day and wrote at night. Morrison began writing fiction, she says, because her circumstances gave her the time. When she moved to Syracuse, NY, after her divorce, she knew that she wouldn't stay long. She didn't, therefore, try to make friends. Random House allowed Morrison to work at home. Creative writing gave her a focus during her solitary evenings. After editing all day and putting her children down for the night, she began to revise a short story that she had written years before while still a student at Howard University. This story became her first novel, *The Bluest Eye*.

Many people have marveled that, while doing important editing work in her full-time job, Morrison simultaneously succeeded in rearing her children and beginning a new career in writing. One of her sons is a sound engineer, and the other an architect. As an editor, she opened doors for many other African American authors. As a novelist, she has achieved international acclaim. Morrison admits that her workload was taxing, but she has no patience with suggestions that she is unusual. Black American women have always been, she notes, "both safe harbor and ship" (Tate in Taylor-Guthrie 161). Morrison sees herself as one in a long line of women who have had dual responsibilities. They had to nurture (be the safe harbor) and to provide financially (be the ship, the way to the safe harbor). Because she is mindful of African American women's history, she disagrees with those who think that a woman must or should choose between rearing children and doing paid work. She characterizes black women as busy and eminently capable: "[W]e're managing households and other people's children and two jobs and listening to everybody and at the same time creating, singing, holding, bearing, transferring the culture for generations. We've been walking on water for four hundred years" (Moyers in Taylor-Guthrie 270).

Being an editor and raising her children did not leave Morrison much time for a social life. Still, she found that being a mother liberated her from many time-consuming social roles. Morrison's sons, she reports, did not need her social self. They had only three expectations of her: she had to maintain order for them, be useful, and have a sense of humor. Though she worked hard at her editing and wrote her first novel while her sons were still pre-schoolers, Morrison is clear on making children the highest priority: "What they deserve and need, in-house, is a mother. They do not need and cannot use a writer" (Washington in Taylor-Guthrie 238).

Morrison does not think that having children early, or being a single parent, necessarily ruins life for either the children or the mother. Like her, such mothers can still become successful professionals. She points out that in her grandmother's time, many women were married by age sixteen. She emphasizes, however, that mothers, especially young mothers, do not bear all the responsibility for children. The community must help these women maintain their multiple roles so that mothers and children remain contributing members of society. All of Morrison's novels explore the relationships between mothers and their children, and *The Bluest Eye* and *Beloved* center on motherhood.

Though it is possible to show Morrison's work as part of many traditions—American, African American, the novel—she remains one of a kind. First, her subject matter has always been original. *The Bluest Eye* deals with the many cooperating forces that make a little black girl come to want blue eyes. *Sula* is centered on women's friendship, a rare topic in literature before 1973. *Song of Solomon* tells of an African American man searching for his roots, but this theme is blended with political issues in a wholly new way. Similarly, *Tar Baby* takes an age-old concern—a woman and a man in love—and makes it new with a landscape where trees talk and political concerns are inescapable. *Beloved* seeks to fill a gap in our knowledge: how did slaves, with their terrible experiences, become free, healthy people? *Jazz* returns to romantic issues. Its protagonists, Joe and Violet, are not the usual young couple, however. They have experienced first-hand the Great Migration and the jazz age, and when the book opens, they are in their fifties.

Perhaps some of this originality stems from Morrison's unusual ideas about audience and plot development. Most writers have a particular audience in mind. Morrison, however, says that she writes for the characters of whatever novel she is working on, not for an external audience. She feels that trying to talk to a particular audience outside the book leads to too much awkward explanation. Her ideas about development of plot and character are similarly unusual. Creative writing programs have made "writing what you know" a cliché. Morrison, on the other hand, writes to find out what she doesn't know (Tate in Taylor-Guthrie

169). So she explores unusual characters who naturally become involved in unusual events. Many readers feel that this aspect of Morrison's novels stimulates their own imaginations.

Since *The Bluest Eye* was published in 1970, Morrison has written steadily, producing a nonfiction book, many articles, a short story, a play, and six more novels. She has definite ideas about the importance of reading and writing novels, and about why people want to hear stories: "That's the way they learn things. That's the way human beings organize their human knowledge—fairy tales, myths. All narration" (Bakerman in Taylor-Guthrie 35). In Morrison's view, folktales and music—spirituals, blues, jazz—were until recently the central expressions of African American culture. Now, because social conditions have changed, the artistic forms to express experience must change too, and so the novel can and must do what spirituals used to do within the black community (Jones in Taylor-Guthrie 183).

Morrison began publishing just after the Civil Rights Movement of the 1960s. During the years when her early novels came out, black women authors experienced intense pressure to write about certain kinds of characters and plots. Some African American readers wanted good role models, for example. Others wanted novels focused on whites' victimization of blacks. The success of Alice Walker's 1982 novel *The Color Purple* resulted in another demand. Some African Americans thought that *The Color Purple* had bought its success by confirming white readers' stereotypes about black males. They insisted that all black writers, but especially women writers, owed the black community positive pictures of black men. These characters would not only contradict white stereotypes but would supply the black community with role models.

Morrison refused to comply with these expectations. She does not base her characters on real people. Using real people makes a writer into what Morrison considers a literary vampire, an author who feeds her novels from others' lives (Schappell 105). Because her characters are not typical African Americans, because their circumstances are often extreme, she doesn't feel that the question of role models should apply. Characters who always display goodness and strength would simply be dull, she feels. Further, she thinks that "no one should tell any writer what to write, at all, ever" (Washington in Taylor-Guthrie 237). Although Morrison resists political demands that she write on particular subjects, or about particular subjects in particular ways, she considers her books very political. In her view, the aesthetic of "art for art's sake"—literature with no social purpose—is useless. In addition, because the idea came on the literary scene only recently (during the late 1800s), it has no tradition or rich history (Bellinelli video). She sees no difficulty in aiming to create novels that are at once beautiful and political (Byatt video).

Morrison sees herself as one of a group of writers developing new subjects. She observes that white male writers tend to be interested in and to write about white men. (In line with her belief that no one should dictate another artist's subject matter, she does not criticize this choice.) Many white women writers share this interest in white men, she says. Perhaps more surprisingly, she finds that African American male writers do too, for they measure their identities and their power against those of their white male characters. Black women writers, she claims, are the only writers who focus primarily on black women and black men (Byatt video).

Morrison often doesn't know what plot will develop out of a new subject when she begins to write. She always knows the ending of a book, she remarks, just not how the characters are going to get there. While she is writing a book, the characters become so real to Morrison that she is sometimes seriously tempted to withdraw from everyday social life. Like real people, these characters have personalities. Morrison notes that if a writer lets a strong character like Pilate (in *Song of Solomon*) have much dialogue, the character will take over the book in the same way that a strong personality can dominate a conversation.

Morrison has taught creative writing and literature at various universities since the mid 1970s. She now teaches at Princeton University. Her advice to those who want to write is direct: "The only advice I have for any writer is to read. It's like any other craft. You have to know the industry and know what has been done. . . . You can't break any rule that you don't know. This is the language that we speak, and one should know all there is to know about it. Everything" (Jones in Taylor-Guthrie 187). Reading other writers doesn't mean imitating them, of course. Morrison comments that her books don't really resemble those of other great writers like James Joyce or William Faulkner.

At the same time, she expresses admiration for three groups of writers. First, the South American "magic realists," such as Gabriel García Márquez and Miguel Asturias, appeal to her. "Magic realism" reproduces the social conditions and routines of ordinary life, like realistic or naturalistic art, but also uses events that would be considered impossible or miraculous by modern Western science. The characters accept these supernatural events, without surprise, simply as part of reality. The contrast of magic realism with North American realism makes us aware that different cultures define reality in different ways. This concept is important because some of Morrison's novels also include events outside the realm of Western science.

Calling them "fearless," Morrison has expressed respect for a group of three women writers: the Americans Eudora Welty and Lillian Hellman, and the South African Nadine Gordimer. All white writers from segregated societies, they have nevertheless done a superior job, she feels, of depicting black characters. Morrison draws attention to both their aesthetic achievements and their moral commitments (Watkins in Taylor-Guthrie 47).

Morrison mentions having learned from several African writers, among them Chinua Achebe, a Nigerian novelist famous for a trilogy of novels about the European invasion and takeover of traditional African society; Wole Soyinka, a Nobel-prize winning playwright from Nigeria; and the Ghanaian novelist Ayi Kwei Armah (Davis in Taylor-Guthrie 228–29). She also admires the novels of Camara Laye, who is from Guinea (Jones in Taylor-Guthrie 179).

Although she admires other writers' works, Morrison thinks that they have had little direct influence on her own writing. Painters, on the other hand, have sometimes contributed directly. Morrison reports that the Norwegian expressionist Edvard Munch's painting, "Spring Evening on Karl Johan Street," contributed to her depiction of small towns in *Song of Solomon* (Watkins in Taylor-Guthrie 47). Like Morrison's novels, many of Munch's paintings communicate an interest in psychology as well as intense emotion. Graphic art is so important to Morrison that her Princeton office displays an architect's pen-and-ink drawing of all the houses in her novels (Schappell 85). In comparing her writing to painting, Morrison notes that both make use of white space. The white space around painted figures defines them, she notes. In her definition, the white space of a written narrative consists of what is *not* written, what is left unsaid for the reader to infer.

Morrison expects readers to be active, to infer a great deal in her works. People understand, she says, that really listening to music—as opposed to just having the stereo on for background—requires concentration, intelligence, and imagination (Caldwell in Taylor-Guthrie 243). Morrison wants her readers to use these traits too: "My writing expects, demands participatory reading. . . . The reader supplies the emotions. The reader supplies even some of the color, some of the sound. My language has to have holes and spaces so the reader can come into it" (Tate in Taylor-Guthrie 164). In Toni Morrison's view, this kind of reader/writer interaction, in fact, defines black literature: "[I]t's not just having black people *in* it or having it be written by a black person, but it has to have . . . the participation of the *other*, that is, the audience, the reader" (Davis in Taylor-Guthrie 231, emphasis in original).

All of Morrison's novels deal with African American characters and communities; several of them have no characters from other racial or ethnic groups. Morrison does not feel that her focus prevents the work from being universal, that is, from communicating things that are true of all human beings to readers of many different backgrounds. Morrison notes that in high school, when she read the great English and European novelists, she was impressed that they could paint their cultures, their specific locales, in such wonderful detail that she could experience, understand, and enjoy them. All good writing, she thinks, communicates an intimate knowledge of specific people and places.

Occasionally, readers who don't share the culture of Morrison's black characters feel intimidated about interpreting the stories. An interviewer once asked Morrison if it was true that white readers who had not read deeply in African American literature—essays and political tracts as well as novels, poetry, and drama—would not be able to understand her novels. Morrison noted that such readers would miss some insider jokes but probably not the whole meaning of her work (Byatt video). In addition, she emphasizes that she and many other black readers have read and understood beyond their original cultures. Morrison feels quite able to interpret and comment on, for example, works by the English writer Jane Austen or the white American poet Emily Dickinson. In a humorous moment, she quipped, "Insensitive white people cannot deal with black writing, but then they cannot deal with their own literature either" (Tate in Taylor-Guthrie 160).

Morrison has said that trying to explain too much ruins fiction; she feels that the necessity to explain to a largely white audience interfered with the art of earlier black writers such as Richard Wright and Ralph Ellison. At the same time, she would like readers to know "black cosmology" and to be aware of what the terms "church," "community," and "ancestor" mean to African American culture (McKay in Taylor-Guthrie 151). The reader of this volume can meet Morrison's wish simply by reading Chapter 2, where these terms are explained. When readers understand the books' cultural premises, they should engage with the novels fearlessly.

Morrison urges individual readers to come to their own understandings of her books. As a teacher, she has been dismayed that students often lack the confidence to interpret without first consulting secondary sources such as interviews or literary criticism. Trust the tale, not the interview, she says (Neustadt in Taylor-Guthrie 85). By this she means that readers must rely on the text of each novel rather than trying to find an "expert" statement that allegedly tells them what she meant. Even authors interpreting their own work often change their minds over time. As readers and interpreters, writers work from their own experience, and that experience changes and grows. Thus, even the same writer interprets differently at different stages of his or her life. In fact, Morrison's interviews show just this sort of change. Speaking of the ending of her novel *Tar Baby* in 1981, Morrison interpreted "lickety split" to mean that the rabbit-character was returning to the symbolic brier patch (Ruas in Taylor-Guthrie 107). In 1983, she interpreted the words to mean that the rabbit-character has a choice of the brier patch or the open road (McKay in Taylor-Guthrie 151).

When an interviewer asked her if her works had sometimes been misinterpreted, Morrison acknowledged that they had. However, she added that she does not know if readers whose interpretations are similar to hers are "any more right than people who see it another way" (Tate in Taylor-Guthrie 169). Morrison does not, therefore, consider the author the final authority on what the text means. No final authority exists in her world. Instead, Morrison values the processes of interaction and discussion that take place in a community of readers.

Interpretations that consider only part of a book or that cannot be supported from the text are not useful, of course. (If an interpretation cannot be supported with quotations and examples from the text, then it is not really engaged with that text.) But because Morrison requires only concentrated, intelligent, imaginative interaction with her novels, she welcomes a wide range of interpretations.

Considerable debate over terminology to describe Americans of African descent has taken place. This book will use "black" and "African American" interchangeably, following the practice of most literary scholars, including the editors of *The Oxford Companion to African American Literature* and *The Norton Anthology of African American Literature*.

2

Literary Contexts

Toni Morrison describes herself as a "black woman novelist" (Caldwell in Taylor-Guthrie 243) but also as "midwestern" (Schappell 119). She sees herself, then, as a writer with a racial/cultural identity, a gender identity, and a national/regional identity. In her interviews and her literary criticism, Morrison enlarges on this point. She indicates that black American writers form a tradition of African American literature while simultaneously contributing to the traditions of American literature as a whole. These three terms—*black, woman,* and *American*—suggest three literary contexts for Morrison's novels.

Black writing in the United States expresses experience that is specifically African American. That is, black literature records the history and cultural response that no other group shares. Although many other racial and ethnic minorities experience discrimination, for example, no other group was forcibly brought to the United States or enslaved. To address this singular historical situation, Toni Morrison has written a historical trilogy. *Beloved* deals with slavery and its immediate aftermath; *Jazz* continues this exploration into the 1920s. The third volume, *Paradise*, extends the examination of history into the 1970s.

This trilogy joins an African American tradition developed largely in response to the available audience. The first audience for black literature in the United States was overwhelmingly white. Slaves were legally barred from learning to read or write, and universal education (free schools for all) came into being only after the Civil War, so that even most free blacks could not afford schooling.

In the nineteenth century, most printed black literature consisted of slave narratives. These narratives, true stories of slaves' escapes to free states or countries, were published by white abolitionists to educate whites about the evils of slavery. Thus, the dominant genre of African American literature in the nineteenth century was heavily influenced by white publishers and white audiences.

After emancipation, the black audience grew slowly. Few states had free public school systems, and even those increasingly excluded black children. By 1900, white publishers still controlled the book industry, but the black audience was large enough to support magazines like *The Colored American*, which had a peak circulation of 15,000 (*The Oxford Companion to African American Literature* 163). Sixty years later, the black audience had grown sufficiently large to allow the Black Arts movement to flourish. (In the Black Arts movement, African American artists and critics promoted subject matter and techniques specifically tailored for an African American audience.) Until very recently, however, black writers had to deal with the expectations of white audiences and publishers.

In many ways, the early black writers' situation simply extended the situation of every black American, as described by W. E. B. Du Bois in 1903. In *The Souls of Black Folk*, Du Bois coined the term "double consciousness" to describe the results for black people of living in a society that devalued them and their culture: "It is a peculiar sensation, this double-consciousness, this sense of always looking at oneself through the eyes of others. . . . One ever feels his two-ness,—an American, a Negro; two souls, two thoughts, two unreconciled strivings; two warring ideals in one dark body" (364–65). To survive, blacks always had to be aware of racist stereotypes that determined how their actions would be interpreted by the white power structure. Simultaneously, they had to retain an awareness of the African American community's more positive definition of black identity as well as its interpretations of particular actions.

As long as white readers made up the bulk of the audience, black writers often concentrated on two subjects. First, they demonstrated the falsity of racist stereotypes of black people and culture. Second, they objected to social injustices such as lynching, segregation, the denial of voting rights, biased legal systems, and other forms of institutionalized discrimination. Until about 1950, the dominant genre of black fiction in this century was called "the protest novel." The depictions of protest novels necessarily concerned the impact of white racism on black culture.

African Americans, of course, did not need to be educated about these issues. As they became a larger part of the audience, black writers were freer to explore black culture and communities in their own right, rather than in relation to the white power structure. (During the 1920s, many black artists did focus on black experience. This movement, called the Harlem Renaissance, was financially underwritten by whites, however, and its presentations were heavily influenced by white stereotypes of black culture as primitive or exotic.) Morrison's novels have been a major contribution to this celebration of black identity and culture.

As part of honoring African American cultural traditions, Morrison revisits both the genres and the themes of earlier writers. In *Beloved*, for instance, she returns to the genre of the slave narrative. Freed from the nineteenth-century problem of controlling white publishers and audiences, *Beloved* carries on the slave narrative—from a black perspective. In *Beloved*, ex-slaves tell one another (and the next generation of black children) the stories of their experiences. Within the novel, then, African Americans speak of the slave experience to a black audience. Through this work, Morrison as a black writer tells the truths of slavery to the mixed-race audience of the present.

W. E. B. Du Bois's theme of double consciousness appears throughout Morrison's works. *The Bluest Eye* shows the damage done to a black child when racist definitions obliterate all positive definitions of her worth. *Tar Baby* explores how double consciousness is manifested in different generations and social classes. Morrison also shows both individual characters and the African American community resisting oppression by using insights from double consciousness.

Historically, African American literature has shown many examples of doubly conscious black characters gaining their own ends by manipulating whites' racist expectations, a behavior called "masking." (Thus, a character might avoid telling whites the whereabouts of a black fugitive by pretending to be too stupid or confused to answer questions sensibly.) Morrison's novels rarely depict black/white interaction, but the issue of masking always arises when the two cultures meet. Thus, for example, in *Song of Solomon*, Pilate assumes the mask of the poor, ignorant countrywoman for the white police in order to free her nephew Milkman. Communities as well as individuals can mask. When whites want to deny the existence of well-educated black people in *Song of Solomon*, they rename a street "Mains" and forbid the community to refer to it as "Doctor Street." The black residents ostensibly conform; henceforth they refer to it as "Not Doctor Street." Masking assumes a prominent place in *Tar Baby*, the Morrison novel with the most interaction of black and white characters.

In addition to adapting historical genres and themes, Toni Morrison has participated in contemporary literary movements. Along with many other artists, Morrison has sought to honor varieties of black American speech, and to amalgamate two elements of African American creativity by infusing literature with the distinctly black music of blues and jazz. In her historical trilogy, *Beloved* is suffused with the ache of the blues aesthetic, while the title of *Jazz* speaks—or sings—for itself.

As a "black *woman* writer" [emphasis added], Toni Morrison pioneered literary exploration of complex black female identities. In 1970, when Morrison published her first novel, most literary characterizations of women had not progressed beyond stereotypes. The nature of those stereotypes differed for white and black women because their historical experiences differed. The nineteenth-century stereotypes of white and black women were complementary. In this racist and sexist folklore, white women became sexless angels, while black women became sexual animals. Many nineteenth- and early twentieth-century black women's novels seem rather prim now because the writers wanted to deny the stereotype by portraying irreproachable heroines.

Black women writers had not only these racist issues to confront, but sexist attitudes that affected all women writers. The white, British author Virginia Woolf noted in *Professions for Women* that women writers were not permitted to tell "the truth of the body." Sometimes the censorship was internalized, so that women never wrote what they knew for fear of male publishers and critics. Often, however, the censorship operated directly. The white American novelist Edith Summers Kelley, for instance, was forced to omit a scene of childbirth from her 1923 work, *Weeds*. Truths of the female body such as pregnancy, childbirth, abortion, rape, and sexual experience simply could not be expressed in literary form because male publishers considered them distasteful. A writer who wanted to express truths about black female bodies had both sexism and racism to contend with.

Most of the little published truth about black women's experiences remained out of print in the late 1960s, when Toni Morrison was writing her first novel. Of the black-authored books available, only a few were by women. Stereotypes remained a problem. In *Black Women Novelists*, critic Barbara Christian identifies three main pre-1970 stereotypes: the bossy and comic Mammy, who nurtures everyone; the mulatta, a mixed-race woman whose life is necessarily tragic; and the Sapphire, who dominates and emasculates black men.

Morrison's first two novels, *The Bluest Eye* and *Sula*, helped to make more realistic black women visible to the American reading public. Both works trace the development of children into adults, and thus belong to the long-established literary genre called the *bildungsroman*. Until this time, however, the *bildungsroman* featured mostly white male characters. Those portraying white females tended to end with the youthful heroine's marriage, or to focus on her experience in a marriage. Morrison extended the genre's range and depth by her attention to specifically black American female experience. In her first two books, Morrison presented menstruation and sexuality, two truths of the female body. Perhaps more importantly, she focused on the truths of black female culture, with its emphases on female friendship and motherhood. And she told the truths of American society in her portrait of racist damage to black children and the African American community. Overturning stereotypes, these novels set a new standard of complex, nuanced presentation for black female characters.

Morrison can revise and expand literary tradition precisely because she knows it so well. Before writing her novels, she completed formal study of American literature at Cornell University with an M.A. thesis on two great modernist writers, Virginia Woolf and William Faulkner. More recently she has published *Playing in the Dark: Whiteness and the Literary Imagination*, which analyzes the critical biases of professional literary criticism. As a self-aware American writer, Morrison has used themes and techniques from two earlier major movements in twentieth-century literature—modernism and postmodernism—like a jazz musician uses a melody, as the basis for original interpretation.

A dominant movement from about 1910 until World War II, modernism was the literary analogue to jazz in the musical world. Jazz has always been recognized as an African American creation, and considerable literary criticism of the 1980s and 1990s has accented the previously overlooked contributions of African American writers to the development of modernism. Literary modernism developed new subjects and new techniques for exploring them. Modernists were interested in exploring the individual's consciousness, and in defining a new relationship to the past. Exploring characters' points of view with what came to be called "stream of consciousness," modernist works often seem frag-

mented. Stream of consciousness writing tries to show the actual processes of the mind. Because we do not feel and think in complete, logical
sentences, works using stream of consciousness contain partial sentences,
many images, and frequent repetition. Their plots do not move forward
in a linear fashion but often circle. Sometimes they revisit the same happenings again and again as a character ponders their meanings, just as
we reconsider important happenings in our real lives.

Sometimes modernist works examine the same happenings from several points of view, to show how individual characters experience them
differently. Because of their interest in individual experience, modernist
novels do not use an omniscient narrator. (An omniscient narrator conveys to the reader what all the characters think and feel.) Omniscient
narrators unify literary works, often commenting to show the limitations
of particular characters' judgments. In modernist works, the reader must
take over many of the functions that the omniscient narrator performed
in earlier fiction.

Self-consciously creating something new, modernist writers naturally
reconsidered their relationship to the literary past, particularly to myths.
In fact, the use of myth became a dominant characteristic of modernist
literature. Different artists found different relationships between their
present and the mythic past. The poet T. S. Eliot thought, for example,
that heroic myths highlighted the shabbiness of contemporary life. James
Joyce and William Faulkner, on the other hand, found heroism in everyday life, which, to their minds, still manifested mythic patterns.

Toni Morrison's early novels are steeped in modernist subject matter,
plot, and technique. *The Bluest Eye, Sula*, and *Song of Solomon* explore
individuals' realities, often re-examining the same experience. In *The Bluest Eye*, for example, although Claudia tells the story from an adult's
point of view, she remembers and presents her childhood perspectives
as well. The novel's second narrator interrupts any linear plot progres-
sion by moving into a character's consciousness to show the past experience that now determines their reactions. The reader is exposed
sequentially to the consciousness of Cholly, Mrs. Breedlove, and Soaphead Church, so that their actions toward the main character, Pecola,
make psychological sense.

When *Sula* shifts between Sula's and Nel's perspectives, the reader
often has to consider a whole new interpretation of an event. When Sula
cuts off part of her finger, for instance, the reader is likely to connect
this action to Eva's heroic sacrifice of her leg. Much later in the novel,

however, Nel remembers the action as simply another example of Sula's tendency to panic. As a modernist work, *Sula* never lets the reader rest easy, with a single and uncomplicated understanding of an event's meaning. Instead, the reader must develop an interpretation that honors a multiplicity of meanings in experience.

Like many modernist works, both *The Bluest Eye* and *Song of Solomon* use myth as their organizing principle. *The Bluest Eye*, however, concentrates on the relationship of everyday life to one myth, the story of Demeter and Persephone. (This myth explains Earth's seasons through a story of mother-love detailed in the alternative reading section of Chapter 3.) *Song of Solomon* incorporates elements of Greek myths, African American slave narratives, and sacred stories from American Indian cultures. Thematically and technically more complex than *The Bluest Eye*, *Song of Solomon* demonstrates Morrison's movement from modernist to postmodernist premises.

"Postmodern" describes the culture of the Western world from about 1965 to the present. In *Flyboy in the Buttermilk*, cultural critic Greg Tate has described postmodernism in terms of the "four p's": parody, pluralism, politics, and popular or "pop" culture. All but parody are central to Toni Morrison's later fiction. Pluralism, politics, and pop culture are intimately connected in *Tar Baby*, *Beloved*, and *Jazz*.

Pluralism means the ongoing presence of conflicting points of view. Postmodernists are pluralists because they have abandoned the modernist idea that a writer can bring a permanent, larger unity out of characters' fragmented experiences. For the postmodernist, all such unities are temporary and artificial. Whether for a single person or for a society, postmodernist meaning is never fixed, but always in the process of being revised. In postmodernist models, different individuals' experiences of the same event can never be resolved into one truth. *Song of Solomon* hints at such a world when Milkman can't resolve the conflict of his parents' stories about their early marriage. *Tar Baby* expands the theme by taking the construction of meaning as one of its primary subjects.

Tar Baby's postmodern exploration works on several levels. First, the characters discuss the tar baby legend, only to disagree about its ultimate meaning. Second, *Tar Baby* draws attention to itself as one of the historical series of tar baby folktales. The novel thus becomes the 1980s revision of a tale told in African villages in the 1600s and in American theatres showing Walt Disney's *Song of the South* in the 1950s. Third, the reader is invited to consider the characters' actions within the framework of the tar baby story. The available evidence is conflicting, however, so that the reader cannot conclusively assign the role of the tar baby to any one character or even abstract idea.

Beloved specifically investigates what happens when a character refuses a postmodernist world—that is, when a character clings to one interpretation, one meaning, of the past. Unable to change her understanding of a painful past, Sethe becomes its prisoner. In the epilogue, the narrator muses on how a community constructs and revises stories, which over time become its histories.

In political terms, the postmodernist understanding of meaning suggests that differing and conflicting views will always exist and that a successful system must maintain peace by acknowledging the legitimacy of these viewpoints. Further, everything is political in a postmodernist understanding. This idea goes beyond the valid and important concept that politics cause certain events, which is present in all of Morrison's works. Every character in *Beloved* experiences life in politically determined ways—the Garners as slave owners; Sethe and Paul D as slaves and then freed people; the Bodwins as abolitionists. Postmodernists see social structures like slavery and their psychic results as only the most visible effects of politics.

Postmodernists maintain that in a less visible but profoundly important way, politics teaches every individual how to make meaning out of raw experience. According to postmodernists, individuals only appear to generate unique interpretations. These interpretations actually originate not in the psyches of individuals, but in their experiences of social structures that are part of a larger political system. For example, until very recently, the legal system of the United States did not recognize rape within marriage. If a husband forcibly had sex with his unconsenting wife, the courts considered the action a private disagreement. Such married women did not, therefore, generally understand themselves as rape victims. In the 1990s, however, the man's action is criminal—rape. The meaning of the action has shifted as society has changed its political structures to recognize the civil rights of women. This change, in turn, affects how women think and feel about their experiences.

The postmodernist understanding of reality as a political construction comes naturally to minority populations. It would, for instance, be part of the double consciousness discussed earlier. In *Jazz*, we see an example of a character realizing the political content of an ordinary event. Felicity identifies a beautiful ring, which might seem a natural thing to want, as a microcosm of white values that she can accept or refuse. No interpretation of meaning, whether of an event or a material object, is "natural" in a postmodernist system; every interpretation has political roots.

Postmodernists see traditional distinctions between high art (such as opera) and popular culture (radio top-forty songs) as oppressive politics. Their artistic creations use elements from a wide range of past artistic productions, without regard to whether their borrowings were originally highbrow or lowbrow. Again, minority populations would tend to anticipate the dominant culture's development of this attitude because their artistic productions would have been defined as lowbrow, even vulgar. In music, for instance, both blues and jazz were originally regarded by most European Americans as primitive and degrading.

African American writers have honored many forms of popular culture. Alice Walker's "Everyday Use" (in her *In Love and Trouble: Stories of Black Women*), for example, reveres the many anonymous women artists who made heirloom quilts. In another instance, Zora Neale Hurston gathered African American folktales for her 1935 collection, *Mules and Men*. And at least since 1926, when Langston Hughes published a book of poetry called *The Weary Blues*, African American writers have experimentally integrated the aesthetics of popular music and literature. Morrison carries on this tradition in *Beloved*, a blues novel, and its sequel in both literary and musical history, *Jazz*.

As a black American woman writer, Toni Morrison uses many elements of American literature. Her works acknowledge and debate with the great modernist and postmodernist writers. The Golden Gray story of *Jazz*, for example, alludes to the plot and characterization of William Faulkner's *Absalom, Absalom!* The scene of *Tar Baby* in which Son and Jadine first enter Eloe echoes a similar scene in Zora Neale Hurston's *Their Eyes Were Watching God*. In addition to recognizing these noted writers, however, Morrison uses her works to "re-memory" people otherwise lost to us—those who died during the Middle Passage (the journey on slave ships from Africa to the United States), or the woman who killed her child rather than have it returned to slavery (*Beloved*). Closely observed, ordinary people like Cholly Breedlove (*The Bluest Eye*), Nel (*Sula*), Denver (*Beloved*), or Joe and Violet Trace (*Jazz*) become extraordinary.

Every character in Morrison's books participates in two continuums. One moves outward in space from the individual to the ever-present surrounding community. The other moves simultaneously backward and forward in time, to connect the present with past and future generations. In this way, Toni Morrison's fiction illustrates exactly what makes African American literature African American.

African American culture and literature work within a concept of the universe that differs from dominant Western ideas. In *Trabelin' On: Journey to an Afro-Baptist Faith*, Mechal Sobel traces this idea to its roots and names it "the African sacred cosmos." Toni Morrison has acknowledged the importance of the sacred cosmos to African American culture by saying that she wants her readers to be familiar with "black cosmology" (McKay in Taylor-Guthrie 151). The African sacred cosmos differs from Western models in three important areas: definition of what is sacred, understanding of time, and concept of the self.

Traditional African religious systems made no distinction between sacred places or activities and profane ones. As in many American Indian societies, every place remained sacred because it had been created by divine will. In the same way, every action participated in the sacred because it happened within a sacred world and was performed by sacred creations. Every act of creation, whether childbirth or the making of a basket, echoes divine creation. Although many of Morrison's characters have lost their sense of participating in the sacred, the strongest and most appealing characters, like *Song of Solomon's* Pilate, rejoice in it. Morrison's everyday ritual for beginning to write demonstrates her own belief in the sacred nature of artistic creation. She watches the dawn break as a way of entering the "nonsecular"—that is, "not worldly, sacred"—space from which she writes (Schappell 87).

The African sacred cosmos incorporates an idea of time that has no counterpart in the West. In Western systems, time is linear and progressive. Westerners understand that one set of events happens when a particular group of people is alive. Then those events are past, those people are dead, and others take their place. Time in the African sacred cosmos has a different sort of continuity. When individuals die, they remain present in their communities in much the same way that they did in life. Their form has changed—they no longer have physical bodies—but their personalities remain unchanged, and they directly influence happenings in the present. When the last person who knew a dead person also dies, the older spirit joins the long-dead, the ancestors. The ancestors and living human beings are joined, however, by the active spirits.

Morrison's fiction reflects the crucial importance of ancestral figures in African American culture as a whole. Ancestor and community are two of the concepts that Morrison has designated as critical for understanding her novels (Schappell 151). In her novels, spirits persist beyond the Western finality of death: both Sula and Pilate's father speak after their deaths. Further, finding the lost ancestor is essential to finding oneself in *Song of Solomon*; the ancestral horsemen of Isle de Chevaliers are the force through which Son must define himself in *Tar Baby*. Memories of her mother, Ma'am, and Ma'am's African language empower Sethe in *Beloved*. And in *Jazz*, the characters must trace the ancestors so they can mature. In Morrison's novels, all individual growth depends on a web of relationships within the larger, living ancestral community.

Just as concepts of past and present are separate in Western thought but united in the African sacred cosmos, so are self and other people inseparable. The self in traditional African societies cannot exist alone; it is made up of a web of shifting relationships to other physical and spiritual beings. This concept of the self's unbreakable connections to others would by itself have made social community important in African American culture. It was reinforced, however, by oppression that insisted on defining black individuals always as members of a racial group. Many states adopted Thomas Jefferson's standard that a person having one-eighth African blood (that is, a great-grandparent of African descent) would be considered black (Dennis 60). This standard persisted in the South until at least the mid-1960s and was reflected in census and survey classifications that did not include a biracial category until the 1990s. Legally defined as a group, African Americans constructed a cultural community. African American literature as a whole recognizes the defining importance of community.

Morrison's novels explore the many influences of the community on individuals. In *The Bluest Eye* and *Sula*, the community fails the protagonists. In *Song of Solomon*, on the other hand, the Southern community enables Milkman to find his roots and himself. *Tar Baby* shows a much-divided community unable to provide role models for contemporary men and women. In *Beloved*, the community at different times betrays and rescues. *Jazz* shows the community becoming politically and artistically active, protesting injustice and creating jazz. In all of Morrison's novels, the community is a primary character, because without it individuals could not exist.

Considering a last quality of this culture may underline the continuity of twentieth-century African American literature with earlier African American and African art. African American culture values orality. African cultures relied on oral performance to conduct the business of everyday life, to educate children, to worship. This emphasis on orality was preserved in America in part because laws forbade teaching slaves to read or write. Also, because even slaves were often allowed their own religious services, and black churches experienced less white interference than any other African American institution, oral performance remained sacred. Many oral forms, ranging from folktale to song, have important thematic roles in Morrison's novels. African American folktales of the tar baby and of flying Africans inform *Tar Baby* and *Song of Solomon*, for example. In another way, the modernist engagement with myth is another form of interaction with the oral. Classical Western myths, which we tend to think of as printed in the works of Greek playwrights, were of course originally recited for their audiences in oral performances. Whenever oral forms are contrasted with print in Morrison's works, the oral forms emerge as more accurate. In *Beloved*, for example, Schoolteacher's book on slavery will clearly perpetuate racist lies. In that same novel, Paul D refuses to trust the newspaper to tell him about Sethe's past, preferring to hear what Sethe herself says. In the Western world, the dominant power has written history, but African Americans are telling it like they see it.

A specific oral form—call-and-response—has both contemporary and historic significance for African American writers. Call-and-response developed in slavery, as one slave organized the energies of others by issuing a verbal call to which the rest might respond. Lack of response meant that the person was not recognized or accepted as a leader. Response gave a leader a suggestion for the direction his or her next call might take. Steady call-and-response helped develop work rhythms— and expressions of African American oral creativity that could survive slavery. African American churches rely on call-and-response in their services. Because these churches were so active in the Civil Rights Movement, and because Martin Luther King, Jr. was a minister, one of the most famous speeches of that movement exemplifies call-and-response. In "I Have a Dream," King used elements of a black minister's earlier speech. That minister had issued a call that King's response incorporated and enlarged to make his call. Since then, King's call in "I Have a Dream" has received many thousand responses as Americans of all races pay tribute to his ideas. Having acknowledged King's importance, speakers and writers then explain their own ideas, and these become the next generation of calls. Call-and-response provides the basic rhythm for much African American music, in gospel singing and some varieties of jazz.

Morrison's fictional works specifically honor call-and-response. Indeed, it is the central path to freedom in *Beloved*. Baby Suggs, whom the community always calls "Baby Suggs, Holy," makes it a central part of her healing ministry. Paul D and his chain gang use call-and-response to escape, while Ella and the community of women use it to liberate Sethe. Call-and-response is an oral manifestation of the self-in-community found in the African sacred cosmos.

But because that living cosmos extends back to the ancestors, call-and-response in a larger sense extends to the real world of writers and literary tradition. As a "black woman writer" in America, Toni Morrison responds to the written and oral calls of her black, white, and American Indian literary ancestors. As she does so, her response to them becomes her call to us.

The Bluest Eye
(1970)

Morrison's first novel establishes both thematic and technical elements that remain important in her later works. The novel realistically explores a black community in a particular time and place—Lorain, Ohio, in the 1940s—and shows that the events there result from wider social realities of racism and poverty. At the same time, the novel connects its characters and events to the Greek myth of Demeter and Persephone. Morrison's later works share this concentration on African American characters and community, and several connect ordinary people and happenings to the larger-than-life patterns of myths.

To explore these subjects, the novel uses a complex blend of narration from an omniscient narrator (one who knows all the characters' thoughts and histories) and a retrospective first-person narrator (in this case, an adult remembering her childhood). As in Morrison's other works, the narration does not proceed in the straightforward chronological order of the events told, but instead moves back and forth in time.

The Bluest Eye shows racism's damaging effects on the black community at large and on black families. As the black community and individual black people absorb the wider culture's racist pictures of themselves, they focus their self-hatred on the most vulnerable character, twelve-year-old Pecola Breedlove. Pecola's tragedy, then, is the culmination of many other tragedies. However, *The Bluest Eye* also contains stories of perseverance and survival. One of these survivors is the first-person narrator, Claudia MacTeer. Through Claudia and the omniscient narrator, Morrison sings a song of praise and grief for all the Pecolas of the world.

SOCIAL AND LITERARY CONTEXT

The Bluest Eye shares concerns with the two most powerful social forces in the United States during the 1950s and 1960s, the Black Power movement and the feminist movement. This period saw the rise of two major organizations of African American political power. Martin Luther King, Jr. headed a Christian, nonviolent, and desegregationist movement that worked through boycotts and demonstrations. Malcolm X espoused a Muslim, separatist philosophy that supported "any means necessary" for self-defense.

As a result of these movements, America's social landscape changed substantially from 1950 to 1970. The civil rights movement culminated in new laws—the Voting Rights Act and the Civil Rights Act. The Voting Rights Act used Federal power to break a century-old system by which Southern states had prevented African Americans from registering to vote. The Civil Rights Act of 1964 ended "Jim Crow" laws—separate schools, restaurants, seating on buses, even separate rest rooms for blacks and whites. (Although these separate facilities were supposed to be "separate but equal," in fact the funding was never comparable, and frequently no facilities at all were provided for African Americans.) By the end of the 1960s, both Malcolm X and King had been assassinated, and the power of their movements had declined. Focusing on a different kind of social and cultural change, African Americans worked to analyze their cultural heritage and its contributions to American civilization. Toni Morrison's editorial work on *The Black Book* (see Chapter 1) typifies this ongoing reclamation of African American history and culture. As African American students claimed a heritage worthy of study, universities formally recognized their culture's existence and integrity with Black Studies programs.

Women's Studies programs developed at about the same time, a product of the women's movement of the 1960s and 1970s. The feminist movement worked for changes in women's economic opportunities and social roles in general. The early movement had three main goals: (1) achieving reproductive rights such as contraception and abortion, (2) ending gender discrimination in jobs, and (3) stopping violence against women. Soon, splits between the interests of white middle class women and African American women of all classes became increasingly obvious. Though all women faced economic discrimination, for example, African American women's opportunities were largely restricted to factory and farm work or domestic labor such as housecleaning and laundering.

Working from different historical experiences and viewpoints, as well as different economic positions, white and black women naturally looked at social roles from divergent perspectives. To claim middle-class white male economic opportunities, white women leaders attacked traditional roles that had made the rearing of children and homemaking their only proper activities. This role had been an option only for middle class white women, however, and what they perceived as a domestic trap seemed an unimaginable luxury for working class white women and women of color. Although the feminst movement was slow to acknowledge its racism and class bias, it did focus public attention on the experiences of women.

Like the Black Power movement, feminism sought to change both laws and culture. Examining universities' offerings, feminists found that courses in history, anthropology, sociology, literature, and medicine often ignored women altogether or offered only stereotypes. As feminism demanded better books by and about women, publishers responded with many new titles in fiction, biography, and autobiography. The call for a new scholarship that would examine women's historical roles and contributions to culture developed into Women's Studies programs.

Black Studies and Women's Studies thus revised university courses. As part of this ongoing creative re-examination, scholars have in the last twenty-five years rediscovered many previously lost or undervalued materials. Oxford University Press, for instance, has published twenty-five volumes of literary works by African American women—works from the nineteenth century, when for more than fifty years, it was a crime for African Americans to learn to read or write.

Literature as well as politics developed both black separatist and feminist movements. In the early 1960s, the Black Arts movement denounced traditional European and Anglo-American forms and techniques as inappropriate for African American experience. These forms did not develop, they argued, to express African American experience and would therefore distort it. The Black Arts movement called on artists to develop new forms for the new themes of black experience, and to create art that would have an immediate political effect. In *Black Art*, for instance, Maulana Karenga called for art to "expose the enemy, praise the people, and support the revolution" (*Norton Anthology of African American Literature* 1974). In its commitment to "expose," this art carried on the tradition of black protest literature.

At the same time, considerable feminist literature critiqued male presentations of traditional subjects or introduced new subjects. Female characters emerged from their traditional secondary positions—the main male character's mother, wife, mistress, or child—to heroines in their own right. As women writers presented female physical experiences previously considered unpublishable, fiction began to include menstruation, pregnancy, childbirth, abortion, and sexuality. Much of this literature protested against the legal and social constraints on women's development.

In joining the Black Arts and feminist protests against racist and sexist injustice, *The Bluest Eye* significantly expanded American literature. Before 1970, American novels about racism had concentrated on adults and literature about incest had remained almost entirely on a symbolic level. *The Bluest Eye* expands these treatments in two ways. First, it analyzes the destructive psychological effects of racism on both children and adults. Second, it explores familial rape much more thoroughly and realistically than earlier novels. In its brilliant synthesis, *The Bluest Eye* shows the interconnectedness of racism, psychological damage, and rape.

The novel develops the emotional rationale for some of the cultural changes sought by the political movements of the 1960s. Activists called for black dolls, for example, to help African American children build self-esteem. The "Black is beautiful" movement enlarged on this idea, advocating pride in black skin and African or African American features. In *The Bluest Eye*, the absence of black dolls—and the inescapable presence of white ones—is presented as part of what makes the main character, Pecola, feel invisible. Further, the novel presents the emotional consequences of identifying ugliness with blackness, and clearly shows that too many beautiful, unique black children are destroyed by racist aesthetics.

Focusing on a twelve-year-old African American girl was an inherently feminist choice because few adult books up to 1970 had considered girls' lives important enough to be a novel's central interest. *The Bluest Eye* delineates how Pecola is repeatedly exposed to psychological violation, and how physical violation completes the psychological destruction. Significantly, this physical violation—rape—is a crime brought to the nation's consciousness by the feminist movement.

Nevertheless, *The Bluest Eye* diverges from what critics call protest literature in important ways. Historically, African American protest literature addressed largely white audiences. Antislavery literature, for example, had to speak to those with legal power rather than to slaves. For that reason, white characters generally figure prominently in such works. In addition, protest literature has often focused on the necessity for a particular political change, an end to slavery or an end to job discrimination, for instance. To reach a wide audience, such works have often been made as simple as possible in literary technique.

Morrison's choices for *The Bluest Eye* stand outside or at least extend considerably the conventional protest novel. The novel's political agenda is not simple because the cultural malaise that it depicts cannot be addressed with a mere law or two. And though the white world generates the racism whose destructive effects are examined, white characters play very minor roles, appearing in only two scenes. However, the black community has internalized the racist standards that these white characters represent. As a result, the community destroys its own most vulnerable members. Finally, although the novel's narrative technique is accessible to many readers, it does not present events chronologically, as most protest novels do. Instead, *The Bluest Eye* uses techniques of involved flashbacks and a cyclical return to particular events.

The social and literary movements of the 1960s provide a context for understanding this novel, but they certainly do not explain it. *The Bluest Eye* focuses on issues of its time, but develops them with transcendent psychological profundity and moral intensity. *The Bluest Eye* goes beyond the mindset of its own time to establish many of the basic terms for subsequent discussions of racism and psychology.

GENRE AND NARRATIVE TECHNIQUE

In *The Bluest Eye* Morrison expands a conventional literary genre, the *bildungsroman*. A *bildungsroman* recounts how an individual, often an extraordinary person, grows up. The *bildungsroman* has sometimes focused on artists, for example, or on especially intelligent or virtuous heroes. Novels focused on more ordinary people often show a world in which their characters are the victims of powerful social or natural forces; individual personality is not the focus. (These novels belong to the literary movement called naturalism.) In Pecola and Claudia, *The Bluest Eye* focuses on ordinary African American girls and claims for them the status of earlier heroines in the *bildungsroman*. At the same time that it illustrates the girls' struggles with the social forces of racism and poverty, the novel embraces individual personality by detailed characterization. The destruction of Pecola's personality is the novel's tragedy; the survival of Claudia's personality, its triumph.

The novel opens with two prologues. In the first, the omniscient narrator foreshadows the progressive destruction of Pecola Breedlove by showing how a familiar story appears to her at three different times. This story—about Mother and Father and their children Dick, Jane, and Sally—comes from primers, books used to teach children to read during the 1940s and 1950s in the United States and Canada. The first telling of the story uses standard spaces and punctuation. The second uses much smaller spaces between the words and omits both capital letters and punctuation, so that the sentences run together. The third version runs together not only the sentences but the words. The breakdown of order in the language of the story suggests the breakdown of order in Pecola's mind. Various parts of the third version of the story reappear throughout the novel to highlight the contrast between Pecola's family experiences and those of the primer's idealized white family.

The second prologue comes from Claudia MacTeer's consciousness. Claudia tells the reader Pecola's eventual fate and suggests that her tragedy corresponds to an interruption of nature's cycle, a spring season in which nothing grows. Noting that the why of Pecola's fate is hard to deal with, Claudia decides to tell only how it occurred. In this way, Morrison's narrative technique tells readers to find the why in the how.

Four sections—"Autumn," "Winter," "Spring," and "Summer"—follow the prologues. Like the prologues, these developmental sections alternate between two viewpoints. Claudia MacTeer speaks in first-person ("I") about experiences in her childhood, particularly those connected with Pecola Breedlove. The omniscient narrator tells the reader about events that Claudia could not have seen (such as happenings in the Breedlove house) or things that Claudia could not have known (the history of Pecola's parents, Pauline and Cholly, for example). Omniscient narration also lets us know what characters are thinking. In "Summer," for instance, the reader overhears what appears to be a conversation between Pecola and another child. The dialogue is printed in italics, however, to distinguish it from other conversations because Pecola is alone. The omniscient narrator has taken the reader into Pecola's thoughts. Driven to insanity by her unmet need for love, Pecola has invented a companion for herself. The italicized dialogue records Pecola's conversation with this imaginary friend. The omniscient narration provides the reader with a descriptive and analytical context for Claudia's personal, emotional memories.

PLOT DEVELOPMENT

As part of the overall contrast between one girl's survival and another's destruction, each seasonal section of the novel includes materials about Claudia MacTeer and Pecola Breedlove. Every section either presents their experiences directly or explores the reasons that their experiences diverge. "Autumn" shows the relationships within the MacTeer family and those in the Breedlove family. In "Winter," both narrators' stories testify to racist damage to the African American community. That community then unconsciously uses internalized racist standards to psychologically injure Pecola. "Spring" has a dual function. First, it shows the vulnerability of the young girls to a largely brutal environment. Second, it explores the histories of the surrounding adults who both make up that environment and are the girls' only protection from it. The shortest section, "Summer," presents the fruition of the circumstances detailed in the preceding three seasons.

"Autumn" contrasts the MacTeer and the Breedlove households, family environments that encourage Claudia and doom Pecola. This contrast is heightened when Pecola stays with Claudia's family for a few days after the Breedloves are evicted from their home. Although Morrison's presentation contrasts the two girls' childhoods, it does not make them into opposites. Pecola's experience is a nightmare, but Claudia's memories of her childhood do not resemble the sugar-candy lives of the children in the Dick-Jane-Sally story. Instead, she remembers that her parents, like all others of that time and place, were verbally rough with their children. She recounts, for example, her mother's rant when Pecola drinks an entire quart of milk—a serious strain on the MacTeer budget. However, Claudia also remembers her parents' emotional commitment to her and her older sister Frieda, a commitment that the Breedloves are incapable of making to the unlucky Pecola.

The omniscient narrator shows the barrenness of the Breedloves' family life, and its origins in racism. The Breedloves do not love themselves or one another. Pecola asks a question that does not generally occur to children who are loved: "I mean, how do you get somebody to love you?" (29). In accounts presented as typical of African American experience, the novel depicts a furniture store forcing the Breedloves to accept damaged goods, for example. In another instance, when Pecola buys candy, the white shopkeeper will not even touch her hand to take her money. These experiences destroy the Breedloves' confidence in themselves. Gradually they accept racism's message that they are ugly and inferior.

The African American community as a whole shares these racist experiences, but some have supports that the particularly vulnerable Breedloves lack. The community senses the Breedloves' self-hatred and encourages it by agreeing that the Breedloves are ugly. This cycle of mutually reinforcing communal disapproval and self-hatred climaxes in "Summer." In "Autumn" the Breedlove family as a whole is scapegoated, but in "Summer," when Pecola alone is chosen as scapegoat, her personality collapses into insanity

"Winter" depicts the black community's internalization of white racist standards, and their effects on Pecola. Claudia recounts the community's idolatry of Maureen Peal, a light-skinned, middle-class child. Significantly, Maureen first befriends and then verbally attacks Pecola. The omniscient narrator shows Geraldine, the middle-class mother of Junior (one of Pecola's schoolmates), projecting on Pecola everything that she is ashamed of, everything that whites use to despise African Americans. When Pecola visits Junior, Geraldine separates the children by throwing Pecola out of their home.

In "Spring" Claudia briefly narrates what happens when the MacTeers' lodger, Mr. Henry, gropes at her sister Frieda's breasts. When Frieda tells her parents, they are enraged and throw Mr. Henry out of their house. Claudia and Frieda believe that they must get Frieda some alcohol, the only force they can think of that will preserve Frieda from being "ruined" (a 1940s euphemism for sexual experience). Their quest for liquor is one of the novel's few comic notes.

The omniscient narrator relates Pecola's far more serious experience of sexual assault. Raped by her father and emotionally abandoned by her mother, Pecola falls prey to Soaphead Church, who promises her what she thinks will make her lovable, blue eyes.

To tell how the Breedlove parents come to fail their daughter Pecola, the omniscient narrator explores their histories and the development of their marriage. Cholly, Pecola's father, has never been part of a family, and he suffers an early, specifically sexual racist humiliation. Pauline, Pecola's mother, also suffers from isolation. Although she comes from a functional family, she loses both that family and the southern black community when she and Cholly move North in search of economic opportunity. Although Cholly and Pauline initially love one another, their love cannot withstand poverty, racism, and isolation from the community. Too countrified to fit into Northern urban women's circles, Pauline spends most of her time at the movies. From these films, she absorbs racist ideas of female beauty and learns to dislike her own appearance. When she looks at her new-born daughter, Pauline "knowed she [the baby] was ugly" (100), for she sees herself in her child.

Emotionally abandoning her own family, Pauline creates an alternate, fantasy-family from her workplace. Pauline does domestic work for a white family, the Fishers. At their home, she has access to beautiful material goods; as their servant, she can use their status to deal with tradespeople who do not respect her in her own right. Pauline's emotional loyalties lie with the white children rather than with her own. When Pecola accidentally makes a mess and burns herself, Pauline knocks her down and runs to comfort the white child frightened by the commotion. Appropriately, Pecola has been trained to call Pauline by a name that does not make emotional claims. To her daughter, Pauline is not "Mother" but "Mrs. Breedlove."

The wider community also fails Pecola. Having absorbed the idea that she is ugly, and knowing that she is unloved, Pecola desperately wants the blue eyes that she understands will make a child lovable in American society. She takes her request to Soaphead Church, a fake conjure man. Because his experience of growing up in the West Indies resembles Cholly and Pauline's experience in the United States, he too lacks a solid sense of self. In fact, Soaphead has so little confidence that he can function sexually only with little girls. Nevertheless, he recognizes how racism has damaged Pecola. Unlike Cholly and Pauline, Soaphead can articulate what has happened to him, and to Pecola. In a grotesquely humorous counterpart to Claudia's narration, he expresses his outrage at racism in a letter to God.

In the first scene of "Summer," Claudia remembers the disastrous events leading to Pecola's madness. The community condemns Cholly, Pecola's father, for raping his twelve-year-old daughter. But the same community also ostracizes her, claiming that she must be guilty in some way. Frieda and Claudia share the community's attitude toward Pecola, but they try to protect her baby by casting a spell. Naturally, their efforts do not succeed. (As the reader knows from the beginning of Claudia's narration in "Autumn," the baby dies.) In the next scene, the point of view shifts from Claudia to the omniscient narrator. Entering Pecola's mind, the reader overhears a conversation. Although the dialogue sounds like a discussion between Pecola and another real person, no one else is present. Pecola has become insane. Lacking love from her family and her community, she has created an imaginary friend who seems real to her.

In the final passage, the viewpoint again moves back to Claudia. An adult now, Claudia considers the lasting damage to Pecola. In a symbolic representation of her ongoing isolation, the still-crazy Pecola continues to live at the edge of the town that rejected her. Seeing her, Claudia meditates on the community's—and her own—participation in Pecola's tragedy.

CHARACTER DEVELOPMENT

The Bluest Eye contains two characters more fully developed than any of the others, Pecola and Claudia. The adult Claudia tells the story of the year when Pecola was twelve, she was nine, and her sister Frieda was ten years old. In most of *The Bluest Eye*, the reader observes the three girls and responds to Claudia's understanding of them. The whole novel concerns the building and destruction of Pecola's personality. Because the novel aims at telling the why of Pecola's life through its how, the agents of her destruction—her parents and Soaphead Church—must remain comprehensible people rather than monsters (round rather than flat characters). In some important scenes, readers simply watch these characters. Generally, however, the omniscient narrator summarizes most of each character's history in direct fashion, and frequently reveals their motivation to maintain the reader's sympathy or understanding.

The secondary characters are types, meant to represent certain traits or responses but not to evoke the intense emotion or complex understanding that comes from fuller characterization. Their importance lies in their interactions with Pecola. At its best, this interaction is merely neutral. The novel's whores—China, Poland, and Marie—entertain Pecola with stories, and she in turn respects them as the more favored children do not. The narrator and her sister, for example, call Marie the "Maginot Line" whereas Pecola calls her "Miss Marie." (The actual Maginot Line consisted of fortifications built by France after World War I. These were intended to protect France from a second German attack. In fact, during World War II the Germans simply went around the fortifications by invading from a conquered, previously neutral country. The nickname "Maginot Line" therefore implies spread-out physique, expense, and uselessness.) The narrator distinguishes these whores from literary and social stereotypes of prostitutes with hearts of gold or prostitutes as sweet victims. The three women tolerate Pecola because she runs errands for them.

More socially respectable characters treat Pecola much more harshly. Maureen Peal symbolizes a life of privilege based on conformity to white ideals of beauty. The entire neighborhood fawns on the little girl with the "good" hair, the long, straight braids. Maureen enjoys her middle-class status, signified most clearly by her new clothing in a neighborhood where almost all children wear hand-me-downs. She cruelly insults Pecola's color and her poverty.

A grown-up, more consciously vicious version of Maureen, Geraldine exemplifies black middle-class hatred of poor blacks. The description of Geraldine in fact begins with "They come from Mobile. From Aiken" (67), making clear her function as the representative of a group rather than an individual. Even children who are outcasts, like Geraldine's son Junior, abuse Pecola. Pretending to be friendly, Junior invites Pecola into his home. He then ridicules her and uses her visit as a pretext for killing the cat that receives all Geraldine's love. Naturally, Geraldine vents her rage on Pecola. Geraldine and Mr. Yacobowski (the racist white shopkeeper who will not touch Pecola's hand) are flat, one-dimensional characters.

Those more important to Pecola receive more detailed characterization. Cholly Breedlove is abandoned by his parents and cared for by his great-aunt Jimmy until her death, when he is thirteen. At Aunt Jimmy's funeral, he meets Darlene, a member of his extended family. Cholly begins to enjoy a sexual experience, his first, with Darlene when they are interrupted by white men hunting in the area. These white men force Cholly and Darlene to continue sexual intercourse while they watch. Darlene removes herself emotionally from the scene, a passive victim. Cholly focuses his rage and humiliation on Darlene rather than on the armed white men, who could kill him for any sign of resentment. In this way, he learns to displace his hatred of racist oppression from white men to black women.

Cholly's alienation deepens when he cannot secure a home after great-aunt Jimmy's death. He undertakes a long, difficult journey on foot to find his father, but is ultimately disappointed. His father, preoccupied with a craps game, does not recognize his son. Although Cholly later marries Pauline and has children, he has no foundation on which to build his family because he has never experienced parental love or had a male role model. Poverty and oppression make family life difficult, and Cholly responds by drinking heavily and physically abusing Pauline. Eventually, in a confused mix of emotions including love, desire for control, and delight in doing a forbidden act, he rapes Pecola. Cholly dies in the poorhouse, separated from his family.

Pauline Breedlove is particularly vulnerable to racism, like Cholly, but for a different reason. As a small child, she acquires a permanent limp that sets her apart from the rest of her family. Initially she loves Cholly and enjoys their sexual life. Gradually, however, her frail self-image erodes under the racist images that she absorbs from movies. By the time Pecola is born, Pauline unconsciously hates herself so much that she cannot love any part of herself, including her daughter. Pauline and Cholly encourage the worst in each other. Pauline uses her religion as a weapon to define Cholly as a lazy, drunken devil; in her mind, his wickedness makes her righteous. Pauline escapes the poverty and squalor of her own home through her job as a housekeeper for a white family, the Fishers. She emotionally abandons her own household and children in favor of the Fishers. Her rejection of her children climaxes in her refusal to believe Pecola's account of being raped by Cholly.

Sammy Breedlove, Pecola's older brother, tries unsuccessfully to establish some order in the Breedlove household. After helping his mother physically defend herself against Cholly, he hopes that she will kill her husband, who has been knocked unconscious. He does not understand that his mother will never eliminate Cholly because her self-image depends on Cholly's continued bad behavior. He does understand, however, that the household dynamics will not alter. He responds by running away from what he cannot change.

The central focus, Pecola Breedlove provides the title of the novel. Growing up in a loveless household, twelve-year-old Pecola longs for the blue eyes that she believes will make her lovable. At the end of the novel, Pecola believes that she has been given these blue eyes, but her belief merely indicates her insanity. Pecola goes mad because nearly every other character victimizes her, and she has no emotional support. As with the blue eyes, Pecola can realize her desire for a friend only in madness. In her last scene, Pecola is carrying on a conversation, but no one else is present. Schizoid, she has separated into two personalities. This madness persists into the novel's present, when Mrs. Breedlove and Pecola still live on the edge of the town.

Although children are cruel to Pecola, their actions would be far less important if adults nurtured Pecola. Pecola's mother, however, explicitly rejects her in favor of the Fishers' daughter, and her father rapes her. Instead of rallying to her support, the surrounding community gossips about whether this twelve-year-old might have been responsible for her father's actions. The community has always accepted the Breedloves' understanding of themselves as ugly and inferior, and its treatment of Pecola simply intensifies that attitude.

Elihue Micah Whitcomb, informally known as Soaphead Church, helps to push Pecola into madness. Like Cholly, Soaphead's core personality has been eroded by white racism. Soaphead comes from a Caribbean island, a former colony of Great Britain. His formal education confirms the self-hatred implied by his family's desire to marry only those lighter in skin color. Racism prevents Soaphead from getting the professional job that his education merits, so he emigrates to the United States, where he supports himself by pretending to be a hoodoo man. Having failed sexually with mature women—his wife leaves him before his journey to the United States—Soaphead uses little girls for his sexual gratification.

Although he does not physically abuse Pecola, he uses her. Soaphead despises a mangy local dog, but he lacks the courage to kill it. Instead, as part of the magic that is supposed to give her blue eyes, he gives the innocent Pecola poisoned meat to feed the dog. Because of his education, Soaphead can articulate racism's damage. He writes a long letter to God, indignantly protesting the conditions that make blue eyes the heart's desire of a black girl.

Mrs. MacTeer, Claudia and Frieda's mother, contrasts strongly with Pecola's mother. Mrs. MacTeer loves her children and provides them with an orderly, disciplined world. Her daughters are not allowed to visit the whores, for instance, whereas Pecola spends most of her free time with them.

To help support her family, Mrs. MacTeer takes in a boarder, Mr. Henry. Mr. Henry proves unworthy of her trust. He not only brings in prostitutes in Mrs. MacTeer's absence, but he sexually gropes Frieda. Mr. and Mrs. MacTeer's active, supportive responses are completely different from Mr. and Mrs. Breedlove's behavior to Pecola.

Frieda MacTeer is Claudia's older sister. By presenting Frieda's psychological reality as well as her own, Claudia depicts a later stage of the process by which black girls react to white standards of beauty.

Claudia MacTeer narrates a considerable portion of the novel. From the vantage point of an adult, she recalls the conditions of her childhood that led to Pecola's lasting madness. Remembering her sister, herself, and Pecola, Claudia retraces their encounters with the racist standards that deny their African beauty. Claudia's portrait of her own family shows the love that was not available to Pecola in the Breedlove household. This love brings Claudia and Frieda safely into womanhood. Looking back, Claudia holds the entire community, herself included, responsible for failing Pecola.

THEMATIC ISSUES

The Bluest Eye studies the powerfully destructive effects of institutional racism on individual African Americans and on the African American community. Institutional racism means something more and different from prejudice in individual people. Personal prejudice is manifested in unjust, cruel actions by individuals. Institutional racism, on the other hand, can be unintentionally perpetuated by people who simply haven't thought about racial issues, or people who cannot progress beyond what they were taught. Institutional racism refers, for example, to systematic exclusion of a whole racial group from cultural studies and histories, or the presentation of the group in a way that makes them seem inferior. When the shopkeeper Mr. Yacobowski doesn't want to touch Pecola's hand because she's black, that's individual prejudice. When the standard textbooks in American schools before 1970 did not mention African Americans, except to say that they were enslaved until 1865—when Pecola has only Dick, Jane, and Sally as models—that is institutional racism.

In *The Bluest Eye*, Morrison makes a major contribution to American culture by showing the psychological damage done by institutional racism. Institutional racism, supported by acts of personal prejudice, erodes the self-esteem of all the characters as they internalize the mainstream's picture of them as unimportant, inferior, and ugly. Pecola's parents and Soaphead learn to hate themselves, and thus lose or never develop their potential to be responsible, nurturing adults for African American children. Even Claudia, who shows the strongest resistance to the attack on her self-image, recounts going through a stage of accepting a racist picture of herself. *The Bluest Eye* shows how institutional racism infiltrates and destroys the psychological health of African Americans.

In the novel, black girls see few images of themselves, and those are demeaning. Only white dolls are available, for instance. Education is implicated in racism immediately by the presence of the all-white primer story at the beginning of the novel, and later by Pecola's dismal experiences in school. Even more important, however, is the informal education conveyed by the movies. The pervasive influence of Hollywood films runs through the novel. The MacTeers' boarder flatters Frieda and Claudia by pretending to mistake them for Greta Garbo and Ginger Rogers, white movie stars. Pecola drinks as much (white) milk as she can from the MacTeers' Shirley Temple mug. (Temple was a white child-star of the 1930s.) Mrs. Breedlove learns to despise her own looks while watching romantic movies featuring Jean Harlow, a platinum blonde actress. When a black person, Bill Bojangles for example, appears in these movies, he literally dances attendance on the white characters. Only one movie with an African American theme is mentioned, *Imitation of Life*, and it concerns the black characters' hatred of blackness. The movies' message denigrates African American women's importance, their beauty, and their worthiness to be loved. In the absence of any other message from school or from home, Pecola yearns to have "the bluest eye," the epitome of white beauty, so that she will be lovable.

The Bluest Eye extends its critique of white racism beyond the United States, to include its effects in the West Indies (the Caribbean), where the British colonized the islands and institutionalized racist ideas. The development of Elihue Micah Whitcomb into Soaphead Church reiterates many of the themes present in Pecola's experience. West Indian society of Soaphead's time idolized light skin; its educational system included only British history and forms.

Racism permeates every fiber of those whom it destroys; no aspect is too private to escape. Even those aspects of humanity usually considered instinctual—sexual drive and protection of the young—are distorted or destroyed in Soaphead, Cholly, and Pauline. The male characters' combination of perverted sexuality and diminished ability to protect makes them particularly damaging to little girls. Soaphead preys financially on his whole community, for example, but he sexually abuses only vulnerable girls. Cholly's sexuality is more obviously violent. The interruption of his first sexual experience by white racists teaches him to connect sex with power, violence, and hatred. In the novel's most horrific example of victims creating new victims, Cholly tries to show love for his daughter, but he ends up raping her.

Black women suffer these same losses, though the manifestations are different. Pauline's sexual loss is greater even than Soaphead's, for she barely remembers sexual pleasure. For women, sexuality is inevitably tied up with pregnancy, so that sexual attitudes must influence motherhood. The supposedly inborn desire of a mother to protect her children has clearly been obliterated in Cholly's mother, who abandons him. Pauline also rejects her child, considering her ugly from the moment of her birth. Withdrawing all emotional support from her daughter, Pauline refuses to believe that Cholly has raped Pecola.

Though *The Bluest Eye* condemns racism, it does not present the problem as limited to white people. The novel includes white characters in only two scenes (the shopkeeper and the three hunters who brutalize Cholly). Much of the damage inflicted on Pecola comes from African American adults who have internalized racist standards—her parents, Geraldine, and Soaphead. The book shows not only black proponents of white racism, of course, but black characters who resist it as well. The MacTeers maintain their marriage, protect their children, and even offer Pecola some shelter. Their daughter Frieda defends Pecola from schoolmates' ridicule. Both Frieda and Claudia want very much for Pecola's baby to live, for a black baby to defy the black community's pronouncement that it would be better off dead. Claudia's strong family supports her early independence—she hates white dolls, for example—and enables her to survive psychically whole.

As an adult reflecting on Pecola's fate, Claudia emphasizes the role of the community in scapegoating Pecola: "All of us—all who knew her—felt so wholesome after we cleaned ourselves on her. We were so beautiful when we stood astride her ugliness. Her simplicity decorated us, her guilt sanctified us, her pain made us glow with health, her awkwardness made us think we had a sense of humor. . . . We honed our egos on her" (159). In the novel's last paragraph, Claudia considers the "assassination" of Pecola: "I even think now that the land of the entire country was hostile to marigolds that year. This soil is bad for certain kinds of flowers. Certain seeds it will not nurture, certain fruit it will not bear, and when the land kills of its own volition, we acquiesce and say the victim had no right to live. We are wrong, of course, but it doesn't matter. It's too late" (160). Perhaps the black community cannot change the land (the society) for its seeds (its children), but it need never call that barren land right and the destroyed child wrong. Pecola's story is an African American female tragedy. But her story is told by strong, surviving voices that are also African American and female, the voices of Claudia MacTeer and Toni Morrison.

A MYTHIC OR ARCHETYPAL READING

Scholars have long known that certain patterns recur in the oral stories and written literature of many different cultures. Joseph Campbell's *The Hero With a Thousand Faces* details one of the best known of these mythic patterns, the heroic quest. In the 1930s, Karl Jung, a psychologist, called these patterns manifestations of "archetypes." Jung believed that human beings share what he called a "collective unconscious," and that the cross-cultural similarity of stories occurs because all artists have access to the same unconscious images.

Literary critics use "archetype" to describe recurring patterns without necessarily believing in the collective unconscious. These critics accept the existence of cross-cultural similarities without knowing their origins. Most myths have archetypal patterns; that is, myths from one culture resemble myths from others. Archetypal criticism assumes that because we are familiar with these patterns already, we experience deep, powerful emotional responses when we encounter new expressions of archetypes. For example, consider a story about a baby born at home to a poor family in the winter because the family lacked money for a hospital. If that child grew to have extraordinary influence over others, and died young to save someone else, a Christian might have a profound emotional reaction to the story because it parallels the story of Christ.

Since early in the twentieth century writers have been aware of and interested in mythic patterns, often using analyses of myths gathered at the end of the nineteenth century, such as Sir James Frazer's *The Golden Bough*. For a group of writers known as the modernists, myth became a central means of exploring the life of their times. Two important facts about Morrison's education combine to suggest that archetypal criticism might be a particularly rich approach to her novels. Morrison wrote her master's thesis on two of the great modernist writers, William Faulkner and Virginia Woolf. As an undergraduate, she minored in Classics. Morrison would thus be familiar with both Greek myths themselves and with modernist attitudes toward myth.

Modernists generally took one of two attitudes toward myth. In his novel *Ulysses*, James Joyce uses the myth of the *Odyssey* to show that, although all the details differ from the original stories, the lives of ordinary people in his own place and time (Ireland in the early twentieth century) participate in mythic patterns. Here, myth is used to dignify and ennoble the everyday. When the poet T. S. Eliot looked at *Ulysses*, however, he did not see the ordinary ennobled by myth; he saw myth debased by what Western culture had become. Eliot himself uses myth to show the degeneracy of modern times in works such as *The Wasteland*. There, the juxtaposition of classical myth with everyday life merely shows the inadequacy of modern society. For Eliot, contemporary people look ridiculous when viewed by mythic standards.

Morrison does not adopt either modernist position on myth but develops a more complex approach. In *The Bluest Eye* and her subsequent novels, Morrison consistently reverses the relative importance of myth and human experience that underlies the modernists' views. For her, the myths are important because our everyday lives participate in their patterns; human beings themselves, rather than the mythic stories, are of primary importance.

The Bluest Eye calls attention to its relation to Greek myth when Claudia begins, "Quiet as it's kept, there were no marigolds in the fall of 1941" (9) and then makes the more general case that "our seeds were not the only ones that did not sprout; nobody's did." The Greek myth of Demeter and Persephone (Ceres and Proserpina in the Roman adaptation) recounts a year when nothing grew. One such similarity is not enough to base a reading on, of course, but two might suffice, particularly if the second is an essential part of both the myth and the novel.

In the myth, Demeter is the goddess of agriculture; she is responsible for the fruitfulness of the earth. Human beings are dependent on Demeter for their ability to grow food. One day, when Demeter's daughter Persephone is picking flowers in a meadow, the god Hades kidnaps her and takes her back to his realm, the underworld of the dead, where he rapes her. Not knowing where her daughter is, Demeter goes into such deep mourning that she ignores the prayers of human beings, and nothing grows on the earth. Seeing that the world will starve, the other gods intercede. They find Persephone and promise that if she has not eaten anything in the underworld, she may return to Demeter. Unfortunately, Persephone has eaten six seeds from a pomegranate. The gods work out a compromise by which Persephone spends six months of the year in the underworld, during which Demeter mourns and we have fall and winter, and six months with Demeter, during which we have spring and summer.

The novel and the myth share much more than a barren season. Pecola has the Persephone role; Cholly recreates the Hades role. The description of his effect on Pecola explicitly connects him to Hades' world of the dead: "But his touch was fatal, and the something he gave her filled the matrix of her agony with death" (159). In both myth and novel, rape is central. Claudia thinks that the reason her seeds will not grow is that Pecola is having a baby by her father—the reason for the failed crop is the same as that in the myth: rape has blasted the earth's ability to reproduce.

Despite those similarities, however, *The Bluest Eye* diverges from the myth in a critical way. The myth is often presented simply as an explanation of why the earth has seasons, but it has less obvious meanings as well. The Demeter-Persephone myth shows the power of the mother-daughter bond and the critical importance of mothers to the earth's prosperity.

Demeter is heartsick, perhaps deranged by her grief for Persephone. Mrs. Breedlove, on the other hand, abandons her daughter emotionally before the rape, most clearly in the scene in the Fishers' kitchen when she comforts the white child and pushes her own injured daughter to the floor. (This scene parallels the rape scene, which also takes place in a kitchen, where Cholly knocks Pecola to the floor.) The mother figures of the myth and the novel represent not just different but opposing attitudes toward the daughters. Because the similarities to the myth are suggested first, the reader expects Mrs. Breedlove to play the Demeter role, but the novel reveals her to be as destructive as Cholly, the Hades figure. Thus, *The Bluest Eye* is structured to increase the reader's sense of the dissonance between the archetypal story and the novel.

The novel thus plays off the definition of an archetypal story. Archetypes were originally supposed to be universal patterns, not only cross-cultural but in the structure of all human beings' minds, in the collective unconscious. Although few now believe in the collective unconscious, many believe that archetypes present our most basic desires and instincts. To many, the appeal of the archetype is that it transcends particular societies and speaks to some shared core that makes us human. *The Bluest Eye*, however, denies the existence of a core that remains untouched or unconstructed by social conditions. Social forces, specifically racism, can distort or destroy even those qualities, like mother-love, that we believe fundamental to humanity.

The world of *The Bluest Eye* is not devoid of mother-love, of course. In archetypal depictions, mother-love is not a domestic quality, expressed in home-baked sweets and interior decoration, but an elemental force. Mrs. MacTeer should be understood in this context: her purpose is not to be genteel or to instill gentility in her children; rather, she must protect them and equip them for survival in a hostile environment. Indeed, Mrs. MacTeer not only nurses Claudia through pneumonia but fiercely protects their home in the Mr. Henry episode. Significantly, Pecola enters physical womanhood under Mrs. MacTeer's tutelage. Although both Frieda and Pecola are subject to sexual abuse, parental engagement and support limit Frieda's vulnerability. (Frieda is groped, but Pecola suffers actual rape.) Mother-love cannot protect absolutely, but it offers essential sustenance.

But against Mrs. MacTeer, the novel presents not only Mrs. Breedlove, but Cholly's mother and Geraldine, who abandon or abuse their children. Geraldine is middle-class and Mrs. MacTeer poor: clearly the destruction of mother-love is not due solely to poverty. The background myth of Demeter and Persephone accents the destructive power of racism, which obliterates mother, child, and—if unchecked—the fruitfulness of the earth.

Sula
(1973)

Toni Morrison's two earliest novels, *The Bluest Eye* and *Sula*, depict the growth and development of female characters. In the first, a black girl named Pecola must bear the consequences of her community's internalized racism, and she is driven to madness. To find hope in *The Bluest Eye*, the reader must focus on the female narrator who grew up with Pecola, and who has survived. *Sula* also examines female identity, but with less vulnerable heroines. Whereas Pecola's isolation leads to her doom, Sula Peace and Nel Wright live in stable families and form a friendship that supports their growth into womanhood. In addition, Morrison's examination of the environment for this friendship, the black community, is much more nuanced and complex than in *The Bluest Eye*. Though it has tragic elements, a simple term such as "tragedy" cannot accurately represent the wide range of experience depicted in *Sula*. Above all, *Sula* concerns persistence—of women's friendship, of individual growth, of spirit.

NARRATIVE STRUCTURE

Sula portrays the friendship of Nel Wright and Sula Peace in the context of their community, called the Bottom. The Bottom was an African American settlement in the hills above Medallion, Ohio, until it was bulldozed for a golf course. Before presenting critical events in the life of the Bottom from 1919 to 1965, the narrator meditates on the meaning of this community's life and death.

Part One contains chapters titled with consecutive years from 1919 to 1923; its final chapter skips to 1927. Part Two's chapters include 1937, 1939, 1940, and 1941 before making a similar jump to 1965. "1919" describes the life of Shadrack, a World War I veteran who creates a peculiar annual ritual, National Suicide Day, to control his fear of death and change. "1920" focuses on the history of Nel Wright's grandmother and her mother Helene, and Nel's realization of her own personhood. (Although Sula is the title character, her name does not appear until near the end of "1920.") In a similar history of Sula Peace's family, "1921" concentrates on the character of Sula's grandmother Eva, who shapes the environment in which Sula grows up. "1922" presents the origins and development of the essential bond between Nel and Sula as well as Shadrack's special regard for Sula. "1923" contains the death of Sula's mother Hannah and the growing estrangement of Sula and Eva. In "1927," Nel marries Jude Greene and Sula leaves the Bottom from the wedding reception, not to return for ten years.

Part Two opens with Sula's return to the Bottom, where she quickly outrages community standards by showing no interest in marriage, putting Eva in a nursing home, and having sex with Nel's husband, Jude. (Jude soon leaves the Bottom.) Against the background of growing community disapproval of Sula's sexual freedom, "1939" examines the course of Sula's only serious romantic relationship. In "1940," Nel visits the dying Sula, and after her own death, Sula reflects that she wants to tell Nel about the experience. "1941" describes a disastrous accident (a collapsed tunnel) that kills many townspeople who have mockingly joined Shadrack's National Suicide Day parade. Shadrack himself escapes. "1965" centers on Nel. Mourning the deterioration of the Bottom, Nel visits the nursing home where the woman who was one of the town's strongest forces, Eva, still lives. On her way home she senses Sula's presence and realizes for the first time that her long mourning for the loss of her husband Jude has been mistaken; she has really been missing Sula. The novel closes with her cry of grief.

NARRATIVE TECHNIQUE

Although *Sula* is arranged in chronological order, it does not construct a linear story with the causes of each new plot event clearly visible in the preceding chapter. Instead, *Sula* uses "juxtaposition," the technique through which collages are put together. The effects of a collage on the viewer depend on unusual combinations of pictures, or on unusual arrangements such as overlapping. The pictures of a collage don't fit smoothly together, yet they create a unified effect. The "pictures" of *Sula's* collage are separate events or character sketches. Together, they show the friendship of Nel and Sula as part of the many complicated, overlapping relationships that make up the Bottom.

Morrison presents the novel from the perspective of an omniscient narrator—one who knows all the characters' thoughts and feelings. An omniscient narrator usually puts the reader in the position of someone viewing a conventional portrait or landscape rather than a collage. (In such situations, the viewer can perceive the unity of the whole work with only a glance.) To create the collage-like effect of *Sula*, the omniscient narrator never reveals the thoughts of all the characters at one time. Instead, from chapter to chapter, she chooses a different point-of-view character, so that a different person's consciousness and experience dominate a particular incident or section. In addition, the narrator sometimes moves beyond the consciousness of single, individual characters, to reveal what groups in the community think and feel. On the rare occasions when it agrees unanimously, she presents the united community's view. As in *The Bluest Eye* and *Jazz*, the community has such a direct impact on individuals that it amounts to a character.

In narrative technique for *Sula*, Morrison draws on a specifically modernist usage of juxtaposition. Modernism, discussed in Chapter 3, was the dominant literary movement during the first half of the twentieth century. Writers of this period abandoned the unifying, omniscient narrator of earlier literature to make literature more like life, in which each of us has to make our own sense of the world. Rather than passively receiving a smooth, connected story from an authoritative narrator, the reader is forced to piece together a coherent plot and meaning from more separated pieces of information.

Modernists experimented with many literary genres. For example, T. S. Eliot created his influential poem *The Wasteland* by juxtaposing quotations from other literary works and songs, interspersed with fragmentary narratives of original stories. Fiction uses an analogous technique of juxtaposition. Each successive chapter of William Faulkner's novel *As I Lay Dying*, for instance, drops the reader into a different character's consciousness without the direction or help of an omniscient narrator. To figure out the plot, the reader must work through the perceptions of characters who range from a seven-year-old boy to a madman. The abrupt, disturbing shifts from one consciousness to another are an intended part of the reader's experience. As with all literary techniques, juxtaposition is used to communicate particular themes. In *Cane*, a work that defies our usual definitions of literary genres, Jean Toomer juxtaposed poetry and brief prose sketches. In this way, *Cane* establishes its thematic contrast of rural black culture in the South and urban black culture of the North.

Morrison, who wrote her master's thesis on two modernists, Faulkner and Virginia Woolf, uses juxtaposition as a structuring device in *Sula*. Though relatively short for a novel, *Sula* has an unusually large number of chapters, eleven. This division into small pieces creates an intended choppiness, the uncomfortable sense of frequently stopping and starting. The content of the chapters accentuates this choppy rhythm. Almost every chapter shifts the focus from the story of the preceding chapter by changing the point-of-view character or introducing sudden, shocking events and delaying discussion of the characters' motives until later. In "1921," for example, Eva douses her son Plum with kerosene and burns him to death. Although the reader knows that Plum has become a heroin addict, Eva's reasoning is not revealed. When Hannah, naturally assuming that Eva doesn't know of Plum's danger, tells her that Plum is burning, the chapter ends with Eva's almost nonchalant "Is? My baby? Burning?" (48). Not until midway through the next chapter, "1923," does Hannah's questioning allow the reader to understand Eva's motivation. Juxtaposition thus heightens the reader's sense of incompleteness. Instead of providing quick resolution, juxtaposition introduces new and equally disturbing events.

Paradoxically, when an occasional chapter does contain a single story apparently complete in itself, it too contributes to the novel's overall choppy rhythm. In a novel using a simple, chronological mode of narration, each succeeding chapter would pick up where the last one left off, with the main characters now involved in a different incident, but in some clear way affected by their previous experience. In *Sula*, however, some characters figure prominently in one chapter and then fade entirely into the background. The first chapter centers on Shadrack, and although he appears twice more and has considerable psychic importance to Sula and symbolic importance to the novel, he is not an important actor again. In similar fashion, Helene Wright is the controlling presence of the third chapter, "1920," but barely appears in the rest of the book. These shifts are more unsettling than if Shadrack and Helene were ancestors of the other characters, generations removed, because the reader would then expect them to disappear. Their initial prominence and later shadowy presence contribute to the reader's feeling of disruption. The choppy narration of *Sula* expresses one of its major themes, the fragmentation of both individuals and the community.

PLOT DEVELOPMENT

Different plot events become important depending on what a reader chooses as the central theme of a novel. *Sula* offers several choices: the functioning and death of the Bottom, three generations of women in the Peace and Wright lines, the growth and development of Sula and Nel as individuals, the friendship of Sula and Nel, and the relationship between Sula and the Bottom. The character Sula unifies these thematic concerns, as the title suggests. Two factors heavily influence Sula's development: her friendship with Nel and her relationship to the rest of the Bottom. In turn, Sula is a defining force in the community and a continuing influence on Nel. (Even after Sula's death midway through the novel, Nel's character develops because of Sula.) *Sula* has a triple plot: the life of the community, the development of Sula, and the growth of Nel.

Sula begins with a wide focus. The novel starts by telling us of the death of a neighborhood, the Bottom. We then learn of its origin and the social conditions (slavery, racism) that created it and always affected it. *Sula* next presents the stories of Shadrack, Helene Wright, and Eva Peace. On the realistic level, Helene governs the Wright household (where Nel grows up) and Eva governs the Peace household (where Sula grows up). These major figures symbolically represent different forces active in the Bottom. The first plot developments thus delineate the environment for Sula's and Nel's lives.

Succeeding chapters present events critical to forming Sula's "experimental" personality, in the immediate context of the Peace household and in the larger context of the Bottom. The first event is Sula's meeting Nel; the second, the girls' involvement in the death of another child, Chicken Little; the third, Sula's overhearing that her mother does not love her.

Sula and Nel provide one another with support crucial to establishing and maintaining their identities in somewhat hostile contexts. Nel escapes her mother's stifling conformity to middle-class norms in the less conventional Peace household. With Nel, Sula experiences the sense of order and control not present in the Peace home, as well as the love that her mother cannot offer her. In a wider context, the girls' friendship originates in their separate discoveries of being "neither white nor male" and realizing that "all freedom and triumph was forbidden to them" (52). Nel and Sula thus join forces to affirm for each other the personal worth that the surrounding racism and sexism deny. When Nel and Sula silently agree to keep their involvement in a playmate's drowning a secret, their reliance on each other is confirmed. For each, the other is the only person who knows her completely.

Sula's connections to Nel and to the community weaken in chapters "1923" through "1941." Nel's path first diverges from Sula's in "1927," with her decision to marry Jude Greene. Sula leaves town directly from the wedding reception. When she returns ten years later, the reader sees that Sula and Nel have continued on different paths. In "1937," Sula and Nel represent two modes of being. Nel accepts usual social roles rather than identifying and acting on her own feelings. Her opposite, Sula consults only her own feelings and disregards all community expectations. Confrontations between these ideas of how to live generate most of the rest of the plot.

The first confrontation occurs by accident (when Nel walks in while Jude and Sula are having sex); the second, by Nel's design (when she visits Sula's deathbed). The third confrontation surprises Nel and is likely to surprise the reader too because it takes place many years after Sula's death, during Nel's visit to Eva in the nursing home.

On Sula's return in "1937," Nel realizes how much she has missed her friend's humor, originality, and emotional support. She does not join in the community's condemnation of Sula's sexual freedom and independence. (Sula insults the town by sleeping once and only once with each of its willing men.) When Nel finds Sula having sex with Jude, however, she too condemns Sula. After Sula is rumored to have slept with white men, she becomes a complete outcast. "1939," the last chapter focused mostly on Sula, shows her inability to maintain a stable, mature connection with a man even when she loves him. Nel sees Sula only once after their rupture, when the thirty-year-old Sula is dying. The visit simply renews their disagreement over values. Sula dies alone.

Although Sula's death occurs in the middle of the novel, she retains her importance as the unifying force of the narrative. Sula's essence remains after her death when the reader overhears her thought, "Wait'll I tell Nel" (149). When she dies, the plot dealing with her development is finished, and her direct involvement with the plot is suspended until the very end. However, her death directly affects the other two plot strands. "1940" and "1941" show respectively Nel's and the Bottom's self-destructive responses to Sula's death. Deprived of both friend and husband (Jude has left), Nel denies her deepest feelings of loss and grief. She lives an emotionally empty life for the next twenty-five years. A considerable part of the community makes an analogous choice to reject its connection with Sula, with similar results. When a significant part of the Bottom celebrates Sula's death, it dies in the collapse of the tunnel on National Suicide Day. The death of Sula leads to the literal death of almost a third of the Bottom, and foreshadows the death of the neighborhood.

Unlike the neighborhood, Nel finally recognizes the centrality of Sula to her self. In "1965," Nel visits Eva in a nursing home. Eva brings up Chicken Little's death, an event Nel has not thought of in years. Eva disturbs Nel by accusing her of having participated as much—and therefore being as responsible—as Sula. On her way home, Nel passes Shadrack, who witnessed the whole incident. Then she feels a breeze, which she identifies as Sula's continuing presence. For the first time, she realizes that she has been grieving, not for the loss of Jude, but for her loss of Sula. Understanding what Sula's death has meant to her completes Nel's growth because it restores her to an authentic, honest life of feeling. Nel's cry of grief for Sula closes the book.

GENRE

Sula is a specifically African American female *bildungsroman*, that is, a novel about the growth of a character into adulthood. (See Chapter 3 for a more extended discussion of the *bildungsroman*.). Because of its genre, then, the development of *Sula*'s plot consists of the development of its characters. *Sula* continues the innovation in the genre of the *bildungsroman* that *The Bluest Eye* began. Like the preceding novel, *Sula* shows two girls rather than concentrating on the single character of the traditional *bildrungsroman*. As in *The Bluest Eye*, only one of the pair survives and continues to develop. *Sula* carries this innovation further, however because it divides its attention much more evenly between the pair. In *The Bluest Eye*, Claudia has only a minor role in Pecola's life and serves mostly as a witness (by narrating Pecola's story). On the other hand, *Sula* shows the girls' importance to each other as fundamental. Traditionally, the *bildungsroman* ends when the main character's most important development has taken place. In the nineteenth century, the *bildungsroman* focused on young female characters' paths to marriage. (Jane Austen's *Emma* and Louisa May Alcott's *Little Women* exemplify this tendency.) *The Bluest Eye* violates our expectations of the *bildungsroman* by arresting its main character's emotional development when she is only twelve. Like several other twentieth-century works, *Sula* constructs another variation by showing Nel's marriage not as the sign of her maturity, as in the nineteenth-century works, but as a sign of her immature willingness to submerge herself in another's identity. (*Sula* does not damn marriage as an institution; it merely presents this marriage as built on wrongheaded ideas.)

In its most important change of conventions, *Sula* extends the traditional *bildungsroman* past the physical death of its main character. In this way, it expresses African American spirituality. As mentioned in Chapter 2, the persistence of spirits of the dead constitutes an important part of the African sacred cosmos that underlies African American culture. In *Sula*, Sula continues to exist after her death. This persistence is not limited to Nel's perception of the spirit near the end, for that might be interpreted as only Nel's wishful thinking. Instead, the omniscient narrator shows us the persistence directly. *After* her death, Sula thinks, "Well, I'll be damned . . . it didn't even hurt. Wait'll I tell Nel" (149). Sula exists, not as a transfigured soul purged of earthly traits, but as the identical personality, with the same curiosity and the same interest in Nel. In *Sula*, Morrison depicts the everyday workings of the African sacred cosmos. Situated in this spiritual context, the growth of female identity—the *bildungsroman*—becomes specifically African American.

Although *Sula* maintains the focus on the internal workings of the black community that *The Bluest Eye* began, it widens the scope of the earlier work. *Sula* shows both primary and secondary characters as more affected by events outside the daily context of the small town setting. Although little is made of Eva's or Sula's travels—not bound by the Bottom's conventions, they need not leave it to imagine other ways to live—a trip to the segregated South is necessary for Nel to conceive of a situation that her mother cannot control. For everyone except Sula, excursions outside the black community are not chosen but instead mandated by external forces. Shadrack and (Eva's son) Plum are both drafted for World War I. After Boy-Boy abandons her, Eva must leave the Bottom in search of a way to earn a living for herself and their three children. These excursions away from the community do severe, permanent damage. Both Shadrack and Plum are psychologically destroyed. Eva returns with only one leg.

Sula revisits *The Bluest Eye*'s concern with the psychological harm done to individuals by white racist culture. It shows this same damage to individual men, through its portrait of Jude Greene, but it traces the damage to specifically economic oppression. Not only Jude but the whole of the Bottom yearns to have a profitable part in building America, symbolized by the construction of the tunnel. The Bottom has been promised participation in this venture, and when whites renege on the promise, the Bottom's rage leads to the attack on the tunnel, its collapse, and many deaths.

Sula works with larger structures in another way too. In the histories of the Peace and Wright households, Morrison presents three generations of women. In each, the traits of the grandmother reappear, with different manifestations, in the granddaughters. As part of her attempt to escape the shame she feels for her mother's prostitution, Helene Wright tries to make her daughter conform to perfect middle-class respectability. Nel and the reader find Helene's mother, Rochelle, much more appealing than Helene, however. The presence of the rebellious, independent Rochelle in Nel's background makes Nel's interest in Sula more credible. In the same way, the Peace household contains a triad: Eva, Hannah, and Sula. As with the Wrights, the second generation does not have much influence on the third, because Eva's independence is reincarnated in Sula. These groupings of three generations are the first expression of Morrison's interest in characterization beyond immediate households. Morrison's next novel, *Song of Solomon*, extends this interest. There, knowledge of past generations constitutes a necessary part of a person's identity. Later, *Beloved* expands the importance of the past still further, making it a considerable, almost controlling force in the present.

CHARACTER DEVELOPMENT

Eva Peace, Sula's grandmother, has three children (Pearl, Plum, and Hannah) and no money when her husband, Boyboy, leaves them all. Realizing that they will starve if she does not take drastic action, she leaves the children with a neighbor and is gone for eighteen months. She returns with only one leg, but a purse full of money. It is rumored that she let a train amputate her leg for the insurance money. Boyboy returns briefly, in a new car, with another woman. Eva knows that she hates him, though she does not extend that hatred to all men, but instead bequeaths her daughters "man-love," Morrison's term for making men the center of the women's attention and activities. Although she never remarries, Eva enjoys male company and spends most of her time playing checkers and chatting with would-be suitors.

Eva represents both the nurturant and the violent aspects of the archetypal Earth Mother. She becomes a mother to most of the Bottom, renting part of her large house to lodgers, supervising newlywed women's cooking for their husbands, and taking in orphans. Eva does not advocate her own unconventionality for other women, and in fact calls Sula selfish for not wanting to marry. Although capable of great self-sacrifice for her children—she throws herself out a window in an unsuccessful attempt to rescue Hannah from a fire—she purposely burns her son Plum to death. Eva and Sula are linked by their great energy and independence. Eva somehow knows that Sula and Nel were instrumental in Chicken Little's death, though she was not present when it happened. When she confronts Nel with her knowledge many years later, she prepares Nel to perceive the persistence of Sula's spirit.

Although Hannah Peace is one of Eva's daughters, she has none of her mother's independence or vigor. Her chief activity consists of having casual sex with the willing men of the Bottom. Unaware that Sula is within earshot, Hannah unwittingly destroys her daughter's peace of mind by revealing to a friend that she does not like her daughter. When Sula is fourteen, Hannah dies in a fiery accident, despite Eva's heroic attempt to help her.

Sula Peace, the central character and driving force of the novel, affects every other character. Sula grows up in the unconventional household run by her grandmother Eva. In childhood, she forms an unbreakable attachment to Nel Wright but loses her faith that others can be trusted when she overhears that her mother, Hannah, does not like her. Shortly afterward, she loses her trust in herself. When her playmate Chicken Little slips from her grasp as she swings him round and round, he drowns in the river as she and Nel watch in paralyzed inaction. (Shadrack witnesses these happenings but does not betray the girls' secret.) From this point on, Sula lives an "experimental" life, paying no attention to social conventions or moral questions. Sula watches her mother burn to death with no apparent grief, for example, only interest in the way that Hannah is "dancing." Her only connection is to Nel.

When Nel marries Jude, Sula leaves the Bottom for ten years. On her return, she enjoys Nel's friendship again but does not understand that Nel might feel differently from her on any subject. When Sula has sex with Jude, she does not intend to hurt Nel, only to experience pleasure. Sula is sad and angry that Nel has accepted conventional social mores instead of identifying and acting on her own emotions. Sula violates every community norm, including the prohibition against black women sleeping with white men. Sula spurs the community to become better simply to spite her—wives pay more attention to their husbands, lest they be tempted by Sula; mothers take better care of their children, lest they be harmed by Sula's "evil eye."

Sula remains isolated from others, unable to make emotional connections. She falls in love with the maverick Ajax but then loses him when she pushes him to trade his independence for traditional domestic security. At thirty, Sula becomes ill with a fatal disease. Even on her deathbed, she remains unrepentant. Speaking with Nel, who is still angry about Jude, Sula reaffirms that the only life worth living is one that explores the self fully, with no limits. Sula is disappointed in Nel's choices, but she does not abandon her. After Sula's body dies, her spirit remains, and she wants to tell Nel about the experience of dying.

Nel's mother, Helene Sabat Wright, was raised by a proper grandmother, Cecile, who trained her to despise her mother Rochelle, a prostitute in New Orleans. As a result, Helene is obsessed with middle-class respectability. Disliking noise, dirt, and sex, she marries a husband whose profession allows him only short visits home. Helene thus has complete control of the household. She is uninterested in their daughter Nel's personality, seeing her only as raw material out of which she can make a model little girl. She makes Nel go to sleep with a clothespin on her nose to make it less broad, less obviously African. Helene's steady pressure might have obliterated Nel's personality as well as her husband's if her daughter had not happened to see the limits of her mother's power. On a train trip south for Cecile's funeral, Nel witnesses Helene's unsuccessful attempt to pacify a racist white conductor with a subservient smile. When Nel sees that the entire car of black people despises her mother's fear and her smile, Helene has lost her stranglehold.

Nel Wright Greene is Sula's friend from girlhood. She finds in the Peace household, and especially in Sula, a release from her mother's stifling conformity. Nevertheless, Nel follows a conventional path, becoming the comforting girlfriend and then wife of Jude Greene. When Sula returns to the Bottom, Nel enjoys her friend's personality and feels the stirring of long-unused parts of her own personality. However, Sula's behavior with Jude affronts Nel's ideas of loyalty and trust. From her point of view, the friendship is over. Nel represses her emotions, however, which take form as a ball of fur hovering just outside her peripheral vision. She turns to her children for emotional sustenance, but this sublimation of her own needs is unhealthy. Nel persuades herself to visit the dying Sula as an act of Christian charity. Nel becomes very angry when Sula attacks her values and feelings, particularly resenting Sula's claim that Nel has "a second-hand lonely" (143). Years after Sula's death, Nel visits Eva in a nursing home. Eva inquires about why Nel participated in Chicken Little's death and dismisses Nel's statement that Sula was responsible. On her way home, already thinking of Sula, Nel sees Shadrack. When she feels Sula's spirit in a breeze that stirs the trees, Nel finally realizes that her longtime sorrow has not really been focused on losing Jude, but on losing Sula. Her cry of grief, "girl, girl, girlgirlgirl," ends the book.

Jude Greene becomes Nel's husband. He attracts her with his need for comfort and sympathy in the face of racism. Jude's ideas of marriage consist of absorbing his wife's personality: "The two of them together would make one Jude" (83). Jude becomes interested in Sula, however, because she refuses to provide the sympathy that he whines for, and she turns his needs into a joke. He has no loyalty to Nel, and in the end nothing to hold Sula's interest. When Nel walks into their bedroom to discover Jude having sex with Sula, Jude makes no effort to salvage the marriage and leaves town soon after.

Almost a male counterpart to Sula, Ajax is fascinated by airplanes and flying, a symbolic suggestion of his preoccupation with freedom and exploration. An attractive character, Ajax genuinely enjoys originality and independence in women. When Sula tries to push their relationship into a conventional marriage, Ajax leaves her. After his departure, Sula finds his driver's license with his full name, Albert Jacks. Sula has thought of him as "Ajax," while really he has been "A. Jacks." Interpreting this mistake symbolically, Sula feels that she has lost Ajax because she didn't really know him.

The other male character truly interested in Sula, Shadrack, bonds with her in a different way. Shadrack comes to the Bottom when, as a shell-shocked veteran of World War I, he is released from an insane asylum without any resources. He lives by himself in a hut by the river. A mystic figure, he develops the yearly ritual of a parade for National Suicide Day to express his fear of death and change. Shadrack likes Sula. Seeing her afraid when Chicken Little disappears into the river, he makes her a one-word promise, "Always" (62).

Shadrack does in fact seem always to be linked to Sula. He does not want to hold his annual parade the year of her death because he misses her. When a large part of the community that ostracized Sula joins the parade to mock him, disaster ensues. The mockers unwittingly commit suicide by entering a tunnel that collapses on them. Shadrack, who didn't enter the tunnel, survives. In a way he has avenged Sula. In the final scene of the novel, Nel sees Shadrack just before she feels Sula's presence

The novel includes several minor characters whose primary importance is to theme rather than plot; they appear in only a few scenes. The Deweys are three orphans whom Eva adopts. Though cared for physically, they receive no emotional sustenance, not even names to recognize separate identities. Their arrested physical and emotional growth shows some limitation in Eva's mothering. An alcoholic, Tar Baby also lives in Eva's house. His ironic name refers to the rumor that he is white. Plum, Eva's only son, comes back from World War I a hopeless heroin addict, as she discovers when she finds the spoon that he uses to prepare the drug. Plum not only steals from the household but regresses to an infantile state. He dies when Eva, after hugging him and crying over him, douses him with kerosene and lights a match. Sula's violence to Chicken Little is much less intentional. While playing with Nel and Chicken Little close to the river, Sula swings the little boy round and round. They lose their grip on one another, and he flies into the middle of the river. Nel and Sula watch quietly as he disappears. Their subsequent silence about the mode of his death bonds them to one another.

THEMATIC ISSUES

Because *Sula* concerns the life and death of a neighborhood and of individuals like Sula, the novel naturally explores what constitutes a healthy, viable community or a sound individual. These are related concerns because individuals and communities always influence each other—in Morrison's world view, individuals are irrevocably part of communities, regardless of whether either side acknowledges it. *Sula* analyzes the health of the Bottom by its treatment of individuals, especially those who, like Shadrack, Tar Baby, Plum, or Sula, don't fit its social norms. Besides examining the relationship between the conventional and the unconventional on the large community scale, *Sula* explores it on the smaller individual level, through the friendship of Nel and Sula. Concentrating on females, the novel asks what makes a girl or woman strong and whether strength is sufficient to make an individual psychologically healthy.

In *Sula*, Morrison has little interest in passing moral judgments on characters. Just as *The Bluest Eye* complicates our understanding of an evil action by declaring that Cholly rapes his daughter from twisted love, so *Sula* makes easy judgments impossible, and perhaps any judgment beside the point. The mark above Sula's eye may be useful as an indication of the novel's approach. Depending on what they think of Sula at the time, the townspeople variously see this mark as a snake, a rose, a tadpole, or Hannah's ashes. Clearly, moral judgment depends on one's own angle of vision and preconceptions. The novel presents several extreme examples of individual decisions that damage others, Eva burning her son Plum, for example, or Sula having sex with Jude. The novel encourages the reader to consider what if any limits should restrain individual action.

At the same time, it presents these shocking actions within specific contexts. By the time Eva kills Plum, she has already been established as a self-sacrificing mother. (She probably gets the money to support her children by sacrificing her leg.) Later, she nearly dies in her attempt to rescue her burning daughter, Hannah. Eva's moral character remains a complex issue. Morrison repeatedly complicates moral questions in this way. When Sula has sex with her friend's husband, her motivations are not what we might initially have assumed. The novel therefore indicates that simple moral judgments will be based on incomplete or incorrect information.

Sula explores the consequences of moral judgment on both the macro and the micro levels. On the large scale, the novel analyzes what happens when the community decides that a person is evil. On the small scale, it depicts the consequences of Nel's decision that she is morally good and Sula bad (after the incident with Jude), delineating the effects on both the women's friendship and on Nel's individual development. Thus, the novel seems more interested in the consequences of moral judgment than in encouraging the reader to exercise that judgment.

Sula delineates the development of Sula and Nel into women. Its central theme, the girls' friendship, plays a crucial part in the formation of their identities. To analyze the friendship's continuing effects, *Sula* examines both social sex roles and relationships between individual black men and black women. Like *The Bluest Eye*, *Sula* indicates that these roles have developed in, and the relationships take place within, economic conditions under white racist control. Black veterans of World War I, Shadrack and Plum are abandoned by the society that has used them. Nel and Sula first come together because they have discovered that they do not belong to either the favored race or the favored gender. Similarly, the nature of Nel and Jude's relationship is based on white discrimination against Jude—and on Nel's response, which has become, Morrison implies, the conventional black woman's response to white victimization of black men. As in *The Bluest Eye*, even intimate relationships take place in a social context.

Inevitably, the friendship between Sula and Nel is affected by their attitudes toward the traditional role for women. In the time in which the novel is set, this role emphasizes motherhood. Repeatedly returning to the issue of motherhood, *Sula* exposes flaws in conventional thinking. Too often, the novel indicates, women use motherhood as an excuse for not facing their own feelings, not determining their own actions. In the deathbed scene, for example, Nel says that if Sula had had children, she would know that she can't claim the male privileges of independence and autonomy. Nel implies here that no real woman could leave her children. This argument is bound to fail with Sula, who can remember Eva's doing just that—for the good of the children.

Although she talks a conservative game in regard to motherhood, Eva lives quite experimentally. Rather than take a low-paying job that would force her to spend all her time away from her children, she literally sacrifices a part of herself. Having left her children with a neighbor for eighteen months, Eva returns to Medallion with enough money to support them—and with only one leg. Rumor says that she lost the leg to a train, and that her money comes from insurance compensation. Later, when Hannah catches fire in a barbecue accident, Eva almost dies hurling herself out a second-story window to try to help. Eva's willingness to sacrifice for her children follows traditional expectations, but the sacrifices themselves lie outside all conventional roles for women.

Eva explicitly rejects the more sentimental aspects of conventional motherhood. In answer to Hannah's question about whether she ever played with them, Eva sarcastically asks if she was supposed to be playing ring-around-the-rosy when her children had worms. Eva has apparently managed well enough to disguise the worst of their circumstances from this youngest child because Hannah continues to prod. Eva's angry rejoinder shows the cost of mothering for poor women: "talkin' 'bout

did I love you girl I stayed alive for you" (69). Some parts of the traditional role, Eva implies, require middle-class money.

Eva sets some limits on self-sacrifice, however. In the most dramatic
example, she burns her son Plum rather than accept his drug addiction
and its consequences. Having returned from the war a heroin addict,
Plum steals from the whole household to buy drugs. Explaining her decision to kill him, Eva says, "Being helpless and thinking baby thoughts
. . . and messing up his pants again . . . I had room enough in my heart,
but not in my womb . . . I birthed him once. I couldn't do it again" (71).
Eva considers that adult children have no right to enjoy the unquestion-
ing self-sacrifice that mothers perform for infants.

Despite her attitudes toward grown children, Eva functions as a
mother toward much of Medallion. (Her name suggests the archetypal
mother of humanity, Eve.) She adopts stray children, such as the Deweys. Her mothering is not always nurturant, however. When she ignores
the three foundling boys' individuality, for example, they do not grow
or mature properly. In her grandmother role, she supervises the young
married women who board in her home, insisting that they properly
perform traditional duties, such as cooking. Although the rules differ,
Eva controls her household as rigidly as Helene Wright does.

Both Eva and Nel accuse Sula of selfishness because she refuses the
role of wife and mother. The novel implicitly asks readers whether Sula
is more selfish than a woman using motherhood for her own ends—like
Helene, or Nel. Nel does not admit her real feelings when she finds Sula
and Jude. Instead, she creates a symbol of these feelings, a gray ball of
fur that for years she forces to a place just outside her field of vision.
She does not want to experience the pain that examining her feelings
would cause. Instead, she uses her children to avoid looking at the ball.
That is, she uses her children to compensate her for the losses of Jude
and Sula, and for the loss of her sexuality. Her love for her children
becomes ugly, perverse, even dangerous to them, "a cumbersome bear-
love that, given any rein, would suck their breath away in its crying
need for honey" (138). Although Nel pretends to live for her children,
she is simply refusing to live her own life and claiming theirs instead.
Nel considers herself, however, a model of unselfishness, and the community agrees. And, the community reasons, if Nel's behavior is good,
then Sula's actions and Sula herself must be selfish and bad.

Although Sula and Nel make opposite choices, the novel does not use
this difference as a grounds for moral judgment. The novel documents
the destructive experiences that follow from Nel's decision to accept a

limiting social role. It also documents, however, the destructiveness in Sula's disregard of all social limits. Like Cholly in *The Bluest Eye*, Sula is dangerously free because she has no firm self; Nel remains Sula's only emotional tie. Sula carelessly flings Chicken Little into the river, where he drowns; she watches without grief as her mother burns to death. Sula has nothing to guide her. Whatever she can imagine, she does. An "artist with no art form" (121), Sula causes death and destruction. But she also "simply helped others define themselves" (95). Nel and Sula are necessary to each other, hence their friendship.

Just as the friends need each other to grow and mature properly, so the community needs all its elements. Attempting to cast out any member of the community—or to repress what that person represents—results in the death of the community. The tunnel disaster shows symbolically that the death of the Bottom follows directly from its rejection of the powerful, independent female spirit embodied in Sula.

At first glance, the collapse of the tunnel might seem to avenge the Bottom's rejection of Shadrack rather than of Sula. Sula, after all, is dead by the time Shadrack leads the procession. Throughout, however, the novel establishes close and continuing associations between the two. The novel bearing her name begins with a description of Shadrack and the experiences that formed him. Shadrack feels a steady emotional attachment to Sula. Her death so depresses him that he can barely summon the energy to conduct National Suicide Day that year. Shadrack lives by the river, whose water is crucial to three important events connected to Sula. First, Shadrack witnesses the drowning of Chicken Little, the experience that binds Nel and Sula. Second, at Sula's funeral, the hypocritical mourners sing "Shall We Gather at the River." Their hymn becomes literal in the third incident: when they celebrate Sula's death by mocking Shadrack, they gather *in* the river, which drowns them in the collapsed tunnel.

If Sula's experimental life fails, the novel nevertheless affirms her rather than those who enjoy their false triumph over her. The mockers of Shadrack and Sula are "other-directed" without being unselfish. Their false hopes keep them working for others, "kept them excited about other people's wars; kept them convinced that some magic 'government' was going to lift them up . . ." (160). The mockers do not seek to know their own desires, much less act on them.

In contrast, the townspeople who do not join the mock parade know "the Spirit's touch" (160). Respecting themselves and their community, they "did not understand this curious disorder, this headless display"

(160). They may not endorse Shadrack's means of dealing with his fear of death, but neither will they mock it. Similarly, they may not enjoy Sula, but they will not blasphemously celebrate her death. They understand that to survive, the community must not destroy parts of itself.

The tunnel disaster conveys important symbolic meanings about women's roles and female power. Though Sula definitely presents individual men abusing women, it never presents women as men's victims. Instead, it shows them largely responsible for their own fates. Significantly, two women (Dessie and Ivy) precipitate the tunnel disaster by laughing at Shadrack. Their laugh begins the mock ritual that denies Shadrack and Sula membership in the community.

Not male rejection of women's independence, but women's rejection of their independent female selves, then, triggers the death of the Bottom. The words describing the mock parade, "headless display," connect Dessie and Ivy to the experience that drives Shadrack mad. ("1919" recounts his seeing a soldier who continues running after his head has been shot away.) Shadrack has seen the horror of an apparently functioning body that does not and cannot know that it is dead. But the soldier's body cannot continue its parody of human existence for long. Neither can the mockers, whose physical death only confirms the spiritual death that they have chosen by their social conformity. Unlike Nel, who eventually wakens from her spiritual hibernation, Dessie and Ivy do not receive another chance.

This difference may be due to the ways in which they reject Sula. Nel's rejection never destroys her love for Sula, and though lengthy, the rejection is not permanent. Further, Nel's rejection is private, for herself. Dessie and Ivy publicly try to obliterate female independence from the whole Bottom, but neither they nor the community can live without it.

The tunnel scene also connects symbolically to Plum's death and its message about the limits of female caretaking. Eva says that she kills Plum because he was, as an adult, trying to return to her womb. Here Eva is using metaphorical language to express Plum's withdrawal into infantile irresponsibility. Concrete parts of the scene in Plum's bedroom also suggest childbirth, however. When Eva tastes what she expects to be strawberry soda, she finds that it contains two elements always present in birth, blood and water.

The people mocking Shadrack and Sula resemble Plum in their irresponsibility. As he relies on his mother for all his needs, so they rely on a government to somehow change their lives. As there are blood and water in Plum's bedroom, so the tunnel collapse mixes the people's blood with the river water. And just as Plum was symbolically trying to crawl up to Eva's womb, so the mockers invade the unfinished "birth" tunnel in the earth. Eva destroys Plum in self-defense; mother earth crushes and drowns the irresponsible Bottom. When individuals and communities fail to take responsibility for discovering, examining, and acting on their own natures, they inevitably become unbearable burdens for individual women and for the archetypal female life force.

A FEMINIST READING OF *SULA*

The term "feminist criticism" now encompasses literary study with many different focuses; several recent anthologies use the word "feminisms" in their titles. Some feminist critics explore linguistic issues (how men and women use language); some concentrate on how gender roles influence our interpretive processes; still others are constructing historical traditions of literature from newly recovered works by women. In addition, feminist perspectives are compatible with many other critical perspectives. There are feminist archetypal critics, feminist Marxist critics, feminist multicultural critics, and so on. To simplify: the defining characteristic of these feminist criticisms is their women-centeredness; all of them investigate issues and questions related to women, from women's points of view.

When Morrison published *Sula* in 1974, no novel considered central to the American tradition of fiction had explored a life-long attachment between women friends. The originality of the novel's subject necessitated originality in its development. Doubling the traditional *bildungsroman*, Morrison shows both Nel and Sula growing into womanhood. What womanhood means—what social roles are open to women—affects the girls' growth as individuals and their friendship. With these primary and secondary concerns, *Sula* is unquestionably women-centered.

Feminist criticism examines historical conditions, the social contexts in which women authors have labored. In the nineteenth century, both legal constraints and a narrow social role affected women writers. "The Cult of True Womanhood" is a term that literary historians use to describe the completely domestic, self-sacrificing role that nineteenth-century society prescribed for white middle-class women. Women were socially educated to consider themselves as wives and mothers only, and their opportunities to become professionals and have good-paying careers were legally blocked.

In the 1920s, when *Sula* begins, women's roles were still controlled by the Cult of True Womanhood. The spiritual stature of a True Woman might be high, but her wages were lamentably low if she were forced to earn a living. Black women's jobs were limited to the lowest-paid factory work and domestic work (housecleaning, cooking, laundering). The True Woman's political position didn't bear speaking of—women did not receive the vote until 1919, and black women could not vote in any numbers until the Civil Rights Act of 1965. Thus, wives and mothers received much praise, but very little actual social support or status, particularly if they were black. Sula and Nel have individually discovered their lack of social status as African American girls by the time of their first meeting. They understand what they are not—white and male. Their next task is to understand what they are.

"1922" contains a symbolic scene depicting Nel and Sula's unconscious understanding of how society defines them. First, the girls "undress" sticks by stripping the bark away. Then they uproot grass and dig in the bare ground with the sticks. Nel "poked her twig rhythmically and intensely into the earth" (58), and Sula imitates her. After combining the two separate holes, the girls fill the larger pit with trash. Critics have interpreted this scene in various ways. Most agree that the holes are a symbolic representation of the girls' sexual beings. Some readers have then interpreted the rest of the scene as meaning that the girls are sexually attracted to each other. Nel's movement of the twig, however, seems a symbol of heterosexual intercourse rather than lesbian sexuality. In this reading, when the sticks break down the separation between the two holes, they symbolize men's refusal to make distinctions between women; that is, in the socially dominant male view, women all have the same social role. The garbage filling the holes symbolically represents the "trashing" of female identity, the low social status of African American women. Nel and Sula have, all of their lives, been exposed to social expectations for women; in this scene, they show that they understand the reality of women's experience not acknowledged in the lofty descriptions of their social role.

Sula presents this traditional role as self-defeating for women, destructive to others, and fundamentally dishonest. The role constructs the households in which both girls grow up. Nel's mother, Helene, values social respectability above all else. For her, being respectable means keeping a clean house, having sex infrequently and quietly, rearing a child, and above all controlling behavior to exclude anything unconventional. Helene has settled on this definition, and this way of life, so that no one in Medallion will ever know that her mother was a prostitute in New Orleans. In patriarchal (male-controlled) social systems, prostitution represents particular shame for women because chastity is the most important virtue for them. To prove that she does not deserve this shame, Helene adopts the middle class female role with a vengeance.

Although the Wright household seems the perfect example of the middle-class nuclear family and Helene appears to embody the True Woman, they are both shams. Morrison shows Helene using the role of the self-sacrificing True Woman to disguise her fear of intimacy and her need to control every bit of her experience—which of course means controlling every person within her orbit. Helene is not so much hostile to her husband Wiley as indifferent. She does not rebel against male authority openly, but she works quietly to control it. Wiley is a "seaman," a worker on a ship, often absent from his home. The novel creates a pun here because in the Wright household Wiley's only role is "semen," providing the seed that produces Nel. Helene tries to recreate Nel in her own image, or rather, in the image of the conventional female role. To become a middle-class housewife, Nel must have certain qualifications. *Sula* indicates how much this role has been determined by class and race when, as part of her training, Helene tries to reshape Nel's too-broad (African) nose with a clothespin. Nel's personality survives Helene's pruning only because she receives crucial support from Sula.

The Peace household is equally, though differently, affected by the pressure of women's social role. Whereas Helene enjoys a man's financial support, Eva's husband BoyBoy is an abusive, womanizing drinker. Eva must confront harsh economic realities when BoyBoy deserts her and their three small, hungry children; the traditional role is no longer open to her. Forced by circumstances to give up major advantages of the role, Eva rethinks it completely. Eva has a nontraditional role forced on her by BoyBoy's desertion, but she also chooses it herself in her unique responses. In some ways like Helene fleeing her mother's shame, Eva overcompensates: to make up for her deviation from the traditional role, she insists that other women conform to it.

Eva disapproves of Sula's decision to live completely outside the traditional roles of wife and mother. When Sula returns ten years after Nel's marriage, Eva and she quarrel about how to live. Eva calls Sula selfish for wanting to remain single, and Sula reproaches Eva with the sacrifice that fed her children. Eva defends the traditional role against Sula's claims for independence and autonomy.

Nel commits to the traditional role, and even Sula tries it. Better socialized by her mother, Nel goes first. She marries Jude Greene to soothe his hurt over economic racial discrimination, and he marries her to be soothed. (Neither he nor any other young black men are hired to work on building the tunnel under the river.) To his mind, marriage will shift the responsibility for his economic position. Married, Jude can become the "head of a household pinned to an unsatisfactory job out of necessity" (83). Single, he remains "a waiter hanging around a kitchen like a woman" (83). Jude considers that the institution of marriage will make him a whole man: "The two of them together would make one Jude" (83). Neither he nor Nel apparently considers what the institution will make of Nel.

When Sula returns, she finds an unattractive, unhealthy, static pattern in Nel and Jude's interactions. Jude is still telling "a whiney tale" (103) about his hard life. He expects that Nel will, as always, "excrete" a "milkwarm commiseration" (103). Because "excrete" is usually a polite substitution for "shit," the narrator's words clearly indicate distaste. The wife is expected to listen to and sympathize with her husband's feelings, and Nel usually does. This time, before Nel can excrete, Sula interrupts with a witty, paradoxical monologue. She makes Nel and Jude laugh, but her perspective nevertheless denies Jude's implicit claim that black men have it tougher than anyone else, their wives included. Jude is still telling the same tale after a decade and Nel is still listening and responding in the same ways. Nel and Jude have not grown as individuals because the role of supportive wife does not challenge either of them.

Given Sula's observation, not only of Nel but of other Bottom women's experience of the traditional role, the reader may be surprised that Sula too tries to fulfill that role. Those who want to reject convention must have a strong sense of themselves to create their own roles. Sula not only has no strong sense of herself, she may have no consistent self at all. Hearing that Hannah does not love her convinces Sula that she cannot trust others; seeing her own actions result in Chicken Little's death, Sula cannot trust herself either. She lives an "experimental" life, but the experiments do not advance any process of acquiring or testing knowledge. Sula accumulates sequential experience, but she really does not change or develop. Thus, when Sula first really becomes interested in a man, she returns to the ideas of possession and control that are the underside of the Cult of True Womanhood. Her lover Ajax originally was attracted by Sula's unconventionality. Probably the healthiest character in the book, Ajax has no need of another to make himself whole. In returning to a conventional role, then, Sula has chosen the alternative guaranteed to alienate him.

In fact, Sula's training in True Womanhood has been so minimal that her attempts to snare Ajax are pitiably obvious—hair ribbons glaringly out of character for her, a nicely set table for a man completely uninterested in traditional domesticity. When Ajax has a run-in with the police, she ignores his interpretation of the experience as an enjoyable adventure. Trying to convert it into a Jude-style racist wound, she whispers, "Lean on me" (133). Sula is left alone to face her life—and her death—when Ajax rejects this clumsy attempt to weaken his competence.

Sula and Nel's deathbed confrontation recapitulates Sula's earlier argument with Eva over women's roles. Like Eva, Nel argues that Sula wants the impossible: "You a . . . a colored woman. . . . You can't be walking around all independent-like, doing whatever you like, taking what you want, leaving what you don't" (142). When Nel triumphantly adds that Sula is lonely, Sula agrees but continues with "my lonely is *mine*. Now your lonely is somebody else's. . . . A secondhand lonely" (143). The unrepentant Sula has the last word as she challenges Nel's standards: "About who was good. How you know it was you? . . . Maybe it was me" (146).

This conversation foreshadows a later confrontation when Eva asks Nel for an explanation of how Chicken Little died:

> "I didn't throw no little boy in the water. That was Sula."
>
> "You. Sula. What's the difference? You was there." (168)

Just as Eva refuses to accept Nel's separation of herself and Sula on moral grounds, so the whole novel rejects the community's similar attempt. Like Pecola's community in *The Bluest Eye*, the Bottom chooses a female scapegoat. And, as in the earlier novel, the scapegoating process accents the femaleness of its victim.

The community scapegoats Sula out of fear and hatred. Sula threatens the Bottom by exposing the weaknesses of its social institutions. Sula neither accepts women's traditional role nor lies about its effects on the women around her. Beautiful when she is thirty years old, she sees about her women soured by living without men and women used up by childbearing and male demands. Through contrasting themselves with her, the women see it too. As a single, independent woman, Sula is perceived as a threat to the institution of marriage. When the Bottom's married men have sex with her, their lack of commitment to the institution is clear. Not surprisingly, the women of the community prefer to blame Sula.

In another instance, community members take behavior that has existed in their families, which is part of them, and claim moral purity by projecting it on Sula and rejecting her. The community despises Sula for willingly having sex with white men. Of course, Sula is not the first woman in town to do so because many families have mixed blood. The men too sometimes choose white partners. Nevertheless, no one will admit the truth that sex between a black woman and a white man might not be rape. Sula may in fact be sleeping with white men, but the case is not proved against her. The Bottom insists that black women choose only black men; Sula insists on choosing for herself. The community retaliates by ostracizing her.

But whereas *The Bluest Eye* shows the scapegoat destroyed by this process, *Sula* shows that when a community rejects its own members, it destroys itself. The least self-reliant, least vital members of the community celebrate Sula's physical death as though it were also her spiritual annihilation. Their victory is short-lived and their spiritual notions shallow: they perish in the tunnel collapse while Sula's spirit survives to inspire Nel. As a community, the Bottom too perishes, though self-reliant individuals survive. So do those with the potential to reclaim themselves, like Nel. And so does the spirit of female independence: Sula.

Song of Solomon
(1977)

Morrison's third novel reached the *New York Times* best-seller list and brought her the acclaim of a National Book Critics Circle Award, her first major prize. Twenty years later, the novel again hit the best seller lists when television talk-show host Oprah Winfrey discussed it on her television book club. Its appeal thus bridges the worlds of academic culture and popular culture. Whereas Morrison's first two novels focus on girls and women and her fourth, fifth, and sixth novels concentrate on men and women's relationships, *Song of Solomon* is transitional: it centers on a male protagonist, Milkman Dead. This novel combines elements of the *bildungsroman* (the story of a young person's growth) and the mystery genre in Milkman's quest to understand his nature, his family, and his place in the world. *Song of Solomon* reiterates themes of the earlier novels while developing a new, more positive picture of African American history and community.

PLOT DEVELOPMENT

Part One briefly sketches the racial conditions in the Michigan city where Milkman is born around 1932, then delineates his experiences up to 1963 and his thirtieth birthday. This first section shows Milkman able to enjoy the middle-class comforts his father has provided, but alienated from the present (his family and community) and ignorant of the past. His dissatisfaction makes him eager to undertake the journey to the South that constitutes Part Two. There he finds his spiritual heritage in the southern settings crucial to his family's history (Danville, Pennsylvania, and Shalimar, Virginia).

Part One depicts several estranged relationships that contribute to Milkman's own alienation. His father and mother, Macon and Ruth Dead, live on rent monies from the black community, but they have no social link to it. Further, they teach their children to despise anyone who is not at least middle-class. Milkman's family exists only as a fragmented collection of individuals. Macon remains distant from all his children, and he has severed connections with his sister Pilate. Milkman has no emotional ties to his two considerably older sisters, First Corinthians and Magdalene. Milkman's parents have a sham marriage, and Milkman views Ruth's consequent hunger for affection as unpleasant and unhealthy. When Milkman hears both his parents' versions of their past history and cannot reconcile the discrepancies, he gives up trying to understand them.

In this emotional desert, Milkman forms two initially sustaining relationships, one with a schoolmate, Guitar, and one with Pilate's granddaughter, Hagar. As the characters age, Guitar distances himself from Milkman, and Milkman wishes to break off his relationship with Hagar. Obsessed with Milkman, Hagar stalks him and threatens to kill him. With his important relationships damaged or broken off, Milkman is bored and restless at the end of Part One. He is eager to take the journey that makes up Part Two.

That journey originates in the rift between Macon and Pilate. Macon believes that, decades earlier, when he and Pilate fled the South after their father's death, Pilate stole a bag of gold from him. Milkman travels south to recover this gold. The novel thus has the general form of a mystery, with Milkman trying to solve the puzzle of the missing gold's whereabouts. Much of Part Two consists of Milkman's attempts to recognize and follow clues, to create a coherent history of the gold's travels. To succeed, he must develop previously latent parts of his character and change his shallow values.

As in a conventional mystery, the successful detective survives many dangers. Milkman never finds the gold, but he does find liberating knowledge. As part of his learning, the city-bred Milkman must figure out the customs of society in the rural South. In addition, Milkman learns responsibility and sacrifice. He has promised half the gold to Guitar, who wants it to subsidize political terrorism. Believing that Milkman has be-trayed him, Guitar repeatedly tries to kill his boyhood friend—and kills Pilate instead, probably by accident. The novel ends with Milkman and Guitar locked in physical struggle.

NARRATIVE TECHNIQUE

Like the rest of Morrison's novels, *Song of Solomon* uses the reader's real-life processes of learning. In real life, we discover others' histories one story at a time, in the context of our present. We learn about people by listening to their stories and witnessing their actions. The novel offers a similar mix of stories from the past and actions in the novel's present rather than an artificial tale in straightforward chronological order. At times, the novel revisits a story that we have heard before, telling the same event from a perspective so different that the story itself is barely recognizable. Macon and Ruth tell quite different versions, for example, of her father's death and its aftermath. Milkman and the reader both have to consider all the stories to move toward the truth. Thus, under-standing anyone's real character—as opposed to simply accepting what another character says—is necessary not only to Milkman's maturation and his solution of the family mystery, but to the reader's overall inter-pretation.

The first chapter includes a mix of techniques typical of the whole novel: third-person omniscient narration (from a speaker who can enter any character's mind), dialogue (the characters' speeches), and direct presentation of the characters' actions. The narrator tells us about the sexual pleasure that Ruth and Macon once found in each other, and then about the events that ended it. However, we watch the scene in which Milkman gets his nickname. We only hear of Macon's presence at Pilate's miraculous birth, but we witness the scene in which Macon disowns her (for the second time). Likewise we see Macon refuse Guitar's grand-mother a desperately needed extension on her rent. Our picture of Macon as a disappointed, bitter, isolated, hard man becomes more complicated by the chapter's last scene. There, Macon stands outside Pilate's home, in the dark, listening to Pilate, her daughter Reba, and her granddaugh-ter Hagar singing together. Clearly, he yearns for their emotional con-nection and spiritual communion. We learn about the other characters in a similar fashion, from the narrator's direct accounts, from listening to them, and from seeing their actions.

Although we gradually assemble our knowledge of the complex characters—and only a few minor ones, like the lucky Reba, are left simple—only a few characters continue to develop. Two of these, Milkman and his sister First Corinthians, suddenly become so dissatisfied with their empty lives that they reach out for new experiences. (Milkman travels south, and the upper-class Corinthians takes a job and establishes a relationship with a working-class man.) These experiences in turn help them identify and develop what had earlier been only potential selves.

CHARACTER DEVELOPMENT

Song of Solomon contains some of Morrison's most original and compelling creations—the major characters Milkman, Macon, Ruth, Guitar, Pilate, and Hagar; and the secondary characters Circe and First Corinthians. Almost every reader will be struck by the characters' fantastic names. The nicknames Guitar and Milkman originate in the boys' behaviors, and thus correspond to parts of their identities.

Several other names come from the Bible. Although Hagar does become an outcast wanderer, the other characters diverge from their biblical counterparts. Pilate does not, like Pontius Pilate, deny responsibility. Magdalena shares nothing with the reformed prostitute Mary Magdalen. Biblically, "First Corinthians" is not a person's name at all, but a section title in the New Testament. All these characters received their names when their parents opened the Bible at random and pointed to a word. This once-common practice helps to locate the family's origins in the rural American South.

Even an apparently unremarkable name, like Susan Byrd, carries considerable meaning. A distant cousin, Susan gives Milkman a vital piece of information when he is tracing his family history. "Bird" ties the family to Milkman's ancestor, Sing Bird. It also identifies the family as Indian. Susan's part of the family conceals its Indian heritage by revising the spelling to "Byrd." This choice aligns the family with Anglo-Europeans and thus the Southern Plantation tradition. Susan reveals the family history to Milkman but is careful not to let Grace Long, a gossipy visiting friend, in on the secret.

Circe, who shares her name with a witch in Homer's *Odyssey*, magically links the generations of characters. Midwife at Pilate's birth, she is already old when Pilate and Macon's father is killed and they come to her for shelter. When Milkman finds her, Circe lives with a pack of dogs in the wreck of the old Butler mansion where she served whites for so long. Milkman at first fears that she is supernatural because it seems impossible for her still to be alive. Circe has survived on her keen enjoyment of vengeance. Having watched her employer's family decay into helpless poverty, she now awaits the complete collapse of their mansion (a symbol of her enslavement and oppression). From Circe, Milkman learns the true names of his grandparents, Jake and Sing.

Jake becomes the first Macon Dead when, in the aftermath of the Civil War, a careless bureaucrat records his birthplace as his first name and his father's death as his surname. He marries Sing, who dies giving birth to their second child, Pilate. Macon acquires land, makes a prosperous farm, and dies trying to defend it from greedy white men.

The second Macon Dead, Milkman's father, farmed with the original Macon and, at seventeen, witnesses his death. He and his sister Pilate then hide, first with Circe, and then in a cave where Macon kills a white miser whom he considers a threat. Macon assumes incorrectly that Pilate has stolen the miser's gold that they should share. Macon moves north, where he is safer, and acquires property in a Michigan city. There he marries Ruth Foster. Here too Macon thinks that he is betrayed because he believes that his wife carried on an incestuous relationship with her father, Dr. Foster. Embittered and alienated, he becomes a greedy landlord and a distant father, contemptuous of the son whom he tried to abort. Macon attempts to enlist Milkman in his war against his wife Ruth. Only in Macon's memories of his youth can the reader see any humanity in him.

Ruth Foster Dead comes from a middle-class family. After her mother's early death, her father, Dr. Foster, becomes concerned that Ruth is focusing inappropriate, possibly sexual affection on him. Therefore, although as a rich man he condescends to Macon, Dr. Foster is secretly glad to let the sixteen-year-old Ruth marry him.

Ruth and Macon initially enjoy their marriage. Macon never forgives Dr. Foster for refusing to lend him money for a business venture, however, and blames his wife. Ruth nurses her father through his last illness, and her behavior on his death reinforces Macon's perception of incestuous involvement. Years later, Milkman discovers that Ruth still makes secret, overnight trips to tend her father's grave. She defends herself against Macon's accusations by telling Milkman her own version of the Dead marriage. The socially inept Ruth has no friends to fill the void of intimacy.

First Corinthians and Magdalena (Lena) are Macon and Ruth's daughters. Their parents assume that they will marry well, but they do not impress suitors as having sufficient gumption to be good partners. Both remain in their parents' home. Their major pastime, making velvet roses for a department store, is the only means of earning money that their gentility allows. Lena is important in only one scene, when she charges Milkman with selfish, ungrateful behavior toward her and First Corinthians. Her diatribe makes Milkman consider his effect on others for the first time.

First Corinthians is a more developed character than Lena. Determined to get out of the Dead home, she works as a maid but tells her parents that she is a private secretary. On the bus to her job, she becomes acquainted with Porter and later sneaks out of the parental home to meet him. When Porter issues an ultimatum that she either act like a grown woman or give up their affair, First Corinthians abandons empty middle-class refinement for love.

The main character, Milkman, is the third Macon Dead. Born into a loveless home, he is caught in his parents' battle. For much of the book he does not remember the origin of his nickname. Eventually, he remembers that the name came from Freddy, his father's handyman, who witnessed him nursing from Ruth's breast when he was five years old. (Ruth has insisted on this; it is her only source of sensual gratification after Macon has sexually abandoned her.) Disliking his father and distrusting his mother, Milkman can find no center. He develops a limp that indicates an internal emptiness.

Milkman has two emotional supports, his friend Guitar and his aunt Pilate. As a boy, Milkman escapes the sterility of the Dead household at Pilate's home, where he enjoys music, food, and emotional connection. Eventually he and his older cousin Hagar (Pilate's granddaughter) become lovers. Milkman has no loyalty, however. Like his sisters, Milkman at thirty still lives with his parents. He works for his father. Bored and unhappy with his parents' war, he recruits Guitar to steal what he thinks is Pilate's sack of gold. He ends his relationship with Hagar in a particularly heartless way. Showing no awareness that he has betrayed them, Milkman is only annoyed at Hagar's persistence and his own mistake about Pilate. (The stolen sack contains only bones, not gold.)

On his journey south in search of the missing gold, Milkman learns his family's true history and matures into a responsible adult. There he acquires the traditional male skills of hunting and self-defense, and at last starts to consider others. When he accepts a sexual offer from Sweet, he treats her like a lover rather than an object. In the first test of his new self, Milkman accepts responsibility for his treatment of Hagar. Similarly, he does what he can to comfort the dying Pilate. The book's last image shows Milkman and Guitar locked together, wrestling to the death. Although the image is violent, it also conveys Milkman's acceptance of Guitar's challenge to engage fully with others.

Guitar Bains, a few years older than Milkman, becomes his best friend despite their difference in social class. Having moved north after the death of Guitar's father in a sawmill accident, the Bains family is poor. (Milkman's father threatens to evict Guitar's family when they cannot pay their rent on time.) Because he thinks that his mother showed undue deference to callous mill officials, Guitar remains suspicious of women. Even so, he understands what Milkman's abandonment means to Hagar and pities her.

Guitar commits himself to a secret political organization called the Seven Days. The Days are seven men dedicated to evening the score for racial violence. When a black person is deliberately murdered by whites, the man responsible for that day of the week avenges the death. The Day kills a white person as similar to the black victim as possible and duplicates the mode of the original murder. Guitar maintains that the Days act out of love for black people, but Milkman points out Guitar's hatred for many blacks as well as whites.

Song of Solomon emphasizes that the white violence motivating the Seven Days is real and reprehensible. Further, the black community cannot rely on the police or the courts to protect or avenge. Guitar needs gold to finance vengeance for the deaths of four little girls who died from a bomb set in their church. (This essential part of the novel's plot refers to the famous 1963 bombing of a church in Birmingham, Alabama.)

The limitations of Guitar's ideas emerge clearly during his pursuit of the gold. Guitar does not value Pilate and is glad to help Milkman rob her. That project fails when the young men are arrested as burglars. Guitar does not recognize Pilate's generosity in rescuing them from the police. Instead, he is furious that she has acted in accordance with the policemen's stereotype of the ignorant black countrywoman to win their freedom. Later, Guitar wrongly concludes from circumstantial evidence that Milkman has cheated him. Despite still loving Milkman, Guitar reacts violently, twice trying to kill his friend. In the second attempt, he accidentally shoots and kills Pilate instead. The novel ends with Guitar and Milkman locked in one another's "killing arms" (337). Guitar's philosophy has caused him to kill one of the most nurturant forces in the black community, Pilate. Further, he must either kill his best friend or give up his own life.

Robert Smith, Railroad Tommy, Empire State, and Porter belong to the Seven Days. In the opening scene, Smith commits suicide by jumping from the roof of Mercy Hospital. Guitar later notes that such an occasional casualty is inevitable because the necessary secrecy of the Seven Days isolates its members from any other community. Railroad Tommy and Empire State remain flat characters, important mostly in showing Milkman's shallowness. Porter, however, plays a decisive part in the development of First Corinthians. Like Guitar forcing Milkman to political and social awareness, Porter makes First Corinthians choose between remaining a child or maturing into a woman.

In Pilate, Morrison has created one of the great original characters of American literature. Milkman thinks at one point that he has never met anyone else like her, and the reader is likely to share his reaction. As the critic Barbara Christian points out in *Black Women Novelists*, earlier African American women characters tend to be stereotypes such as the all-nurturant Mammy, the loose woman, or the tragic mulatta (woman of racially mixed blood). Pilate exists completely outside of these categories, indeed outside almost all social categories. In the earlier novels, characters like Sula had already transcended these stereotypes. However, ordinary social roles provide much of Sula's motivation: they are what she does not want to be, what she will not do. Pilate is so striking precisely because social roles are not annoying or confining for her, but simply irrelevant.

Although Pilate has some fantastic elements—she is born *after* her mother's death, and unlike every other human being, she has no navel—she must nevertheless live in a recognizable social world. She must, for example, earn a living. Pilate learns early that she has two options. Because other people are inevitably terrified by her physical difference, she can either hide it (and her real self) or give up any expectation of being accepted.

Pilate sees her social marginalization not as victimization and exclusion but as freedom to explore her self. She alone is unconstrained by social expectations of women. Pilate "threw away every assumption she had learned and began at zero" (149). She then constructs her own world view from her own experiences. Refusing to romanticize this process, the narrator notes that Pilate is "hampered by huge ignorances" and that she "[arrived] sometimes at profundity, other times at the revelations of a three-year-old" (149). Nevertheless, she is the only character who never stops learning, loving, and developing.

Isolated from society, Pilate maintains contact with the spiritual world. Her values provide an alternative for Milkman's imagination, which is stifled by his father's materialism and Guitar's single-minded politics. In *Song of Solomon*, Pilate is the voice of black love. That love is like Mrs. MacTeer's in *The Bluest Eye*, fiercely protective. Pilate puts a razor to the throat of a man threatening her daughter Reba, for instance. Her words too can be harsh, as when she ends a silly argument between Ruth and Hagar over who loves Milkman more. At the same time, Pilate consistently supports the weaker characters, like Ruth, Milkman, and Hagar. When Hagar dies, Pilate first sings a song to comfort her dead granddaughter and then witnesses to the world, "And she was *loved!*" (319). Dying, she says, "I wish I'd a knowed more people. I would of loved 'em all" (336). In Pilate, Morrison has created a wise, strong, earthy embodiment of African American spirituality.

Pilate, her daughter Reba, and her granddaughter Hagar revisit the three generations of women in *Sula*. Pilate recreates Eva's most positive traits without her arrogance. Like Hannah, Reba remains flat rather than rounded, characterized mainly by her enjoyment of sexuality and her luck, which unfortunately cannot protect Hagar. Despite being raised in a loving, protective atmosphere, Hagar does not develop healthy feelings of self-respect. When Milkman jilts her, Hagar stalks him and makes clumsy, not completely serious attempts to kill him. She cannot follow through when Milkman dares her to stab him. When Milkman verbally knifes her, Hagar does not examine his worth, but her own. Like Sula, she clumsily tries to remake herself in the image of True Womanhood. She hopes Milkman will love her reincarnation as a middle-class woman with designer make-up, clothing, and coiffure. She dies still believing that she has failed. Guitar, who understands her better than anyone else, comments that she could not cope with the social isolation of her grandmother's household. Hagar was the kind of person, he explains, who needs an entire community—blood relatives and a church group—to support her personality.

GENRE

Song of Solomon participates in one of African American literature's most important traditions, the slave narrative. Published and edited by

white abolitionists for political purposes, slave narratives recount an individual's life in slavery and his or her escape. The critic Robert B. Stepto
suggested in *From Behind the Veil* that many twentieth-century African
American novels repeat patterns initiated in nineteenth-century slave
narratives. These narratives, he found, display one of two dominant patterns in depicting African American experience—ascent or immersion.

Narratives of ascent tell stories of men and women ascending from
the South of slavery, through literacy in the dominant culture, to a North
of comparative freedom. "Literacy" here means not only the ability to
read and write (literacy in a print culture), but a wider cultural literacy
including the dominant customs, religion, and so on of European American society. In the North, the newly literate escaped slave lived without
his or her family and thus became, in Stepto's phrase, "an articulate
survivor." Milkman's father, Macon, experiences just such a journey. Macon Dead has become literate, and therefore successful, in the business
world of the white North. He also suffers from the problems of an articulate survivor—separation from his original community and its culture.

Stepto proposes that after emancipation, the immersion pattern of narrative emerged. In this pattern, the main character leaves the isolation of
the North for a southern black community, acquires communal literacy
(knowledge of its customs, manners, religion, and so on), and becomes
"an articulate kinsman." He is now a full member of his community, but
the community is enslaved or oppressed.

Song of Solomon presents Milkman's successful quest to become an articulate kinsman. At thirty, in Michigan, Milkman initially feels isolated,
particularly after his relationships with Hagar and Guitar cool. In the
East and the South, Milkman reestablishes contact with the communities
of which his family was once a part. To become communally literate, he
listens to stories from men who shared his father's youth, learns what is
polite and what insulting in this new context, and participates in the
male ritual of a hunt. Returning to Michigan as an articulate kinsman,
he brings liberating knowledge for Macon, Pilate, and himself.

Song of Solomon thus revises the African American tradition by combining previously separate patterns of ascent and immersion. The earlier
tradition implicitly depicted a terrible choice—either individual freedom
without a context to make it meaningful or membership in a community
denied freedom. *Song of Solomon* enlarges the options. The isolation of
the protagonist in the historical ascent pattern (Macon) is moderated by
the next generation's re-immersion (Milkman's journey).

THEMATIC ISSUES

Song of Solomon reiterates several themes found in *The Bluest Eye* and *Sula*. This reiteration differs from simple repetition, of course. First, *Song of Solomon* presents a more sympathetic portrait of the black middle class than the earlier novels. In many ways, Ruth Foster resembles Helene Wright. Both women are middle-class, manipulative, and exploitative of their children for their own emotional needs. But whereas Helene never engages our sympathy, Ruth is depicted so that we sympathize with her in her sexual loneliness and her social isolation. Ruth's daughter First Corinthians also shares social position with Helene and Nel of *Sula* and with Geraldine from *The Bluest Eye*. The earlier books' presentation of the middle class concentrates on the emptiness of women's social role and cruelty born of the desire to set oneself apart from poor black people. Ruth may share Nel's passive acceptance of a role, but First Corinthians shows considerable courage in breaking out of it. Further, the central character, Milkman, also is middle-class. Although he begins with many of the obnoxious traits of the earlier characters, he grows beyond them to appreciate his people and his culture.

Song of Solomon plays another riff on the central theme of *The Bluest Eye*, the destruction of black girls and women by racist ideas of beauty. Hagar shares Pecola's desire to conform to a white ideal of beauty. *Song of Solomon* analyzes the contribution of social class to this self-hatred. Hagar's home can't really be said to belong to a class because Pilate's unique lifestyle cannot be fitted to any social norms. Through her brother Macon, however, the reader sees the middle class's damning judgment of Pilate, and by implication her granddaughter. When Milkman tires of Hagar, she tries to regain his love by remaking herself in the image of the middle-class women she sees him escorting. Too old to believe in Pecola's dream of blue eyes, Hagar focuses on the clothes and makeup carried by upscale department stores. Whereas Pecola wants simple social acceptance and familial love, Hagar is driven by obsessive romantic love. Once Hagar internalizes a standard of beauty that defines her as ugly, even Pilate can't keep her alive.

Like *The Bluest Eye*, *Song of Solomon* presents both female failure and success. If Hagar dies trying to achieve the middle-class role, and Ruth lives a diminished life within it, First Corinthians makes good her escape. At forty-two, Corinthians chafes at the narrowness of her life in her parents' home. Corinthians has a college education that she has never used. Instead of beginning a career, she waited for a proposal of marriage that never came. Her position has not changed since her childhood, when Macon took the family out for a Sunday ride in his Packard—not to give his family pleasure, but to show off his possessions, including his well-dressed daughters.

Desperate to replace the tedious, useless, but home-bound and therefore genteel work of making velvet roses, Corinthians takes a job as a maid. She lies about the nature of her work, of course, because the Deads would never accept her menial job as suitable for their daughter. On the bus to work, she meets an attractive working-class man, Porter. Interested but unwilling to bring a working-class man home, Corinthians meets him secretly and hides their relationship. Finally, Porter insists that she either live with him openly or give him up entirely. Her acceptance of his terms is absolute: she lies across the hood of his locked car to prevent Porter from driving away. Although she has to some extent merely exchanged one male authority for another—Porter for her father—she is opting for love, for passion, and for a fuller life.

Song of Solomon's themes grow from its central choice to present a male *bildungsroman* in the context of African American history. As Morrison's earlier novels concentrated on girls and women, so this novel highlights male friendship and bonding in addition to exploring father-son relationships through several generations. Unlike Pecola or Sula, Milkman develops into an adult capable of a mature sexual relationship. To become this adult, Milkman must claim his African American heritage.

Through Milkman's quest, *Song of Solomon* introduces its most important new theme, the central importance of orality to African American culture. "Orality" means the transmission and perpetuation of information by speech rather than print. (Instead of books, oral cultures use spoken poetry, stories, and song.) In an oral culture, children are taught to listen closely to others, particularly the elders, as their primary means of learning to live in the world. Milkman initially lacks this ability to listen, as Guitar often tells him. To excavate his family's history, Milkman must listen to precisely the people whom he has treated most disrespectfully, women. Circe and Susan Byrd reveal the facts that allow him to reconstruct his family line (see genealogy diagram).

As a boy and then as a young man, Milkman accepts all the privileges of being male without consciously realizing that there are any. Not until Lena informs him that he has "pissed" on them for the last time does he have any idea how casually disrespectful he has been to his sisters (216). He acts in a similarly sexist way in his sexual relationships, dis-

GENEALOGY FOR *SONG OF SOLOMON*

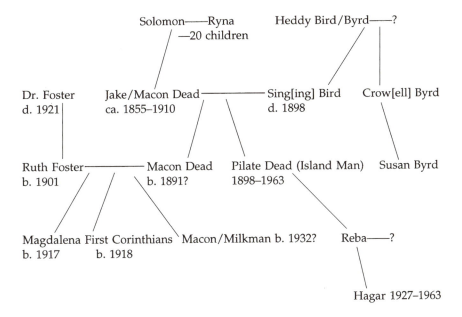

carding Hagar with a thank-you note. As his journey south educates him in historical lore, so too it deepens his understanding of human relationships. For the first time, with Sweet, he tries to give as well as to receive pleasure. Milkman's new perspective cannot undo the harm of his previous actions, however, because Hagar is already dead. Like Pilate, Milkman accepts responsibility for having killed another human being. She carries bones in a sack; he carries the container Pilate has made for him, a shoe box full of Hagar's hair. Milkman's newly recognized sense of emotional connection and responsibility goes far beyond romantic relationships or even family, as *Song of Solomon* deals with an African American community extended over geographic space and time.

Whereas *The Bluest Eye* considers fully only two generations and *Sula* three, *Song of Solomon* shows a three-generation history affecting the fourth generation: Milkman, Magdalene, First Corinthians, and Hagar. Three generations ago, Milkman's ancestors were living in slavery; two generations ago, they became free only to endure Reconstruction; Milkman's father came of age just as Jim Crow (segregationist laws) returned African Americans in the South to near-slavery conditions. Macon remembers witnessing the death of his father, murdered by whites for trying to protect his land. This experience shapes Macon's whole life, from where he lives to what he values. His journey to Michigan was part of the Great Migration of southern agricultural workers to the industrial North. *Song of Solomon*'s historical sweep, then, makes the earlier novels' exclusive focus on the black community impossible because white control of African Americans themselves and white invasions of black communities are inescapable historical facts.

Song of Solomon insists on the centrality of continuing racist violence to American culture. Among its abundant examples are two references to well-known actual happenings. In the first, the men in Tommy's Barbershop discuss the 1953 Mississippi lynching of Emmett Till, a boy visiting from Michigan, for whistling at a white woman. Later, Guitar works to avenge the bombing of a Birmingham, Alabama church that killed four girls attending Sunday school. *Song of Solomon* depicts this violence as a tool of political oppression in its 1960s setting. The novel shows that, for much of earlier American history, racist violence was an openly acknowledged tool for control. By the 1960s, however, the perpetrators had to remain anonymous.

Song of Solomon displays a variety of African American strategies to resist this violent oppression. Milkman's great-grandfather, Solomon, simply leaves. His grandfather (the original Macon) fights back with direct, open, answering violence. Circe believes that white practices are so inherently evil that, given enough time, whites will destroy themselves. Milkman's father tries to beat whites at their own game by avoiding white people but adopting many of their economic practices. Guitar and the other Seven Days create a variation of grandfather Macon's tactics. They practice retaliatory violence, their actions as close as possible to every instance of white attack, but they operate in secret.

Although these strategies are employed in widely separated times and places, *Song of Solomon* examines them all through Milkman's discovery of each of them. The novel explores the consequences of these strategies for individual African Americans and for the black community as a whole. When Solomon leaves, for example, his wife Ryna grieves to death. When Guitar commits himself to his cause, he kills Pilate. By the time Milkman begins his travels, some of the older stories about resistance have been lost. Milkman finds them accidentally, when he stops looking for gold and begins researching his family history. His important rediscovery changes his idea of African American history from a simple tale of oppression to a more complex saga of oppression and creative resistance.

If its rediscovery is accidental, the disappearance of African American history was not. When a drunken white soldier writes Milkman's grandfather's name, Jake, he changes it to Macon. This event symbolically indicates print culture's contempt for and inevitable distortion of oral culture. Trying to leave the painful past of slavery behind, the first Macon accepts what the soldier writes, "Dead," as his surname.

Orality preserves part of the historical past, however, even under unfavorable conditions. Thus, in *Song of Solomon's* opening scene, Pilate sings a verse from the song that Milkman later recognizes as the story of his great-grandparents. Importantly, Pilate is preserving the past without perfectly understanding it because she doesn't know the song's personal applications. In a similar way, when the spirit of her father says to her, "Sing," she understands his word as a command, and sings, finding comfort in music. With Susan Byrd's information, Milkman understands that the spirit may have been saying her mother's name, Sing Bird. Milkman discovers more of his family's real history through another example of orality, a children's jump-rope song. At the end of the novel, Milkman demonstrates his understanding of the heritage bequeathed to him when he sings the children's verse as Pilate's death-song. Easing Pilate's transition to the world of the ancestors, he simultaneously claims his own place as their son.

A MULTICULTURAL READING

As literary critics use the word, "multiculturalism" means an awareness of the many overlapping cultural contexts that produce a literary text. In turn, the text may reflect and participate in several different cultural traditions. When Toni Morrison describes herself as "a black woman writer," she indicates contexts for her work. Alert multicultural critics try to respect her self-definition by examining it in the contexts of black writing (including African and Afro-Caribbean traditions), of African American writing, of women's writing, and of African American women's writing.

A multicultural critic recognizes not so much an American tradition of literature as American traditions. As a nation of immigrants, the United States has birthed numerous traditions from its contributing cultures. African American, American Indian, Latino, Jewish, European American, Asian American—these just begin the list because each of them includes several traditions. Chinese, Thai, Vietnamese, and Japanese are all Asian, for instance. Each ethnic group has not only its unique originating culture, but unique experiences within the United States. Only African Americans experienced slavery, for example, while only Japanese Americans were interned in concentration camps in the United States during World War II. Each group's literary traditions reflect its unique historical experience.

Song of Solomon calls for multicultural criticism in its evocation of the mythic journey because it draws the reader's attention to at least three cultural traditions: European, American Indian, and African American. Multicultural analysis illuminates both the novel's central plot, Milkman's questing journey, and the closely related imagery of flying. The novel strongly invokes Greek myth by having a character, Circe, share a name with the witch Circe in Homer's epic, the *Odyssey*. As one of the earliest epics in the literature of Europe, the *Odyssey* set the pattern for later epics.

Song of Solomon clearly participates in the epic tradition. Epics tell the adventures of great heroes. The *Odyssey* is named for its main character Odysseus, a great warrior. Like other epic heroes, Odysseus meets many supernatural beings, among them Circe. Circe lives on an island populated with pigs (really men she has bewitched); Milkman's Circe, with her dog-filled house, is a clear analogy. At first sight, Milkman mistakes her for a witch from a fairy tale. Circe seems both very old and ageless because men in their seventies remember her as already ancient when they were boys. Nevertheless, *Song of Solomon*'s direct reference to the *Odyssey* claims epic status for Milkman and his quest. Although he seems ordinary at first, Milkman becomes a hero of great stature. Just as Odysseus' journey had critical importance for his island kingdom of Ithaca, so will Milkman's journey have crucial meaning for the African American community.

At once archetypal and culturally specific, *Song of Solomon* draws on both cross-cultural and African American patterns of narrative for its depiction of Milkman's journey. (As discussed in Chapter 3, an archetype represents a cross-cultural pattern that elicits emotional response partly because of its familiarity.) Critics long ago noticed the frequency of journeys in many different cultures' literatures and drew up paradigms (descriptions of patterns) of the archetypal features. The most famous of these is Joseph Campbell's *The Hero with a Thousand Faces*, which delineates the following stages: trouble in the community, the call to adventure, crossing the threshold from the known to the unknown, ordeals that test the hero, and return to the original community.

Clearly, Milkman's journey conforms to the paradigm. The Dead household has troubles sufficient for several quests. Hearing the call to adventure in Macon's story about the gold, Milkman crosses the threshold by flying east. His many ordeals include the fight in the gas station and the hunt, as well as Guitar's attacks. Milkman returns to Michigan with peace-making information about the episode that alienated Macon and Pilate. *Song of Solomon* participates in archetypal patterns; however, it simultaneously uses patterns specific to African American literature. (See this chapter's earlier discussion of Genre.)

A multicultural perspective reveals *Song of Solomon*'s participation in an extension of these patterns and offers insights about the novel's images of flying. *Song of Solomon* invokes three mythic traditions about flying—European, African American, and American Indian. The novel's opening scene alludes to the European myth of Icarus. (The Icarus story comes from Greece, but can be designated more broadly as European because the Romans spread its influence. In addition, the myth's elements appear in numerous European works of literature, from antiquity to our own time.) In the myth, the builder Daedalus and his son Icarus are imprisoned. They fashion wings of wax and feathers, then fly over their prison walls. Daedalus makes good his escape, but Icarus is carried away with the joy of flight and, ignoring his father's warnings, flies too close to the sun. When the sun melts the wings, Icarus falls into the sea and drowns. As commonly understood, the myth cautions against presumptuous artistic ambition.

The opening of *Song of Solomon* reiterates the Icarus tale. Robert Smith, one of the Seven Days, has homemade wings of blue silk when he flies from the roof of Mercy Hospital. They serve him no better than Icarus's wings, and as Freddie inelegantly says, Smith goes "splat." The opening image of flying from oppression, then, shows a failure. Evidently, the single artist cannot craft wings to carry himself beyond his prison without great loss. However, Pilate (a pun on "pilot") suggests another strategy when she sings *"Sugarman done fly away ... Sugarman done gone home"* to Smith (6).

Pilate's Sugarman belongs to African American myths of Africans flying off from slavery and returning to their homes in Africa. In Virginia, Milkman learns the other verses of the song, which is the key to his family heritage. Over time, the name of the male African ancestor of the

whole Dead family, "Solomon," has become "Sugarman." Solomon succeeded where Smith failed, for he "done gone home," from Solomon's
Leap, a cliff in Virginia. The issue here is not whether the novel indicates
that people can literally fly. If Solomon flew in exactly the same way as
Smith, with exactly the same physical result, the spiritual meaning still
would be different. In the African sacred cosmos, Solomon's spirit endures and completes its journey home to Africa.

   Song of Solomon suggests problems in this tradition, however. As in
the European myth of flying, the airborne person here is male. Solomon's
leap into the air leaves behind Jake (whom he drops), twenty other children, and his wife Ryna. Ryna's eternal grief—Milkman hears her sobs
in Ryna's Gulch—goes beyond a lament for a personal betrayal. If men
fly away, women must remain earth-bound, to care for the children.
(This mythic pattern in fact reflects a historical reality. Male slave narratives often tell the story of a lone escapee; female slave narratives often
recount a woman waiting until she can take her children with her.) The
men's Leap, then, creates the women's Gulch. Freedom for the male individual—leaving as a strategy of resistance to oppression—abandons
the whole community of women and children to the oppressor, the white
people known as "Buckra." In the Sugarman/Solomon song, a woman
singer begs her flying man not to leave his family in the land of cotton,
not to leave her with "Buckra's arms to yoke me" (303). Left an orphan
by Solomon's departure and Ryna's death, baby Jake—Milkman's grandfather Macon—is taken, as the Sugarman song continues, *"to a red man's
house"* (303). The novel then shifts to an American Indian concept of
flying.

   Throughout the novel, *Song of Solomon* suggests parallels between African American and American Indian experiences. Guitar mentions, for
example, that the ground is saturated with black blood, and was soaked
with Indian blood before that. Milkman ruminates that the name of the
state he lives in, Michigan, comes from the Algonquin words for "Great
Water," "michi gami" (329). African American and American Indian cultures literally blend in Milkman's family, when Jake marries Singing
Bird, the daughter of his Indian foster mother, Heddy.

   The impasse suggested by comparing European and African American
myths of male flight—one either dies or abandons family and community—is resolved in the American Indian understanding of flying. Although "Indian" covers a huge diversity of indigenous cultures in the
Americas, some overarching similarities can be located. The following

generalizations bear the same relationship to any particular tribe's beliefs as the African sacred cosmos bears to any specific African people's beliefs.

American Indians' traditions hold that all of creation is sacred and living. What European culture defines as dead, or simply inanimate (never having been alive), remains vital to American Indian cultures. Even rocks and soil are alive. Spiritual energies flow among the various living forms as, for example, people eat food or plants grow. For a time after human beings were created, they could take on animal forms at will, and they were able to communicate with animals.

Song of Solomon confirms this world view through Milkman's thoughts during the hunt. Resting, Milkman hears the variety of sounds that the dogs and men make: "The dogs, the men—none was just hollering, just signaling location or pace. The men and the dogs were talking to each other" (277). This recognition is crucial to Milkman's transformation into an articulate kinsman. A little later, Milkman receives a vital communication from an unexpected source:

> Down either side of his thighs he felt the sweet gum's surface roots cradling him like the rough but maternal hands of a grandfather. Feeling both tense and relaxed, he sank his fingers into the grass. He tried to listen with his fingertips, to hear what, if anything, the earth had to say, and it told him quickly that someone was standing behind him and he had just enough time to raise one hand to his neck and catch the wire that fastened around his throat. (279)

The earth has enabled Milkman to survive Guitar's first attack. The image of the tree as a grandfather suggests the interpenetration of landscape and humanity central to Indian thought. Both the myths of Icarus and of Flying Africans are built on the necessity of leaving an oppressive place. American Indian myth suggests, on the other hand, that the place itself is not oppressive but sacred. One does not fly away from a land but up from it. Freedom does not depend upon leaving a place but on being in harmony with the whole of creation.

Song of Solomon closes with two affirmations of this spiritual concept. By the time that he recreates Solomon's leap, from the same cliff, Milkman knows that one cannot conquer natural forces. Instead, he "knew what Shalimar knew: If you surrendered to the air, you could *ride* it"

(337, emphasis in original). Having become communally literate, having learned the wisdom of the ancestors, Milkman has already become part of the spiritual world. Death matters very little because it will change only the form of his participation in the sacred world.

Beautifully melding African American and American Indian traditions, the finale confirms Milkman's perception that he participates at all times in a spiritual universe. The novel's presentation of Pilate's death and its aftermath demonstrates the process that Milkman may undergo if Guitar succeeds in killing him. Milkman himself connects Pilate to the American Indian sense of place and freedom: "Now he knew why he loved her so. Without ever leaving the ground, she could fly" (336).

The novel offers the reader further connections between African American and American Indian thought in the gleam of Pilate's earring. A famous book connecting African and African American culture, *Flash of the Spirit*, reports that in West African societies, glints of light are thought both to attract ancestral spirits and to testify to their presence. (For this reason, African Americans in the South still make "bottle trees"—barebranched trees with bottles of different colors over the end of the limbs—to bring the ancestors home.) The glint of Pilate's earring draws an ancestral spirit to her grave, so that she is welcomed into the spirit world.

This spirit, a bird awakened by Milkman's singing his "Sugarman" tribute to Pilate, flies into the grave, then moves off with the earring holding Pilate's name. Singing Bird, Pilate's mother, has returned to claim her child. Living ancestors welcome a living Pilate into a sacred landscape.

Tar Baby
(1981)

Toni Morrison's fourth novel expands into new thematic territory. Set largely on an imaginary island in the Caribbean, Isle des Chevaliers, by implication *Tar Baby* meditates on the whole of the African diaspora (the dispersal of originally African peoples through the slave trade). Through the white character Valerian Street, the book shows the United States' economic control of the Caribbean. The novel is therefore grounded in reality, past and present. At the same time, its world contains many mythic elements—talking trees, an old woman whose breasts remain forever milk-filled, and phantom warriors. Whereas only Pilate in *Song of Solomon* perceives spirits, the narrator of *Tar Baby* presents an environment that is conscious, aware of itself and of the characters. In another departure from naturalistic depiction, the title itself suggests a correspondence between its characters and those of a folktale.

What occurs in this mytho-historical setting also differs from the subjects of the earlier novels. Whereas they are stories of children becoming adults, *Tar Baby* in a sense begins where they leave off, with the clash of already-formed adults. The novel focuses on three couples associated with various cultural conflicts. In the white couple, Valerian and Margaret Street, Morrison exposes the dynamics of white American sex roles. (*Tar Baby* is the only one of Morrison's novels to deal extensively with white characters.) Through the first black couple, Sydney and Ondine Childs, *Tar Baby* shows the difficulties of African Americans in educating even their most privileged children in a European-controlled context. The second black couple, Son and Jadine, embody the conflict between traditional, rural southern African American culture and a less defined hybrid culture with elements from Africa, America, and Europe. The relationships among the couples illustrate many contemporary problems of race, class, gender, and national power.

PLOT DEVELOPMENT

Tar Baby opens with an unnamed black man swimming from a ship to the shore of a Caribbean island. This is Son, the "disturbing" element who exposes the problems in this apparent paradise. The island is populated by rich whites who winter there, and their servants. The novel centers on the household of Valerian Street, who has decided to live on the island year-round. Valerian's establishment in many ways resembles an updated Southern plantation. A retired capitalist, Valerian inherited a candy factory, which, as Son points out, uses sugar from Caribbean mills. Akin to the stereotype of the plantation mistress, Valerian's wife Margaret has no particular responsibilities or interests, and merely wanders about vaguely. Occasionally she meddles with the African American servants, Sydney and Ondine, as they perform most of the practical labor of running the household. The heavier yard and house work is performed by Thérèse and Gideon, black natives of a nearby island.

Into this household comes Sydney and Ondine's niece Jadine, whom Valerian has given an expensive education. A top model in Europe, she has come to Isle des Chevaliers to consider whether she wants to marry a European. Just before leaving Europe, she sees a lovely, perfectly self-possessed black African woman dressed in yellow. When the woman spits at her in apparent disgust, Jadine finds herself unable to shake the memory. She expects no such shocking incidents at Isle des Chevaliers.

In this organized world, everyone understands his or her social place. No one speaks honestly of that place except to someone else who shares it. For instance, Sydney and Ondine talk meaningfully to each other, but not to those socially beneath them (Gideon and Thérèse) or to those above them (the Streets). Jadine's place remains unclear, however. As the servants' niece, she would naturally share their status, but she has a much better formal education than they—or than Margaret. She sits at the dinner table with Valerian and Margaret to eat the food that Ondine has cooked and Sydney has served. The routines are well-established, the atmosphere pleasant as everyone evades serious questions

Tar Baby uses the Christmas season, a quintessential family gathering time, as an ironic setting. Previous to Son's arrival, the only dissonant note is the Streets' quarrel over whether their son Michael will return for Christmas. The holiday highlights the fundamental problems in the Street family, in the employer-servant relationship of the Streets and the Childses, and in the Childses' relationship with Jadine.

Son's outsider status destabilizes the superficial harmony. Son initially approaches the Streets' house to find food, but he stays there, hiding, because he is so attracted to Jadine. When Margaret leaves the dinner table and stumbles on Son concealed in her closet, the first crisis is precipitated. The drunken Valerian asks Son to dinner, offending his frightened wife as well as Sydney and Ondine. Son's short stay provokes Margaret to make openly racist comments, Sydney and Ondine to reveal their distaste for his lower class status, and Jadine to admit an ambivalent attraction to him. With little shared experience and few shared values, Son and Jadine nevertheless establish an intense and sexual relationship.

The second crisis occurs at Christmas dinner. Valerian has insisted that the household abandon its customs so that Sydney, Ondine, Son, and Jadine should all dine formally with him and Margaret. At the table, Son remarks that it's too bad Gideon can't join them for the good food. The others know Thérèse and Gideon only by the disrespectful generic names, Yardman and Mary. When the confusion over names is cleared, Valerian reveals that he has fired them for stealing. Ondine becomes extremely angry that she has lost her everyday help without even being consulted. Son is angry that Thérèse and Gideon have lost their livelihood for taking what he thinks was stolen from them first. As the quarrel worsens, it reveals ugly truths about power.

At first, Valerian and Son simply face off. Valerian has been amusing himself with Son's presence, but he does not respect Son and underestimates him. Each feels righteous; each aligns himself with his version of the legends of Isle des Chevaliers. In Valerian's view, the phantom warriors are French soldiers, with a European system of law (the Napoleonic code) to defend. In Son's view, the warriors are blind African horsemen, miraculously escaped from their drowning captors, with their symbiotic relationship to the land to offer as strength.

Gradually the others around the table are drawn into the argument. Valerian fires Sydney and Ondine. When Margaret becomes physically violent, Ondine retaliates in kind—and also tells an old secret. Margaret, she reveals, physically abused her helpless son until he grew old enough to talk. That abuse accounts for his emotional distance from his parents, and his absence from their Christmas table.

Early the next morning Son and Jadine flee the aftermath of the Christmas quarrel, but their own climactic argument is the novel's third crisis. To try to work out a life, they visit both New York City (where Jadine is at home) and Eloe, Florida (Son's tiny hometown). Each finds the other's home ground sterile, even suffocating. Son dislikes urban life and the upwardly mobile jobs that Jadine wants him to prepare for. Jadine doesn't even consider living in the rural South, with its traditional roles for women. In Eloe she has a sort of waking nightmare in which she is visited by spirits of traditional women from Eloe, her aunt Ondine, Thérèse (though she is now old), and the African woman dressed in yellow. Jadine rejects the traditional roles they represent yet feels incomplete and inadequate.

More than personal, their quarrel concerns what constitutes African American culture. To each, the other's values make up a tar baby, a white-designed trap. Son claims to embody authentic black culture and more than once implies that no matter what Jadine's skin color, she is essentially European. Jadine sees Son's refusal to consider usual kinds of employment as effectively choosing poverty and ignorance, and then calling the result true blackness. Unable to live together or even agree on a place to try, Jadine and Son part.

Tar Baby then briefly presents the consequences of the various quarrels. The truth releases Margaret, who becomes active and self-confident, but it destroys Valerian. Unable to accept the knowledge that he chose to be willfully ignorant of Margaret's abuse of Michael, Valerian becomes senile. Jadine returns to Isle des Chevaliers to pick up her belongings. There she must listen to Ondine's reproaches. From her aunt's perspective, Jadine abandoned Ondine and Sydney after Valerian fired them, then matter-of-factly returned without any apology or explanation. Ondine accuses Jadine of not understanding what a daughter owes her surrogate parents, her caretakers. Having found all her relationships unsatisfying, Jadine decides that only she can keep herself emotionally safe, and she leaves for Europe.

In the final scenes, Thérèse pilots a boat through fog to land Son on the shore of Isle des Chevaliers, a replay of the beginning of the novel when he swims there. Son has decided that he needs Jadine and returns to the island without knowing that she has left. He will have to choose whether to follow her or to join the phantom warriors of Isle des Chevaliers. In an ending even more ambiguous than that of *Song of Solomon*, Son is last seen, like Brer Rabbit of the tar baby story, running "lickety split" over Isle des Chevaliers.

CHARACTER DEVELOPMENT

As compared with Morrison's earlier novels, *Tar Baby* has little interest in character development in the sense of presenting characters who develop or change. Instead, the novel introduces the reader to the range of traits within a character by briefly relating his or her history. Then, as the plot develops, different traits emerge as dominant. In this novel, plot tends to reveal characters to themselves, to make them more self-aware, rather than forcing them to acquire new traits. *Tar Baby* does not ask if Son and Jadine can change each other so that their relationship endures, although they assume that this is what must happen. Instead, it asks if they can agree on a way of life that respects both their identities.

Tar Baby generally lets the reader see the characters interacting and then presents their histories. Thus, Chapter 1 shows Valerian and Margaret at their breakfast table, followed by Sydney and Ondine at theirs, with Jadine soon joining them. The narrator describes the characters' families, including the economic situations central to their motivations.

Valerian Street, a retired capitalist, initially wields the most social power. As a wealthy white man from the United States, he enjoys his estate on Isle des Chevaliers. He has inherited wealth from a candy factory that his uncles ran as a patriarchy, with the workers as a sort of extended family and the male owners in the position of an all-powerful father. Although Valerian considers his uncles foolishly sentimental, he runs his household on exactly the same paternalistic basis.

Although he is not a loving man, Valerian is profoundly shocked when his first wife divorces him. He marries a second time primarily to prove to his ex-wife that he is capable of emotion. In the magical Isle des Chevaliers, where all of nature is alive and spirits roam, Valerian sees his first wife. However, knowing that she is dead by now, he believes this manifestation to be a hallucination. His inability to perceive her as a reality shows his alienation from his environment and his spiritual sterility.

Valerian regrets the emotional distance between himself and his son Michael, but he does not initially understand its origins. As the story opens, he is genial, even generous, unless crossed. If opposed, he uses his power in destructive ways. Later, his personality collapses when he is forced to realize how and why he has failed his son. Valerian's senility, however, does not obliterate his personality traits but simply expresses them differently. Throughout his life, Valerian has unconsciously failed to pay attention to life around him if he fears learning something unpleasant. Thus, he did not recognize Margaret's abuse of Michael because, fundamentally, he did not want to know about it. He is horrified when he recognizes this pattern, but his senility is just another form of withdrawal, another way to deny responsibility. When the novel ends, he is a helpless invalid.

Valerian's second wife, Margaret, is a beauty queen much younger than he. Margaret's subjection to Valerian comes from more than women's place in a social structure that gives men more power. Valerian comes from a rich, established family, and Margaret from the working class. With her working-class education, Margaret is badly out of place in Valerian's aristocratic circles. In addition, she has never enjoyed love because her parents were too awed by her beauty to understand her ordinary emotional needs. Initially, Margaret seeks relief from her isolation in friendship with Valerian's servants, especially Ondine, but Valerian forbids her this emotional connection. Margaret learns that childbearing is her only hope of sustaining her social position. Consequently, she resents her only child, their son Michael. Secretly, she physically abuses him, stopping only when the toddler begins to talk and might be able to tell someone.

At the beginning of the novel, although she is only in her forties, Margaret is vague, almost senile. Her energy and concentration are drained by living the lie of the happy family. Released when Ondine tells the truth, Margaret becomes a much stronger, more assertive character. Nevertheless, she still has tendencies to deny her own responsibility. For example, she maintains that Ondine should have stopped the child abuse, and she insists that Michael is not damaged.

Michael, the Streets' adult son, does not appear except in the characters' recollections. Valerian considers him a feckless drifter because he has not settled into any profession. As a baby, he suffered the physical abuse of cigarette burns and pin pricks from his resentful mother. At one point, Valerian discovered him huddled under a sink, but did not draw the obvious conclusions about the boy's fear. The Streets' different expectations about Michael point to their own characters. Though he has made no commitment and never visits, Margaret expects him for Christmas dinner; Valerian knows that he will not come. Thus, Valerian appears to be the realist and Margaret living in a fantasy world. Valerian's reality is very partial, however, given his desire to remain ignorant of unpleasant realities.

African Americans, Sydney and Ondine Childs have served the Streets as domestic workers for many years. Their work is made difficult by their employers' personalities. Both are aware of the shallowness of Valerian's commitment to them. They tolerate their situation because of the steady work, good pay, and the side benefit of a superb education for their niece Jadine. The Childses share some of their employers' prejudices toward Caribbean natives. They refuse to learn the names of those hired for the hardest labor, for example, or even to look at them closely enough to recognize them. Son despises Sydney and Ondine as the equivalent of house slaves who have no loyalty to their own people.

They are, however, extremely loyal to Jadine, whom they have reared. Jadine's education has made her experience quite different from theirs, however, and they do not understand her now. Ondine is particularly hurt that Jadine abandons them by leaving with Son immediately after Christmas dinner, without even knowing whether her aunt and uncle are still employed. On Jadine's return, Ondine confronts her and talks about the responsibilities of being a daughter.

Jadine, also called Jade, has returned to Isle des Chevaliers from Europe in part to visit her aunt and uncle, but mostly to decide whether she should accept a marriage proposal. Though her wealthy European suitor sends her fabulous presents, she clearly does not love him. She considers this marriage to protect herself emotionally. Safety first became important to Jadine when, as a child, she saw a female dog mistreated because it came in heat. That incident has made Jadine fear sexuality as the force that makes women vulnerable.

Jadine is attracted to Son, but she has upper-class expectations and is therefore unable to respect his choices. Jadine wants Son to acquire a college education and a professional job. Her own education has made her consider European culture and art superior to their African counterparts, and she has complete contempt for the rural, Southern, African American culture that Son comes from and loves. Jadine's career as a professional model in Europe symbolically raises questions about who controls her actions and even her body.

Two incidents highlight Jadine's fears about her role as a woman. While she is still in Europe, an African woman in a yellow dress spits at her. Jadine has already noticed and admired the woman's beauty and self-possession. The woman's action shows Jadine as irrevocably separated from African culture. But she seems no more connected to African American or Afro-Caribbean culture. In Eloe, she has a nightmare vision of traditional women including the African woman, Thérèse, her aunt Ondine, and many anonymous countrywomen all reproaching her. Literally an orphan without a family, Jadine is symbolically a cultural orphan. With no sustaining culture, Jadine rejects any traditional idea of family ties. She is deaf to Ondine's discussion of duty to those who have cared for you. Jadine sets out for Europe determined to rely only on her own strength.

Son jumps ship to swim ashore at Isle des Chevaliers. There he disrupts the apparently stable social order by exposing the racial and class tensions. Son considers himself clear-sighted and truthful, but his sentimental notions about women cover his distrust of and violence toward them. He remembers Eloe, the tiny Florida town where he grew up, as the home of all-nurturant women who staff the pie tables at church suppers. This romantic memory is far more powerful than the recollection of how he left Eloe—a fugitive avoiding arrest for his wife's death. He may not have meant to kill his wife Cheyenne, but he is responsible for her death. (To punish her for being with another man, he drunkenly drove a jeep through the wall of their house. Cheyenne died in the resulting flames.) Since then, Son has wandered. He maintains one tie with Eloe—he sends his father, Franklin Green, money orders, although he never adds a letter or even a note.

Son considers all those who accept the social structure, from Valerian through Sydney and Ondine, to be exploiters and liars. He trusts only those at the bottom of the social scale (Gideon and Thérèse), or those who, like himself, do not participate in it at all. Son does not value luxury items such as Jadine's fur coat, seeing them as products made by the suffering of others. He stays on Isle des Chevaliers only for Jadine's company.

Son cannot tolerate life in Jadine's chosen place, New York City. In Eloe he is oblivious to Jadine's problems with traditional roles for women. When Son and Jadine quarrel repeatedly about the values that they want to live by, Son resorts to violence. Too late, he understands how much he wants her love. Looking at Jadine's photographs of Eloe, he sees it through her eyes and realizes its limitations. Son follows Jadine back to the Caribbean and, against the advice of Thérèse, lands on Isle des Chevaliers to look for her. Given that Jadine has already left for Paris, and that Son will certainly be unwelcome on the island, his fate remains uncertain.

Thérèse, a Dominican, does the part of the hard labor defined as "women's work" for Valerian's household. Ondine refuses to learn her name and calls her Mary. Thérèse has her vengeance, however, in refusing to speak to American blacks and refusing to admit that whites exist at all. She believes, for instance, that American women use products manufactured from vital physical materials (such as those expelled after childbirth, the "afterbirth") for trivialities such as hair conditioners. Thérèse sees American culture as predatory and cannibalistic.

Thérèse has breasts that are magically always full of milk, though she is in her sixties, perhaps a sign of her nurturing capabilities. Particularly aware of the island's supernatural forces, Thérèse loves to make up stories. She intuits Son's presence on the island before anyone else sees him, and she and her nephew Gideon leave food for him. Thérèse originally thinks that he might be one of the island's chevaliers; at the end, she hopes that he will abandon his search for Jadine to become a chevalier

Only two years younger than his aunt Thérèse, Gideon tries to make his fortune first in Canada and then in the United States. He returns home because Thérèse has repeatedly lied, asking him to help her manage some nonexistent property. Gideon is not unduly bothered by Thérèse's deception, having lied about his own success abroad. He is more practical than she, happy enough to be home in Dominica even without material success. Valerian's household refers to Gideon as Yardman because he works as their gardener.

The swamp women and the avacado tree are two of the many parts of the island's natural scene that are conscious, that think and even speak. The swamp women consider Jadine odd, unnatural in her desire to be different from them.

Because *Tar Baby* examines myth-making, the reader must be particularly careful not to accept any character's evaluation of any other character at face value. Each character oversimplifies the others to maintain a myth that gives him or her emotional safety or comfort. As part of this process, the characters must also oversimplify themselves and their roles. Seen in context, what appears to be the narrator's statement often turns out to be the characters' points of view. For example, consider the statement about Valerian and Son during their confrontation at the Christmas dinner table: "The man who respected industry looked over a gulf at the man who prized fraternity" (205). The narrator appears to present very simple descriptions of the two, and to indicate that their values are completely opposed. The reader knows, however, that Valerian and Son do share some values. Both men consider jokes demeaning black women as acceptable humor, for instance. The wider context for the dinner table description, then, includes the men's earlier actions and interactions. The context indicates that the apparently objective description is not only subjective, but wrong or at least incomplete.

The events framing the confrontation further undercut the idea of any objectivity in the statement. Clearly, the narrator is describing the characters' self-concepts rather than the reality. Each character has a stake in thinking of himself as a representative of industry or of fraternity. If Valerian's self-image reflects industry, then he can understand Son in stereotyped terms, as the primitive and lazy black male. Son, in turn, can see himself as representing humane values and understand Valerian through stereotypes of the cold-blooded exploiter of black labor. In their struggle over who will control, the two men develop progressively more reductive images of each other as bad and of themselves as good; the industry/fraternity statement comes midway in the process.

The characters offer these stereotyped statements about one another most frequently when they are angry or frightened. (The fear need not refer to physical safety. Much of *Tar Baby* depicts the risk and difficulty involved in giving up a false story that seems to guarantee emotional safety.) Because the plot develops through the crises of arguments, many such confrontations take place. Jadine and Son accuse each other, for example, of stereotypical male irresponsibility and female sexual betrayal: "Mama-spoiled black man, will you mature with me? Culture-bearing black woman, whose culture are you bearing?"(269). The reader must always understand that these statements may be partially or wholly false, and that they often let us know more about the speaker than about the person allegedly described.

THEMATIC ISSUES

The epigraph at the beginning of *Tar Baby* declares one of its major themes: "For it hath been declared unto me of you, my brethren, by them which are of the house of Chloe, that there are contentions among you." From the first book of Corinthians, chapter 1, verse 11, this biblical quotation acknowledges divisions within a community. Remembering that Toni Morrison's real name is Chloe Wofford, the reader sees that "the house of Chloe" is the black community, and *Tar Baby* the bringer of news that it is divided. *Tar Baby* shows quarrels broader than individual disagreements. In its portrait, the black community is split by gender

(Son vs. Jadine), by generation (Jadine vs. Ondine), and by class (Ondine and Sydney vs. Thérèse and Gideon, Ondine and Sydney vs. Son, Jadine vs. Son). In addition, although whites economically dominate the fragmented black community, the white world itself is divided by gender (Valerian vs. Margaret) and generation (Margaret vs. Michael). Of Morrison's novels, only *Tar Baby* includes fully developed white characters. Valerian and Margaret all but disappear in the last third of the novel, however, as *Tar Baby* concentrates on black characters, particularly Son and Jadine.

Beginning with its title, *Tar Baby* investigates the relationships between power and stories, particularly folk tales or myths. The novel examines power in many intersecting structures, including at least nationality, geographic setting, race, class, and gender, each of which becomes a thematic issue. Many of the novel's themes thus center on actual social arrangements. The world that contains these arrangements, however, differs markedly from what readers might expect. All of it living, the natural world in *Tar Baby* resembles the spiritual cosmos of American Indians. It differs from the American Indian conception, however, in seeing natural forces as personifications. In other words, when Jadine falls into the swamp, the narrator describes the mire as not simply alive in itself but inhabited by female spirits:

> The [swamp] women hanging from the trees were quiet now, but arrogant—mindful as they were of their value, their exceptional femaleness; knowing as they did that the first world of the world had been built with their sacred properties; that they alone could hold together the stones of pyramids, and the rushes of Moses's crib; knowing their steady consistency, their pace of glaciers, their permanent embrace, they wondered at the girl's desperate struggle down below to be free, to be something other than they were. (183)

To make satisfying lives, the American black characters must honor their spiritual heritage and recognize the sacredness of the surrounding natural world; at the same time, they must adjust to the industrialized society into which they were born.

To some extent, then, the disjunction between the animated natural world and the social world functions thematically in the novel. If the characters could easily integrate the two worlds, Son and Jadine would have fewer difficulties in their relationship. Most critics think, however, that Toni Morrison had a technical difficulty in writing *Tar Baby* similar to her characters' experiential difficulties in reconciling the two worlds. In the critics' view, she presents a living, active natural world that remains too separate from the social world to be believable.

Tar Baby presents the current social world as a barely changed continuation of historically unjust social and economic structures. In a reprise of European invasion and domination of the Americas, the novel shows that only whites and their servants live on this Caribbean island. Native Indians were, of course, obliterated in the first years of European contact, and the Africans brought to replace them have been pushed off the most desirable land. Gideon and Thérèse, for example, could never afford to live on Isle des Chevaliers.

The strong continuity between past and present is explicit. As Son notes, the Street family's candy factory uses Caribbean sugar, so that Valerian's wealth is founded on poorly paid Caribbean labor. In addition, from the seventeenth until the early nineteenth century, the manufacture of sugar in the Caribbean used slave labor in a system even more devastating than that in the United States. Sugar was exported to the United States, which used it to make whiskey, and the whiskey was then traded to Africans for more slaves—the so-called "iron triangle" of the slave trade.

The whole set-up of Isle des Chevaliers recalls a plantation. Like many large plantation homes, the Streets' mansion has a name: l'Arbe de la Croix. "Croix" is French for a cross used for crucifixion. The identity of those crucified is suggested by its origins—the house was built by Haitian laborers without a union. Valerian's vision of Isle des Chevaliers shares with the antebellum South a self-aggrandizing mythology of knights and chivalry. Valerian defines the chevaliers of the island's name as Napoleonic soldiers, thus linking himself with past imperial glories. Under Valerian's management, the island shelters only rich Americans and the "aristocracy" exiled from other empires. (Valerian's only crony, the French dentist Dr. Michelin, was run out of France's one-time colony, Algeria, by the independence movement there.) With its artificiality, its dependence on black labor with a white master presiding, Valerian's greenhouse is a symbolic plantation.

Valerian exercises a master's power on his household. His will determines his wife's movements, for example. Margaret dislikes living on Isle des Chevaliers and would like to return to the United States, but Valerian simply ignores her wishes. And, of course, his decisions about where to live determine his employees' residence also. Although Sydney and Ondine are not enslaved, they are economically dependent on him, particularly as they age. Valerian has been generous to the Childs family, educating Jadine, for example. However, the proverb "Be just before you are generous" accurately describes the problems with such generosity. Sydney and Ondine are not themselves empowered to act for their niece, and they cannot leave Valerian's employment without sacrificing her education. Further, Valerian's generosity is whimsical, subject to recall without notice. Sydney must ask, for instance, if he and Ondine still have jobs after the disastrous Christmas dinner.

Tar Baby does not present Valerian as personally responsible for all social injustice, but it does indict the group that he represents by showing the far-reaching effects of its abuses of power. Even those who try to opt out of the economies controlled by others like Valerian cannot escape. Such people are not free to define themselves because they must define themselves against the dominant political and economic system. Thus, Son is an "undocumented" man, without any national identification such as a social security number. Like a slave fleeing without a pass, Son is a fugitive without a passport.

Although European domination and African slavery provide the underlying structure for social interaction, personal identity is more complex than the roles of master and slave. Every dominant nation, race, social class, or gender places social limitations on others. These factors individually affect a person's identity, and each particular effect may be either submerged or pre-eminent depending on the situation. That is, in one situation a character might act from her understanding of herself as a woman; in another, she might react from a definition of herself based on social class or on race. Often, she reacts from a combination of these structures, say, as a white woman or as an upper-class woman.

Margaret's experience demonstrates the complications of power. As the young white wife of a rich white American, she has more power than Valerian's black servants, Sydney and Ondine. Yet in considerable measure, what class and race distinctions give her, gender takes away. Her husband Valerian controls her behavior, forbidding her intimacy with Ondine, for example. Valerian also mocks the mistakes that come from her limited formal education, the result of her working-class origins. Told by a friendly woman of Valerian's acquaintance to "get busy" making babies, Margaret naturally resents being valued only for her reproductive capabilities. Isolated by new upper-class status (which is not hers but only hers as Valerian's wife), she takes out her anger at her class-based and gender-based powerlessness on the only person with less power than she, her child.

Characters may share positions in one or two of the power structures yet be widely separated by their experiences in another. Margaret and Jadine, for example, share gender and class, but not race. Thus, as unusually beautiful women, and as hangers-on to the upper class, Margaret and Jadine can initially agree to reject Son as lower class, but Margaret makes Jadine uncomfortable when she adds racial stereotypes by calling him a gorilla. In fact, Jadine frequently experiences discomfort "with the way Margaret stirred her into blackening up or universaling out, always alluding to or ferreting out what she believed were racial characteristics. She ended by resisting both . . ." (64).

Although any single aspect of identity—gender, race, or class—may be dominant at one time, the others do not vanish. Jadine is simultaneously female, and black, and attached to the upper class. In another instance of overlapping identities, Valerian and Son laugh over "three colored whores who went to heaven" (148). Here, their being male matters more than any other factor. Almost always, however, race and class separate them, as when Valerian thinks of the Isle's phantom warriors as Europeans and Son thinks of them as Africans. Identities are not composed of discrete elements that simply "turn up," as playing dice have six sides but only one number "up" on any given throw. Instead, identities are more like trees in bloom, where the trunk, the leaves, the buds, and the blossoms are all simultaneously functioning parts of the tree.

Examples of the complications of power and identity abound. *Tar Baby* does not present a "real" self or person that is influenced by the "outside" pressures of class, gender, and other factors. Instead, it presents the self as a construction made by experiencing one's particular combination of these factors. Because of his class and his rural background, Son can establish a relationship with Thérèse and Gideon. Their identities do not completely coincide, however, because their nationalities differ, and their nations of origin have vastly different amounts of power.

Each nation or class or gender thus acquires characteristic patterns of behavior. For years, Son has been traveling outside the United States, and he is repulsed by the consistency with which generous, courageous people are killed there. (In real life, the period of Son's travels is just after the assassinations of Martin Luther King, Jr., and Robert Kennedy. Son perceives that the country is killing people before they reach King's or Kennedy's level of influence and power.) In exile, Son sees himself as separate from the violence of the United States. *Tar Baby* shows clearly the self-deception in Son's ideas. As an "undocumented" man (166), Son resists many traditional violent uses of power. He cannot, however, remain unaffected by them all, and he participates in some of them.

A seemingly trivial fishing incident illustrates his character's overlap with traditional American male roles. In a small boat off the coast of Argentina, Son and two companions—a Swedish man and a Mexican man—are fishing for snapper. The other men have been enjoying considerable success one entire afternoon whereas Son has been luckless. When he lands a large fish, it looks as though his luck has changed, and the other men congratulate him. The fish shows unexpected resistance, however, and manages to jump into the air and slap Son's face with its tail. The Swede and the Mexican are vastly amused, until Son dismembers the fish by placing its head on his knee and smashing it with his fist. Son's grotesque violence does not result from self-defense; the only thing at stake is his sense of dignity.

The reaction of Son's companions demonstrates, in miniature, international perceptions of the United States. The Swede laughs at him, but the Mexican man identifies him as *"Americano. Cierto Americano. Es verdad"* [Translation: American, certainly American. Truly.] (167). As a distant and European country, Sweden has had mostly amicable dealings with the United States. The Swede is therefore amused, not threatened, by Son's violence. As a bordering nation, however, Mexico has experienced American violence first-hand—in the nineteenth century, the United States forced Mexico to give up one-third of its national territory. Historically, the United States has invaded Central America (though not Mexico) many times. Predictably, the Mexican is not amused by Son's temper and sudden violence. The Mexican man's reaction does not display prejudice because he actually sees Son commit a violent, vengeful act against an animal. Instead, the reaction is based on the obvious connection between Son's socialization as an American male and his day-to-day behavior. And Son has participated directly in his nation's violence because he has been a soldier in Vietnam.

America's training for men echoes in Son's everyday actions. Violence characterizes not only his interactions with men but his emotional experiences with women. He leaves the United States to flee the legal consequences of his part in his wife Cheyenne's death. Like the other characters, Son remains static. Far from learning from the experience that exiled him, he re-enacts it with Jadine. As critic John Duvall points out, a careful reading of Son and Jadine's last quarrel indicates rape. Son has accused Jadine of sexually betraying him and the entire black race by even considering marriage with a white man. He tears off his shirt while reciting the tar baby story to her, and the scene is full of her protests, "Don't touch me!" and "Quit! Leave me *alone!*" (270). Son leaves Jadine "slippery, gutted" (271)—raped. The word "gutted" connects Son's violence toward Jadine with his earlier brutal killing of the fish. At times, then, even the "undocumented" Son reacts in ways characteristic of the extremely aggressive American male role.

In the world of *Tar Baby*, identity is always complex. First one factor, then another, sometimes combinations of two or three factors, determine one's social status at the moment. This social position in turn constructs our perceptions because we have no choice but to see from where we are standing—and what we see already implies an interpretation.

Tar Baby examines the connections of social position and interpretation through the folktale of its title. The novel depicts the characters' various implied interpretations of the tar baby story, and the reasons for these different interpretations. Myth functions differently in *Tar Baby* than in Morrison's earlier books. In *The Bluest Eye*, Claudia narrates another person's experience in terms that parallel the Demeter/Persephone myth. In this novel, the ways that the characters interpret the tar baby myth are the ways in which they understand their own experience too. What one sees in the myth, then, corresponds to what one sees in actual experience. The characters' interpretations not only differ but clash. These disagreements stem, Morrison shows, from the interpreters' very different social positions.

On another level, *Tar Baby* goes beyond showing characters' readings of the tar baby story. Joining many other versions of its title myth, *Tar Baby* retells the folktale and issues a triple invitation to readers: (1) to become aware of their own interpretation of the tar baby story, (2) to refine this interpretation by comparing it with those of the characters, and (3) to see what understanding emerges if the values implied in one's interpretation are applied to the novel's version of the myth—who or what do you, from the vantage point of your particular and complex identity, see as *Tar Baby's* tar baby?

AN INTERTEXTUAL READING

Intertextual readings, as the phrasing suggests, concentrate on the relationships of a particular text to other texts. Intertextuality assumes that a particular book is always related to the texts of its own time, and to earlier texts. To some extent, this way of reading resembles the older critical approach of connecting a work to a literary tradition through studying the influence of one writer on another. Thus, both intertextual readings and influence studies might discuss *Tar Baby*'s connection to Zora Neale Hurston's *Their Eyes Were Watching God* (1937), a novel central to the development of African American fiction. In Hurston's work, a romantic couple, Janie and Jody Starks, settle in the rural, all-black Florida town of Eatonville. Morrison has chosen in "Jadine" a name that recalls "Janie." More importantly, Jadine and Son's trip to Eloe clearly parallels Janie and Jody's venture. In addition, the dialogue of *Tar Baby* in the first Eloe scene closely follows that in the analogous scene of Hurston's novel. Both intertextual criticism and influence studies would note these parallels. Their discussions would diverge, however, because their premises differ.

Intertextual criticism comes from a branch of literary theory. Rather than providing interpretations of individual texts, "theory" investigates the ways that we read. Literary theory covers issues such as how we choose what's important in a text and how we decide on the meanings for what we have chosen. Intertextual criticism defines "text" much more broadly than the essays, fiction, and poetry that constitute traditionally defined literature. Newspaper editorials, letters to the editor, advertisements, television programs—all the materials of popular culture—are considered texts.

Furthermore, intertextual criticism's understanding of identity and experience differs sharply from that of traditional criticism. Intertextuality is based on the premise that both actual people and literary characters experience reality as a series of stories, of texts. They "read" their experience by constructing stories and meanings. Most people are familiar with the idea that interpretations of a story may differ and even contradict one another. Extending this idea, intertextualist critics believe that people's interpretations of the "same" real event may differ so much that they have different experiences. We react to actual events, and literary characters react to fictional events, by making up a story. Stories, then, are how we structure our reality to make sense. Stories connect and explain the events that we choose as meaningful in our experience.

How we choose and arrange the events that are the raw materials of our stories depends upon what patterns we know. These patterns come from the stories that we've heard and read previously, the texts that our culture has provided. All experience consists of texts that we read in the context of the texts that we already know. In a sense, all of us are following "scripts" that have been socially provided for us.

This view implies a paradox about human experience. On one hand, people seem less free than in a traditional view because they process their experience through the scripts that they have unconsciously absorbed from previous texts. On the other hand, in this view reality is far more malleable. Because reality isn't simply "there" but is always an interpretation, people can understand their experiences in several different, valid ways. Experience becomes richer, and individual growth more likely, because we are not burdened with an unchangeable past or a static identity. Taking advantage of the system's flexibility relies, however, on having a wide variety of texts available—and on being conscious of which of these texts we select to make our experiences meaningful.

An intertextual reading of *Tar Baby* approaches the novel in two contexts: (1) the texts of African American culture in general, and (2) the texts of earlier versions of the tar baby tale. In *Playing the Changes*, critic Craig Werner has traced the development of the tar baby story and discussed the various meanings that its readers have constructed from it. The basic plot, he says, has remained fairly consistent across four hundred years and a move from Africa to the United States. The story begins as Brer Rabbit or another trickster figure sees Tar Baby. (Tar Baby consists of tar shaped to resemble a human figure.) In some versions, Tar Baby has been made and placed in Brer Rabbit's way by the rest of the animals; in others, by a white farmer. Brer Rabbit greets Tar Baby, who of course does not reply. Angry at this insult, Brer Rabbit hits the Tar Baby, and his paw sticks tight. As the cycle of perceived insult and retaliation repeats, Brer Rabbit gets progressively more stuck to the Tar Baby. Finally those who made Tar Baby appear to torment him with their cleverness and his helplessness. Brer Rabbit appears to be humble and submissive, but he fools his captors. Torture him in any way, he begs, but do not throw him into the nearby brier patch. Of course, rabbits live in brier patches, which are their best protection. Wanting to hurt him as much as possible, his captor throws him into the brier patch. From the safety of his home, Brer Rabbit taunts the captor, who has not only allowed the escape but has been used as the means of escape.

Readers of this text have made many meanings from it. In nonracialized contexts, for example, a reader might interpret it as a story about a child confronting adults' power, or about a person confronting his own repressed desires. Werner examines the text first in the nonracialized context of West Africa before European contact, then in the racialized context of the American South.

In West African societies, the trickster figure was an individualist who often harmed the community at large. Although his cleverness might be admired, it was also feared. "Readers" of the text (listeners, of course, because the cultures were oral) would highlight the costs of the behavior, both to the trickster and the community. As the context shifts from West Africa to the United States—that is, as readers have different social texts available—the nature of the trickster figure and its meaning also shift.

In the dramatically racialized society of the United States, the tar baby tale became a racial allegory. (In allegory, each character stands for an abstract trait.) In this reading, the white farmer represents the white world's power to enslave blacks, and Brer Rabbit stands for African Americans. Directly struggling against this power merely leads to disaster (Brer Rabbit stuck to the tar). Instead, blacks must learn to fool the white masters by wearing a mask—playing the part that the whites expect (in this case, the frightened, stupid captive). Using what they know of the master (in this case his desire to be as cruel as possible) ultimately leads to freedom (the brier patch). The costs of Brer Rabbit's trickery would no longer be paid by a valued community but by the slave masters. Accordingly, the selfish individualist of the West African tale became in the oral folklore of African Americans a much more positive figure of survival and resistance to white control.

White America did not *hear* the Brer Rabbit story, however. Instead, beginning in 1880, whites read it in Joel Chandler Harris's Uncle Remus tales. Harris's stories have a "frame." They are not presented directly; instead, the reader overhears the stories told by an old black man to a white child. The frame thus promotes the plantation myth; its picture of racial harmony clashes with many of the stories' plots. Although the frame unconsciously denies the history of enslavement that the tar baby represents, in their time the Harris versions were socially useful. Increasingly, as the nineteenth century wore on, the Ku Klux Klan and its ilk presented texts defining black men as rapists, beasts. The countertext of Harris's kindly "uncles" and "mammies" provided an alternative.

The 1948 Walt Disney version of the Tar baby story, Werner argues, presented a more extreme version of Harris's text. And given the texts produced during the seventy intervening years, Harris's uncles and mammies were no longer useful in changing the nation's social climate. The Disney version, in fact, made Uncle Remus and the white child "real" and Brer Rabbit a cartoon figure. In effect, this made the trickster, the figure of black resistance, merely imaginary. In the Disney text, the nation's history of enslavement and exploitation could be hidden behind the portrait of Uncle Remus, the happy black person primarily concerned with nurturing and entertaining white children. Black resistance and triumph? A figment of the imagination. The Disney version was the last major reworking of the tar baby story before Morrison's novel.

Even today, Tar Baby remains a quintessentially racial text in the racialized society of America. The enslaved black community, Harris, and Disney all produced racialized texts. The larger context of racial awareness does not limit readers' interpretations, however. Various readers have understood the tar baby to mean anything from white racist stereotypes (which it is futile to spend time denying) to the materialism of European-American culture. Depending on the interpreter, the brier patch has meant the whole of the U.S. black community, part of the black community, or Africa. Morrison takes advantage of the tale's many possibilities by showing that the actions of *Tar Baby*'s characters imply their different readings of the text.

The simplest readings come from the Streets and Thérèse. Almost the only thing that Valerian and Margaret can agree on is the need for safety, and they both define safety in terms of controlling black people. Neither of the Streets would see Brer Rabbit as a black trickster; for them, only the ugly and dangerous Tar Baby is black. Valerian's need for control is obvious—forbidding Margaret to befriend Ondine, firing Thérèse and Gideon, firing Sydney and Ondine despite their many years of service. The Streets project everything that they fear onto blacks. Margaret displays this tendency most obviously when she assumes that Son is hiding in her closet in hopes of raping her. At the same time, the Streets live on a kind of re-created plantation. Both Margaret and Valerian expect their black servants to be responsible for their care. Margaret even expected Ondine to take responsibility for Margaret's abuse of her child. To the Streets, Brer Rabbit's return to his brier patch is just what they would have anticipated, a preference for an uncivilized wilderness.

Thérèse's reading of the tar baby is equally simple, a countertext to the Streets' interpretation. Thérèse views the tar baby as any contact with the white world, or any contact with a black person who has absorbed the values of that world. Once get involved with whites, and you're stuck. She urges Son to consider Jadine a tar baby who has "forgotten her ancient properties" (her meanings as a black woman). Thérèse's alternative is the marginalized existence of the brier patch—either living on the island next to Isle des Chevaliers, or joining the phantom warriors.

Both of these simple readings have obvious problems. Fixated on safety, the Streets have no idea of the reality around them, of how Sydney and Ondine think of them, for example. Gideon points out that Thérèse's vision also obscures reality. When Thérèse makes up a story about Son in Valerian's home, Gideon objects that crucial elements are missing: "While you making up your story about what this one thinks and this one feels, you have left out the white bosses. What do they feel about this? It's not important who this one loves and who this one hates . . . if you don't figure on the white ones and what they thinking about it all" (111). Thérèse has forgotten a critical element of the tar baby tale. Brer Rabbit escapes by knowing the farmer's weakness (his cruelty)—only knowing the whites, not ignoring them, can lead to liberation.

With years of employment in the Streets' home, Sydney and Ondine have had years to learn about whites. Their interpretation of tar baby, in fact, shows too much white influence, too much agreement with Margaret and Valerian. Sydney and Ondine consider Valerian the farmer who has unwittingly imported the tar baby, Son, who threatens their niece Jadine. To them almost as much as to the Streets, Son personifies ignorance, poverty, and potential violence. Nevertheless, their reading diverges from the Streets'—they would not see *every* black man as the tar baby.

Son and Jadine develop more complicated readings of the text of tar baby. Son makes his explicit during their last quarrel: Jadine is the tar baby, ostensibly black but really created by and serving white interests. He sees himself as Brer Rabbit, the heroic individualist. By the end of the novel, however, he has confronted the limitation of his reading. Eloe had been his brier patch, his safe home. Loving Jadine, however, he suddenly becomes aware of its thorns. Eloe no longer seems everything desirable. At the end of *Tar Baby*, Son is searching for Jadine. Brer Rabbit would not seek out the tar baby a second time. Son has changed his reading of the tar baby text.

Jadine's reading is harder to discern. For a while, Jadine accepts Son's presentation of himself as Brer Rabbit without realizing or accepting that she is cast as the tar baby. Jadine's tar baby may be Son's original brier patch—Eloe, and the limited, traditional roles that it offers black women. Jadine's description of nighttime in Eloe foregrounds its blackness. As the "blackest nothing she had ever seen" (251), it threatens her deeply.

When that black is populated, it's even worse, because she is visited by the spirits of traditional black women, all of whom despise her. If Jadine's reading is certain of its tar baby, however, its brier patch remains as unclear as Son's, and for the same reason. She had hoped that New York would prove to be the brier patch, a place where she and Son could make a home. When that fails, she leaves for Europe, in effect giving up the effort of reading tar baby in the American context. Nevertheless, her attitude shows that her reading can change: "The same sixteen answers to the question What went wrong? kicked like a chorus line. Having sixteen answers meant having none. So none it was" (290). If she is not able to construct a reading of her experience, at least she is not oversimplifying it. She has sixteen possible versions, and hence no authoritative version. The text of her experience has many possible readings; the book of her life is still open.

Having examined the characters' readings of the tar baby tale, the reader has still another task—constructing his or her own reading of *Tar Baby*. A reading of Jadine as the tar baby oversimplifies. *Tar Baby* itself might seem to confirm that interpretation because when Jadine falls into the swamp, she emerges covered with tar. That text can be read another way, however. After his escape, Brer Rabbit sits in the brier patch and licks tar from his fur. Jadine may, then, be Brer Rabbit. Son is certainly Brer Rabbit because in the final scene the narrator describes him as moving with the same sound as the Brer Rabbit of the fable, "lickety split." Two Brer Rabbits? Perhaps Margaret is a third, stuck all those years to the tar baby of her secret—not the secret of her child abuse, but the secret of its cause, her real social position. Margaret's brier patch seems to be a home in which Valerian has been forced to know who Margaret is, and thus forced to relinquish his control.

Tar Baby offers several Brer Rabbits, I think, but only one tar baby: oversimplifying oneself or others for a false dream of safety. Given the characters'—and our—racialized context, the characters' oversimplifications generally rely on racial terms. Valerian cannot qualify as Brer Rabbit because he alone can't change his reading. Confronted with the truth about Margaret, and the related truth about himself, he can't make a new story. Instead, he collapses into an invalid, a white child taken care of by an older black man, Sydney. Valerian has withdrawn from the Brer Rabbit story itself and moved into the Harris frame for it. Sitting in his greenhouse, Valerian literally is no longer where the action is. Margaret is active, folding clothes. Jadine is on a plane to Paris. Son is running over the ground of Isle des Chevaliers. The novel's last images show all of them in motion, presumably moving toward the brier patch.

Where is the brier patch? Could be anywhere. Nowhere, if you can't change your ideas about where it might be. Not where you thought it would be? Reread the text of your experience. Not satisfied with this interpretation of *Tar Baby*? Reread that text too. Put it up against other texts, change its contexts. "Lickety-split. Lickety-split. Lickety-lickety-lickety-split" (306).

Beloved
(1987)

Morrison's critically acclaimed novel *Beloved* probes the most painful part of the African American heritage, slavery, by way of what she has called "rememory"—deliberately reconstructing what has been forgotten. The novel is set after the Civil War and emancipation, during the period of national history known as Reconstruction (1870–90). Much of the characters' pain occurs as they reconstruct themselves, their families, and their communities after the devastation of slavery. They cannot put slavery behind them by a simple act of will. As the novel opens, the past literally haunts the present. Visible only as red light, a spiteful ghost harasses the main female character, Sethe, and her daughter Denver. When the main male character, Paul D, expels the ghost, it returns in human form as the character Beloved. The past cannot be exorcized; it demands recognition in the present. The recognition involved in rememory requires more than the work of individuals; it is a continual, communal process.

Beloved continues the earlier novels' exploration of themes such as the black community, motherhood, and the relationship between a man and a woman. At the same time, it enlarges the scope of its investigation by exploring each theme in relation to slavery. The novel depicts a group attempt to escape from slavery. Although several people die, Paul D, Sethe, and Sethe's children find their separate ways to freedom. In examining their lives as slaves, their escapes, and their experiences in freedom, *Beloved* joins one of the oldest written African American literary traditions, the slave narrative.

Dealing with slavery, emancipation, and Reconstruction, *Beloved* begins what Morrison has planned as a trilogy exploring African American history and culture. Morrison's next novel, *Jazz*, concentrates on the early twentieth century, the historical era immediately following that of *Beloved*. The title of the third novel, *Paradise*, suggests the scope of Morrison's project by recalling the work of the fourteenth-century Italian poet, Dante. In the three volumes of his *Divine Comedy*, Dante recounts his spiritual journey through hell, purgatory, and paradise. Dante's trilogy works on two levels. *The Divine Comedy* contains many details about the politics of Dante's own time and place, the fourteenth-century city-state of Florence. It also depicts a whole cosmology, exploring themes such as justice, punishment, and the individual soul's relationship with God. By invoking Dante, Morrison signals that her trilogy will consider such heroic themes in the specifics of African American experience.

PLOT DEVELOPMENT

Beloved contains three formal parts that tell many gradually emerging stories simultaneously. Set in 1873–74, Part One covers events from Paul D's arrival at Sethe's home to his departure when he hears that many years before Sethe killed her daughter Beloved. As the book opens, Paul D and Sethe have not seen each other for eighteen years, since their escape from Sweet Home and slavery in 1856. A beautiful Kentucky plantation, Sweet Home originally houses a white couple, Mr. and Mrs. Garner, and nine slaves: Baby Suggs and her grown son Halle, six men named Paul A through Paul F, and Sixo. Mr. Garner runs an unusual plantation. His male slaves have no legal or social standing as men, but Garner allows them many male privileges. They are allowed to make some independent decisions and to carry weapons, for example. Garner also permits Halle to buy his mother's freedom. To replace Baby Suggs, the Garners buy a fourteen-year-old girl, Sethe. Two years later Sethe and Halle "marry"—the law does not recognize slaves' marriages—and have children. When Mr. Garner dies and a cruel man called Schoolteacher becomes the master, the slaves attempt a group escape. At least two Pauls and Sixo die. Schoolteacher's nephews brutally abuse Sethe sexually, sucking milk from her breasts and whipping her back bloody. Halle and Sethe's three children—two sons and the two-year-old daughter later known as Beloved—reach safety in Baby Suggs's home in Ohio, a free state. Halle is lost, however, and Sethe just manages to reach Baby Suggs. On the journey, she gives birth to a daughter whom she names Denver, after the runaway white servant girl who has helped her.

Aided by a black man named Stamp Paid, Sethe and baby Denver come to Baby Suggs's healing house. By preaching and living love, Baby Suggs ministers to all that is wounded—Sethe's body, individuals' self-images, and her community's sense of its collective worth. When Sethe and Baby Suggs have enjoyed twenty-eight days of being a family united in freedom, Baby Suggs gives a party to celebrate. Although the surrounding community enjoys the feast, it also envies Baby Suggs's comparatively whole family and her prosperity. Poor and without most of their own families, the rest of the community decides that Baby Suggs's party constitutes bragging. By the next day, the community's envy has overwhelmed its loyalty, and no one warns Baby Suggs that School-teacher and his men are on their way. When they ride into Baby Suggs's yard, Sethe tries to kill herself and her children rather than return to slavery. (Under the Fugitive Slave Act, Schoolteacher can reclaim Sethe and her children, even from a free state.) Sethe is stopped after she cuts two year-old Beloved's throat with a hand saw. The child dies. The community's betrayal mortally hurts Baby Suggs, who takes to her bed and slowly dies.

Sethe receives only a short jail sentence for killing Beloved. Because she will not agree that she did anything wrong, however, she and her remaining three children receive a larger penalty from the black community—complete social isolation for the next eighteen years. Only one visitor calls on Sethe's household, the ghost who drives off her sons, Buglar and Howard. Although Denver at one point attends a school run by Lady Jones, she becomes deaf when the children tease her about her mother's deed. She does not hear sound again until the ghost arrives. Paul D enters this static situation and immediately sets events in motion by evicting the ghost.

Like Sethe's experiences, Paul D's life after Sweet Home is presented in a series of flashbacks. In Georgia, Paul D suffered a second enslavement, a chain gang. Holding life-and-death power, the guards sexually abuse the prisoners. Paul D copes by shrinking his emotions and refusing to remember. The prisoners escape together, still chained, during the confusion and danger of a flood and mudslide. The escapees spend several weeks with a group of Cherokees, themselves fugitives from U.S. soldiers herding them westward after the latest broken treaty. When Paul

D leaves the Cherokee camp, he begins the wandering life that brings him to Sethe's door.

Almost immediately Paul D rids Sethe's house of the harassing ghost. (Sethe and her daughter Denver assume that the ghost is the spirit of Sethe's dead daughter, known only by the incomplete inscription on her tombstone, "Beloved.") Later, Sethe, Paul D, and Denver return home to find a mysterious young woman who, the narrator tells us, walked fully clothed "out of the water" of a creek behind Sethe's house. Referring to this woman as "Beloved," the narrator describes Sethe's first meeting with Beloved in terms that suggest birth: Sethe's body gushes water, a parallel to the breaking of waters just before labor.

Beloved has both mental and physical peculiarities. Parts of her body threaten to fall off; some teeth do fall out. She has a scar on her throat. Her infrequent speech is childish. Though apparently a stranger, she knows intimate things about Sethe, including the lullaby that Sethe sang for her babies.

The rest of Part One revolves around the characters' developing relationships with Beloved. Denver identifies the woman as the returned ghost and welcomes her as a sister. Soon, however, she is frightened to discover that the spirit is covertly attacking Sethe. For example, while pretending to massage Sethe's neck, Beloved tries to choke her. In the meantime, Paul D dislikes Beloved but finds her supernaturally, irresistibly sexually attractive. Under a kind of spell or compulsion, he has sex with her. The ghost's presence thus disrupts every relationship. Stamp Paid adds the final destabilizing element to this volatile mix by telling Paul D how Beloved died. When Sethe confirms the truth of the events, if not the common interpretation of them, Paul D reproaches her in a particularly hurtful way that recalls a racist stereotype. Earlier, Sethe had overheard Schoolteacher telling his nephews to make two lists describing her, one for her human traits and one for her animal traits. Paul D implies the same accusation, that Sethe has acted in an animalistic way, when he tells her that she has "two legs, not four" (273). Unable to accept Sethe's past, or her attitude toward it, he leaves.

Much shorter, with many fewer events in the present, Part Two explores several characters' states of mind. This section matter-of-factly depicts shocking happenings in the present that connect to the painful past. For instance, Stamp Paid finds a clump of hair with a red braid in the river and knows instantly that a little black girl has been murdered by whites. In trying to assimilate this experience, he misses Baby Suggs's healing. Moving from present to past, he remembers that he failed to help Baby Suggs when she was grieving over the community's betrayal. Stamp Paid also revisits the past when he reveals to Paul D the slave experience that led him to choose his unusual name. His master had sexually exploited Stamp Paid's wife, Vashti. Like other enslaved men, Stamp Paid could not protect his wife nor attack his master. To avoid transferring his anger to Vashti, he separates himself from her. He becomes "Stamp Paid" as a way of saying that he's paid his dues. Every time someone calls his name, then, this past experience is evoked.

If the past preoccupies Paul D and Stamp Paid, Sethe's household is living entirely in a past-controlled present, with no thought of the future. Caring less and less about her adult responsibilities, Sethe plays with Denver and Beloved like a child. To examine this unusual household, Part Two sequentially explores the minds of all three women with a technique called stream of consciousness. Through stream of consciousness, an author presents a character's thoughts and feelings directly, to communicate the immediacy of experience. Stream of consciousness presentations usually contain passages without conventional sentences or paragraphs, sometimes without any punctuation. In this way, writers attempt to convey the internal working of our minds, which tend to use images and phrases rather than the formalized patterns of speech or writing. Similarly, a stream of consciousness passage does not offer ideas in a logical order but instead in an associative order: one idea reminds the character of another because of that character's individual experiences.

Denver's and Sethe's minds are not difficult to follow. They exult in Beloved's return, feeling that part of themselves has come back. Beloved's mind, however, presents a challenge because her consciousness jumps from topic to topic. Further, she is thinking about experiences far removed from the reader's. Beloved remembers separating from Sethe when she died, for example, and joining many other bodies under water. She also remembers things that don't seem to belong to baby Beloved's experience, for example, being on board ships. Presumably these are the ships that brought enslaved Africans to the United States. Readers can interpret thoughts and images in Beloved's consciousness in several different ways. Often the writing makes it impossible to settle on a definitive meaning. Beloved is, after all, a spirit with experiences of a different world.

A brief section, Part Three opens with Sethe's household in desperate trouble and ends with a reunion between Sethe and Paul D. To make this reconciliation possible, both must come to terms with the past; symbolically, the ghost must leave. As the section opens, Sethe, Denver, and Beloved are starving because Sethe has lost her job and she doesn't care. With her two-year-old understanding of her own death, Beloved berates Sethe for having left her. Sethe cares only about explaining that she loved Beloved and never intended to abandon her. As Beloved assumes more and more authority, Sethe acts like a fearful child. Neither Beloved nor Sethe takes any notice of Denver.

In this emergency, Denver gathers courage to ask her old schoolteacher, Lady Jones, for help. To reach Lady Jones, she must leave the yard alone for the first time in years. As she wavers, terrified, she hears Baby Suggs's voice reminding her of her ancestors' courage. When Denver worries that she can't be safe because there's no guaranteed self-defense, Baby Suggs agrees and maintains that, nevertheless, one must venture into the world.

Denver's venture secures help from the community in two ways. Acting on Lady Jones's information that Sethe is unwell, neighbors leave food in the yard—their first contact with Sethe in eighteen years. Through Lady Jones, Denver gets a job with elderly whites, the Bodwins, who had been abolitionists. She can thus take on the adult role of supporting her family. Another of the Bodwins' domestic workers learns the true situation in Sethe's home and tells the community. Remembering how circumstances forced them to act in the past, the women of the community move beyond judging Sethe for Beloved's death. They gather at Sethe's gate, determined to defend her.

This climactic scene resolves several thematic tensions such as Sethe's relationship to her community, Sethe's ability to change, and the proper relationship of past and present. From the gate, the assembled women see Sethe and the pregnant Beloved standing in the doorway. Some begin to pray, and then a leader, Ella, "hollers." The others join, neither singing nor speaking, but making a wordless sound of terrific spiritual power. Just then, Denver's employer Mr. Bodwin rides up. Psychically frozen in time since she killed Beloved, Sethe cannot distinguish between Mr. Bodwin in the present and Schoolteacher in the past. She sees only that a man is riding into her yard. Determined to do now what she could not do before, she protects her children by attacking the man with an ice pick. Fortunately, the women pull her away before she damages him. Misunderstanding, Beloved thinks that her mother has once again abandoned her. She leaves, and a boy reports having seen a woman with fish in her hair walking toward the creek from which Beloved had emerged months before.

With the ghost out of the house, Paul D returns. He finds Sethe crushed by grief because she has lost Beloved again. Sethe seems to be unconsciously responding to overwhelming sorrow in the same way as Baby Suggs, by taking to her bed and making no effort to live. Paul D offers not only love but wisdom. In the last scene, Sethe mourns that she has lost her children, her best things. Paul D responds, "You your best thing, Sethe. You are" (273).

The novel concludes with a two-page meditation by the narrator on the story of Beloved. Sethe's community—symbolically, black American culture—decided that "It was not a story to pass on" (274), a line that is repeated. Then the narrator says that eventually they "forgot her" and comments, "This is not a story to pass on" (275). Still, behind Sethe's house, Beloved's "footprints come and go, come and go" (275). The narrator's present-tense verbs imply that Beloved still exists, and the novel's last paragraph consists of one word: Beloved.

CHARACTER DEVELOPMENT

Character development is inextricably linked with the central theme of *Beloved*: the movement from slavery to freedom. The stasis of one character, Beloved, contrasts with the development of the three main characters—Sethe, Paul D, and Denver. Beloved represents the past, the whole unchangeable pain and loss of slavery. Sethe, Paul D, and Denver illustrate the possibilities of the present as they evolve from slaves into free men and women.

The Garners own a planation called Sweet Home, the environment that shapes the main characters. A permissive slave holder, Mr. Garner allows his slaves unusual activities, such as using guns. Mr. Garner seems less concerned with his slaves' welfare, however, than with egotistically taunting his neighbors. He makes no special provision in his will for safeguarding the slaves. When he dies unexpectedly, ownership passes to Mrs. Garner. Mrs. Garner has some empathy, clearly feeling sorry that Sethe cannot legally marry, for instance. However, physically ill and emotionally unequipped to run a plantation, she brings Schoolteacher to run Sweet Home. On her deathbed, she hears Sethe's account of the bloody, only partially successful escape. Physically unable to speak in reply, she cries. Like Mr. Garner, she appears at first a sympathetic character. Like him, however, she has been unwilling to grant humanity to her slaves by freeing them. Her tears merely demonstrate a useless, shallow sentimentality.

Schoolteacher becomes master after Mr. Garner. An educated but cruel man, he subjects the blacks of Sweet Home to all the degradations of conventional slavery. He allows his nephews—in his sight—to rape Sethe and suck the milk from her breasts when she is nine months pregnant. After her escape, Schoolteacher tracks Sethe to her home in a free state and tries to re-enslave her and her children. He is thus responsible for Beloved's death as well as the events of the escape: the assault on Sethe, Halle's madness, and the horrible deaths of the other Sweet Home men. His name suggests the falsity of "learning" that can justify butchery.

Pauls A through F (Paul A, Paul B, etc.), Sixo, and Halle are all men enslaved at Sweet Home. Except for Paul D, the Pauls remain minor characters, important mostly for showing the tragedies resulting from Schoolteacher's reign. Though enslaved, the African Sixo is never a slave. Sixo resists all adjustment to his situation. He insists on choosing his own mate, for example, despite the inconvenience of loving a woman from a distant plantation. Sixo is burned for his part in the rebellion against Schoolteacher, but he dies laughing and yelling, "Seven-o," meaning that his lover is expecting the child who will embody their resistance.

Accommodating to slavery as best he can, Halle takes advantage of Mr. Garner's leniency to work hard and buy freedom for his mother, Baby Suggs. Chosen by Sethe as her man, Halle tries to escape from Schoolteacher's tyranny with his family. He disappears in the turmoil surrounding the failed escape, and Sethe never sees him again. Paul D later tells Sethe that he saw Halle simply sitting and rubbing butter in his hair. By putting together their information, Paul D and Sethe surmise that Halle went mad from witnessing Schoolteacher's nephews sexually attack Sethe.

The only partially sympathetic white character, sixteen-year-old Amy, is herself escaping when she meets Sethe fleeing from Sweet Home. Amy's mother had been an indentured servant. Her mother's employer is exploiting Amy, probably illegally, to pay her dead mother's debt. Amy has been mistreated and she is malnourished. Her spirit has not been broken, however, as she vows to experience pleasure (get herself some soft velvet material) and see some sights (get to Denver). Amy calls Sethe by the words that she has been taught, "nigger" among them, but she does her best to offer aid. She massages Sethe's torn and bleeding feet back to feeling, for example, and more important, helps Sethe give birth to a daughter. Sethe names the child Denver after the city that is Amy's destination.

Stamp Paid and Baby Suggs, survivors of slavery, do their best to help others to freedom. Both have lost their families, and both become symbolic parents and elders in their community. Stamp Paid helps fugitives traveling on the Underground Railroad. (The Underground Railroad was the system of safe houses that hid and supported runaway slaves until they could reach free states or Canada.) Stamp Paid makes sure that families in the area have what they need to survive. He acts from wrong motives only once, when he interferes in Paul D and Sethe's relationship. His meddling in their newly formed family may testify to his continuing agony over losing his own wife.

As Stamp Paid handles the practical aspects of freedom, Baby Suggs works for a free spirituality. In the community, she is called "Baby Suggs, Holy." Her preaching ignores conventional Christian religious practices and doctrines. Instead, she offers services in a pretty area of the woods and urges the worshipers to love the beauty found in themselves and their children. Baby Suggs welcomes her fugitive grandchildren and daughter-in-law Sethe. When the community betrays her by not warning of Schoolteacher's approach, Baby Suggs loses the will to live. She spends her time in bed, still trying to enjoy freedom, but now in an individual, sensual way. (She asks Sethe to bring her samples of intense colors.) After her death, Baby Suggs continues to safeguard her family, and her voice gives Denver support at a crucial moment.

Baby Suggs makes up part of the nurturing female ancestry that sustains Sethe. Sethe's mother, Ma'am, a field worker on a large plantation, is hanged for taking part in a rebellion. From her mother's friend Nan, Sethe learns Ma'am's history and grounds her personality in mother-love. When life at Sweet Home deteriorates, Sethe shows enormous strength in trying for a better life for her children. Despite being nine months pregnant, losing track of her husband Halle, and suffering rape from Schoolteacher's nephews, she manages to get to a free state.

Paradoxically, Sethe's commitment to her children's welfare leads her to kill one of them, Beloved, to avoid returning them and herself to slavery. Sethe's ferocious pride and independence isolate her from her neighbors, who expect her to express remorse for her action. (Her commitment to her children remains unshakable—she trades sex to a stone-cutter in exchange for a word on the dead child's gravestone, "Beloved.") She is further isolated by her mother-in-law's death and the malicious ghost. Time stops for Sethe. To move forward, Sethe must accept Halle's absence, greater distance from Beloved, and new love from Paul D. All these depend in turn on whether Sethe can develop a new self-definition that honors motherhood but does not make it the only measure of her worth.

Paul D establishes a relationship with Sethe after a long separation. An escapee from both Sweet Home and the chain gang, he develops a two-fold strategy for survival. First, he limits his emotional involvement. Second, he shuts away difficult memories. (Morrison symbolizes this repression by imaging his heart as a rusted-shut tobacco tin in his chest.) Paul D has led an unsatisfying, vagabond life and wishes to establish permanent family ties with Sethe and her daughter Denver. To do so, however, he must first come to terms with his past—and Sethe's. He leaves after learning about Beloved, but later returns to love and affirm Sethe.

Howard, Buglar, Denver, and Beloved are all Halle and Sethe's children. Howard and Buglar are afraid of Sethe because they remember that she tried to kill them when Schoolteacher appeared. Each leaves Sethe's home early, driven off by the malice of the spiteful ghost of Beloved. Denver and Beloved coexist for most of the novel. Their relationship changes as Denver matures and Beloved remains the two-year-old she was when she died.

Whereas her brothers' response to trouble is active, Denver passively withdraws. For example, when a boy at school tells her the unpleasant news of how Beloved died, Denver loses her hearing for several years. Deafness solves the immediate difficulty of hearing unpleasant things, of course, but it isolates her. Denver, Sethe, and the ghost live by themselves, without visitors, until Paul D's arrival when Denver is eighteen. Denver is accustomed to having all her mother's attention and is jealous of Paul D. She is just beginning to accept him when her hunger for emotional contact is rechanneled.

Denver is the first to recognize the disheveled young girl in the front yard as a re-embodiment of her sister, Beloved. She ecstatically claims Beloved as her compensation for losing her mother's exclusive attention. Soon, however, she perceives that Beloved is trying to kill Sethe. Shy and inexperienced, Denver nevertheless forces herself to leave the family home and find a job to support her mother, who will otherwise starve. Denver's change from wholly dependent child to independent, caring adult is facilitated by her former schoolteacher, Lady Jones.

Lady Jones teaches school to those most disadvantaged in the black community, those with the darkest skin, to make up for the undeserved privileges that her own lighter skin brings her. Lady Jones helps Denver find a job and communicates her story to the wider community. Women begin leaving food for Sethe's family in the yard, a first step toward Sethe's reentry into her community. Implicitly, Lady Jones's goodness contrasts with Schoolteacher's wickedness. Lady Jones demonstrates that education need not be a tool of the oppressor.

Beloved has several incarnations. First, she is the two-year-old daughter whom Sethe kills when Schoolteacher enters Baby Suggs's yard. Next, she is the angry spirit who haunts Sethe's household for years, driving off Howard and Buglar. When Paul D drives her out, she returns in the body of a young woman. Although Beloved's form changes, her character does not.

Because she personifies the past, and no one can change past events, Beloved cannot change or develop. Beloved always remains a two-year-old, with a two-year-old's understanding. Amoral, she has no consciousness of doing wrong in trying to fulfill her own needs. She remains unaware of others' needs. Thus, she tries to monopolize her mother's attention, even attempting to kill her so that they will be dead together. Her first step is to separate Sethe from Paul D and Denver. She uses her sexuality magically to make Paul D impregnate her, but this pregnancy cannot come to term because of who Beloved is—the past creates the present, but it cannot give birth *in* the present. Birth would change both Beloved (the past) and the present. The past is past: it has created the present but cannot change the present.

Beloved sees only the past when she looks at the present. She cannot comprehend Sethe's attack on Mr. Bodwin as protective of her and Denver. Instead, she understands it as a repetition of what she experienced as maternal abandonment—the separation that occurred when Beloved died and Sethe kept living. Although she is mistaken about Sethe's motivation for attacking Bodwin, Beloved's mistake leads to her acceptance of a permanent separation between herself and her mother. When Beloved leaves Sethe's house, the past has assumed its proper role—not completely gone, but no longer dominating the present.

A powerful leader of women, Ella directs community response to Sethe. First she ostracizes Sethe for killing Beloved and showing no remorse; later she carries on the process that Denver and Lady Jones begin, freeing Sethe by bringing her back into the community. For the eighteen years after Beloved's death, Ella holds aloof from Sethe. On hearing that Beloved has returned and is trying to kill Sethe, however, she organizes a rescue attempt. Ella believes that the terrible past of slavery must not be allowed to reclaim anyone. She leads a group of women to Sethe's yard, where they plan to pray. Instead, they make wordless sounds of primal female power. Paralleling Baby Suggs, Ella re-members forms of black female spirituality.

THEMATIC ISSUES

Beloved explores the effects of slavery on individual men and women, on black families, and on the black community. It documents both slavery's horrifying destruction and the survival of African people and culture. First, its title pays tribute to those who perished in slavery and whose names remain lost to us. The epigraph, "Sixty Million and more" refers to the largest approximations of how many Africans died on the Middle Passage, the journey from Africa to the Americas. (The number of deaths is a matter of intense scholarly debate. Many historians consider sixty million an irresponsibly high estimate.)

Beloved demonstrates that slavery was never benign, no matter how "good" the master. Most importantly, slavery removed Africans from their cultures. On slave ships and later on plantations, Europeans purposely separated slaves from the same geographic areas or tribal groups to make communication more difficult. Because most plantations were small, few slaves on any one of them spoke the same African language. The history of Sethe's mother, Ma'am, suggests the fate of African culture in the Americas.

Having forgotten almost everything about life before Sweet Home, Sethe in middle age suddenly "rememories" her mother. At first, Sethe recalls only being shown a mark under Ma'am's breast as a way of identifying her mother. This mark is probably the result of ritual scarification, an African rite that recognizes an individual's transition to adulthood with a visible sign that he or she belongs to a particular tribe. When Ma'am is lynched and burned (probably in a failed revolt), her body is too badly damaged for the mark to show. Symbolically, slavery has obliterated African identity. Another crucial part of identity and culture, language, also has been lost to the slaves. Sethe eventually recollects Nan's stories of Ma'am: "Nan . . . used different words. Words Sethe understood then but could neither recall nor repeat now. She believed that must be why she remembered so little before Sweet Home. . . . What Nan told her she had forgotten, along with the language she told it in. The same language her ma'am spoke, and which would never come back" (170). Slavery has irrevocably destroyed a great deal of African culture.

Having made African identity impossible, slavery also prevents Africans from developing tenable American identities. It damages individuals by interfering with the expression of every human need; it damages African American culture by dividing black families and separating members of the black community.

Black sexuality is controlled or deformed by slavery. At Sweet Home, Sethe has more choice of a sexual partner than many slaves, but she does not have a choice about whether to mate or to produce children. With no human outlet for sexual expression, five of the remaining six men use animals. The exception, Sixo, walks fifteen miles to the neighboring plantation for a half-hour liaison with his chosen woman.

Further, slavery's breakup of black families weakens individuals' knowledge of their families and of traditional roles. Traditional societies in western Africa tended to have extended systems of family and kinship. These were not recognized, much less respected, during the European conquest. In the United States, slaves were not permitted to maintain the nuclear families of white cultures. Many slaves knew so little of their parents or siblings that Sethe's minimal knowledge seems comparatively lucky: She saw her mother, knew her fate, and heard the story of her own birth. With the exception of Halle, Baby Suggs lost all of her children so early that she could not possibly recognize them later; they, in turn, can know nothing of her. Family heritage is thus destroyed. Because families are disrupted, the passing down of knowledge from generation to generation is interrupted. Individuals must then cope by themselves. With no other mother at Sweet Home, for instance, Sethe must guess at the best child-rearing practices. Similarly, men lack role models for fatherhood. Slavery destroys not only individual families but the whole concept of the family.

As the microcosm of the family is torn apart, so the macrocosm of the community suffers too. Morrison's earlier novels tend to show the black community in one of two ways. Community either clearly participates in the oppression of the main character (*The Bluest Eye, Sula*), or, as in *Song of Solomon*, clearly nurtures him. More complex, *Beloved* traces the evolution from slave community to a "free" community still legally and economically constrained by whites—and by the psychic damage of slavery. It shows a community ambivalent about supporting even its most generous, productive members like Baby Suggs. The end of *Beloved* suggests that the women of the community, in gathering to help Sethe, may be progressing toward unity.

Individuals as well as community must change to become free. In fact, to succeed, individuals must re-form their identities within new families within the community. Sethe, Paul D, and Denver illustrate this process as they develop new identities to form a family supported by the surrounding black community.

At the outset of *Beloved*, both Sethe and Paul D are controlled by the past of slavery; in effect they are still enslaved. Sethe lives in complete isolation, except for her daughter Denver and the ghost. Sethe once suggests to Baby Suggs that they move to escape, but Baby Suggs replies that the evils of slavery have made all houses haunted. Sethe remains in the same house, then, almost literally fixed in and by the past. Paul D, on the other hand, tries to outrun the past. This strategy proves futile because he carries the past within him (symbolically, the rusted-shut tobacco box in his chest). Unable to settle, he wanders until he finds Sethe.

Sethe and Paul D become partners, completing each other in many ways. Paul D can tell Sethe, for example, why Halle never arrived at Baby Suggs's house—he went insane. Sethe can tell Paul D the meaning of his last glimpse of Halle, when Halle simply sat and rubbed butter on his face. Halle must, she says, have witnessed Schoolteacher's nephews stealing her milk during the rape. With their pooled information, Paul D and Sethe can bring closure to their experiences at Sweet Home.

Each needs more than the other to become free, however, because each must change internally. Traits important to survival in slavery may be harmful in freedom. For an enslaved mother, keeping her children with her was the ultimate goal. But when Sethe adheres to this definition of motherhood in freedom, she calls the ghost into her home. The ghost disrupts all ongoing life and development (it maims the dog and drives off Sethe's sons). Sethe resents Paul D's eviction of the ghost, however, because she feels that he has banished her child. For Sethe, accepting the past's domination of the present offers the only way of keeping her dead child.

Being with her children has always been Sethe's first priority. *Beloved*'s depiction of a mother killing a child recalls *Sula*, but the resemblance is only superficial. In *Sula*, Eva murders Plum to protect herself from his exploitative demands. When Sethe kills Beloved, she intends to kill the rest of her children and herself too, then join her dead mother, Ma'am. Sethe is not defending an independent self, as Eva is, but is instead protecting the integrity and unity of her family against slavery. In making her children the ultimate measure of her own worth, however, Sethe devalues herself. Her self-definition echoes that of the slave master, who values her only as a breeder. To survive free, Sethe must develop other definitions of motherhood and of herself.

Initially, Paul D is as much possessed by the past as Sethe is. He appears freer, but whereas Sethe's house is inhabited by the past, Paul D's body is possessed. To make a life with Sethe, to "put his story beside hers" (273), Paul D must open the rusted-shut tobacco box in his chest. He does not do this willingly any more than Sethe gives up Beloved willingly. When Beloved compels him to have sex with her, the tobacco box breaks open. Paul D's sexual union with Beloved should not be understood as a betrayal of Sethe, as it would be if Beloved were simply a woman. When Paul D has sex with Beloved, he is symbolically accepting the past. This process takes him some time, and before he is finished, Stamp Paid forces on him the knowledge that Sethe killed her daughter. Paul D bolts. Too fully occupied with his own past, he cannot at first accept Sethe's reasons for killing Beloved. For a time he withdraws, even from the community, but when Sethe's need is greatest, he returns. His wandering is over.

Because slavery damaged black men and women in different ways, their means of recovery must also be different. To comprehend the past fully, Paul D must acknowledge not only his own male experience but that of black women. As long as he feels able to abandon Sethe because she has killed her daughter, he denies a part of her reality. Slowly he abandons the need to judge her. When he returns to Sethe, he understands her decision in the context of the enslaved past. Fully knowledgeable about her past and his own, he affirms her present self: "You your best thing, Sethe. You are" (273). He is finally able to "put his story beside hers" (273).

Like Sethe and Paul D, Denver is circumscribed by the past; like Beloved, she is initially frozen in an early stage of childhood. Eighteen years old, Denver literally does not leave the yard without being accompanied by an adult. (Interestingly, just as she follows Sethe's pattern, Sethe's sons Howard and Buglar follow Paul D's pattern by leaving.) Denver cares to hear only one story of her mother's past, the story of her own birth. Possessive in her self-centeredness, she resents Paul D's appearance almost as much as Beloved does.

Unlike Beloved, however, Denver can learn. Seeing that Beloved will kill Sethe if nothing is done, Denver goes to her formal source of learning, Lady Jones. Denver secures both charity from the community and, through her job, the means of supporting Sethe. She finds the courage to accept adult responsibilities through Baby Suggs, whose voice directs her to leave the yard. Clearly, the spirit of Baby Suggs persists, just as the spirit of Beloved does. Each remains what she was in life, Beloved a demanding two-year-old and Baby Suggs a wise healer. Denver has started the maturation that will eventually make her an empowering ancestral spirit like Baby Suggs.

In part, these characters find the strength to change through African cultural practices. Having evolved in particular cultures in particular physical environments, these practices must be adapted to new circumstances and places. Sixo's life illustrates the problems in attempting to maintain unchanged African practices. Sixo's African identity cannot long survive enslavement in a European system. His African sense of time, for example, allows him only the briefest contact with Thirty-Mile Woman. He can, however, perpetuate his resistant spirit. His death cry of "Seven-O" implies that Thirty-Mile Woman is pregnant and will give birth to a seventh generation.

Sixo's success remains limited in part because he must operate as an individual, outside of the community that helps to define a traditional African sense of self. (See Chapter 2 for a discussion of the African sacred cosmos.) When individuals can use African practices *in community*, they succeed more often. Call-and-response, for instance, frees both Paul D's chain gang and Sethe. In call-and-response, a leader issues a "call," which might consist of a word, a phrase, or a sound. When a group responds to this call, the leader issues a new call that incorporates the initial communal response, and a new cycle begins. Paul D and his fellow prisoners use verbal call-and-response every day to maintain their community. Later, even though they are still chained together, they escape both the mudslide and their jailors because they signal one another with an adapted call-and-response. Similarly, Ella's "holler" calls forth a unified response from the women attempting to free Sethe. In 1856, facing slavery without community support, Sethe could only think of killing her children and herself. In 1874, facing white oppression with the community's call-and-response, she directs her attack at the white man, Bodwin. Although she has mistaken the proper target, her move to defend self and family is healthy. Even partially recovered African communal practices thus empower individuals and the community.

Beloved begins with death and stasis, but ends with life and growth. Throughout, the novel shows love as a power that reconstructs and inspires. The novel deals with many manifestations of love: love for oneself, mother-daughter love, romantic love, and the love of a community for its individual members. As in the rest of Morrison's books, love's power cannot heal instantaneously or painlessly. Love can neither remake the past nor save every character. Here, as in *The Bluest Eye*, "love is no better than the lover." Badly damaged by slavery, these lovers express themselves erratically, sometimes withholding their support at crucial times. No completely balanced self or perfect mother or ideal community develops, but the book shows the miracle of love making the cruelest experiences bearable. *Beloved* shows the tremendous costs of slavery and celebrates the survival of the African American self, family, and community.

AN HISTORICIST READING

Most readers are familiar with the idea of reading a work in its historical context. In textbooks, introductions to literature train us to be aware of this context by telling us what events and people are referred to. If the work has autobiographical elements, we learn about the writer's life. "Historicism" designates a school of literary criticism that extends this idea. Rather than seeing writers' personalities as the shaping force behind literary works, historicism considers social and economic conditions as the prime movers. Historicists ask why a particular work appeared at a particular time—what made this subject interesting at that time? What made a publisher decide that it would be profitable? What in the social world affected how the literature resolved its thematic issues?

An historicist critic tries to understand why particular literary texts emerged from the social context of their times. This social context includes the era's understanding of earlier literary traditions and political–economic forces. An historicist reading of *Beloved*, explains, in terms of its 1988 social context, (1) why Morrison chose to rework the nineteenth-century genre of the slave narrative and (2) what her specific changes to the genre suggest about and for that social context.

In the nineteenth century, white abolitionists published slave narratives to persuade white readers to do away with slavery. The narratives were shaped to show the cruelties of slavery as an institution and to demonstrate the intellectual and moral worthiness of individual African Americans who had escaped it. Slave narratives shared particular elements because they were designed for a specific purpose and with a specific audience in mind. Slave narratives almost always told the story of only one person's escape because more slaves escaped by themselves than with their families, and because abolitionists wanted to emphasize slavery's destruction of African American families.

Many social conditions had changed during the 150 years separating *Beloved* from the first widely known slave narrative (by Olaudah Equiano). By 1970, the enlarged black audience and the civil rights movement had made it possible for African American writers to tell the truth about the "happy plantation" pictured in *Gone with the Wind*. Two instances of this revisionist work, Alex Haley's semi-historical volume *Roots* (1976) and Ernest Gaines's novel *The Autobiography of Miss Jane Pittman* (1971), became enormously popular television productions.

Beloved, then, joins many other novels in reviving and revising the slave narrative tradition. Other examples include Margaret Walker's *Jubilee* (1966), Gayl Jones's *Corregidora* (1975), Octavia Butler's *Kindred* (1979), David Bradley's *The Chaneysville Incident* (1981), and Sherley Anne Williams's *Dessa Rose* (1986). Part of the revival may have resulted from the general rise of interest in black and female history as the result of the black nationalist movements and the feminist movement. The need for knowledgeable people to educate the reading public about African American experience was no less pressing in 1970 than when slave narratives developed in the early 1800s.

In the 1980s, the decision to focus on slavery rather than on contemporary experience might have come from the intersection of several factors. First was the sense that the truth about slavery could at last be published. Second, in traditional African American culture, honoring the ancestors is a spiritual duty. (Until the black pride movement, however, these enslaved ancestors were often perceived as a source of shame rather than a resource of spiritual heroism.) If these reasons explain the re-emergence of the slave narrative in the 1970s and 1980s, we still have the question of why *Beloved* is set during the 1870s. Writing about the problems of the present in terms of the past has the advantage of not making the audience immediately defensive. *Beloved*, for example, can discuss splits in the black community—and how to heal them—without using the specifics of particular leaders and situations about which readers already have strong opinions.

The situation of African Americans in the 1980s in many ways paralleled that of the 1870s and 1880s. In the 1980s, the African American community faced many serious problems—worsening poverty, weakened family and neighborhood structures for raising children, and stereotypes to justify political neglect. Like the 1880s, the 1980s followed a period of drastic change for African Americans. As the 1860s witnessed emancipation, so the 1960s saw the culmination of the civil rights movement. As the black community of the 1870s lost leaders like Baby Suggs, so did the black community of the 1960s lose the leadership of Malcolm X and Martin Luther King, Jr.

In the 1880s, the rise of organizations like the Ku Klux Klan threatened to re-enslave the black community. The KKK and other groups circulated vicious stereotypes to justify their violent oppression of African Americans. The 1980s saw an analogous political backlash. No new approaches to poverty or racism developed in national political discussion; instead, presidential campaigns invoked stereotypes of black men as criminals and black women as lazy, irresponsible "welfare mothers." In both Reconstruction and the Reagan era, black communities had to rely entirely on their own resources. *Beloved* opens with a divided, leaderless community; debilitated families; and exhausted, isolated individuals. This "stuck" emotional and political state roughly parallels the predicament of the African American community of the 1980s when Toni Morrison wrote and published the novel. *Beloved* depicts the problems of the 1880s in terms applicable to the African American community of the 1980s.

In an historicist view, *Beloved*'s revisions of the slave narrative speak to various political forces active from the 1960s through the 1980s. *Beloved* changes the genre's conventions in both subject and plot. Rather than focusing on a single individual's escape, *Beloved* presents an escape by a man, one by a woman, and one by a group of men. Whereas the slave narrative often ended with the fugitive separated from his family and friends, *Beloved* shows both the African American family and community symbolically reunited.

Beloved's reconfiguration of the slave narrative comments indirectly on the dominant political movements of the preceding two decades. The early feminist movement tended to ignore racially specific experience and to prize independence above participation in the community. The movement's critique of patriarchy (a system in which men hold the social power) tended to show women and men as having opposed interests without paying much attention to the race of the men. Black nationalist movements, on the other hand, tended to perpetuate sexist structures by insisting that black women show their racial loyalty by being subordinate to black men as white women were subordinate to white men. Critiquing these simplistic positions, the plot and theme of *Beloved* present group unity while respecting differences between men's and women's experiences.

Despite their limitations, the black power and feminist movements raised questions that could not be dismissed. Does acquiring a good education simply mean that the student accepts racism and patriarchy along with knowledge? Is it possible to take a traditional role like motherhood without accepting the patriarchy's demeaning definitions of women? *Beloved* considers these ideas by re-examining aspects of the slave narrative.

As historicist critics have established, nineteenth-century slave narratives had to deny two different sets of gender-based stereotypes of African American inferiority. Racist stereotypes held that African Americans' inferior intelligence made educating them impossible. *Narrative of the Life of Frederick Douglass*, a famous slave narrative, set the pattern for attacking the stereotype by highlighting how Douglass had become literate. In these narratives, "literacy" acquired a meaning broader than simply reading and writing. "Literacy" meant being able to perceive and reproduce the customs of white culture. In thus proving that he could "fit in" with white culture, a literate African American man could deny a crucial racial stereotype.

Racist stereotypes of black women focused on their sexuality rather than their intellects. These stereotypes claimed that the mixed-race children on every plantation resulted, not from rape, but from unchaste female slaves' animal sexuality overpowering the masters' moral scruples. To secure the sympathies of their white female audiences, African American women narrators had to show that all women shared the same values of sexual purity and motherhood.

Like many other women's narratives, Mary Prince's 1831 *The History of Mary Prince* and Harriet Jacobs's 1861 *Incidents in the Life of a Slave Girl* address these issues. Both show slavery disrupting mothers' care for their children. Jacobs, in fact, delayed her escape from slavery for seven years, until she could take her two children with her. Both stories show the narrators' constant, heroic resistance to a master's sexual advances. (*Incidents* offers many apologies for its narrator's sexual experience outside marriage—even though slaves were legally prevented from marrying.) Both Prince and Jacobs present their reverence for sexual purity as stemming from religion. In these narratives, the woman slave's experience was presented to and shaped for a white, female audience.

Beloved re-examines the slave narrative's traditional presentations of motherhood, sexual purity, and literacy from an African American perspective. The feminist movement empowered writers to present women's experiences without having the victims, in effect, apologize to the audience. Sethe describes in detail being sexually abused, and trading sex for a carving on her child's tombstone. In the most emotional part of her memories, Sethe mentions repeatedly that during their assault on her, Schoolteacher's nephews "took my milk" (17). Her statement brings together the issues of sexual abuse and racist control of black motherhood because breast milk is Sethe's only means of keeping her babies alive.

In addressing motherhood, *Beloved* entered a tumultuous debate. The role itself had been vigorously questioned by the feminist movement of the 1970s. Many feminists resented motherhood's primacy in the social role for women. Many others objected to the conditions of child-rearing. At the same time, resurgent stereotypes presented African American mothers as lazy and irresponsible. *Beloved* affirms the centrality of loving motherhood to African American women's experience without accepting it as the very definition of womanhood.

With motherhood, as with other aspects of the slave narrative, Morrison's work preserves the traditional issue, but with a difference. In *Beloved*, African American women experience some of slavery's worst evils through motherhood. Baby Suggs loses all of her children except Halle, for instance. At the same time, mother-love offers the strongest defense against slavery. When Nan tells Sethe that her Ma'am chose to conceive and bear her, Sethe acquires the base on which to build feelings of self-worth. Like traditional slave narratives, *Beloved* pictures not only motherhood but nurturing female relationships over generations.

Unlike the earlier narratives, *Beloved* critiques traditional attitudes toward motherhood as confining and destructive. For Sethe to have a tolerable life in freedom, she must move away from the definition of herself as only, or even primarily, a mother. To be a free woman, she must accept Baby Suggs's religion of self-love and become, as Paul D says, her own "best thing" (273).

In a similar way, *Beloved* accepts another core value of the slave narrative—literacy—but redefines its meaning in freedom. Literacy was in itself a positive value in the nineteenth-century narratives. In *Beloved*, however, it is highly suspect, at best a tool with a variety of uses. Because in the world of the novel's setting, print literacy is white-controlled, it often damages the black community. First, the system that teaches literacy is immoral, actively promoting slavery, as Schoolteacher's name symbolically implies. Even more important, accepting the authority of white-controlled literacy potentially threatens the black community. On the micro-level, it interferes with black relationships. Paul D refuses to consider a newspaper clipping about Beloved's death because he knows that newspapers print only what reflects badly on African Americans. He believes the story only when Sethe orally confirms it. The reader sees, however, that his interpretation of the event accepts the values of white reporting rather than Sethe's values. As a result, the couple separates.

This same potential for splitting apart exists on the macro-level. Light-skinned blacks have the most access to formal education, and the most chance of using literacy, broadly defined, to pass into white society. Lady Jones, who is Denver's teacher, has this light skin and hence might profit individually by separating from the black community. Rather than using literacy for her individual benefit (and consequently oppressing other African Americans), Lady Jones redefines literacy as a tool for advancing the whole black community.

The end of *Beloved* extends this portrait of African Americans deter-mining how to use their own forms of literacy for their own purposes. In the final pages, the narrator meditates on what later happened to the story of Beloved. Because it was "unwise" to remember her, the com-munity decided that hers "was not a story to pass on" (274), a phrase taken up and twice repeated by the narrator. Like the novel's use of slave narrative conventions, these must be repetitions with a difference, how-ever, because Morrison *has* passed the story on to us—and in print form. "Pass on" has many meanings, including "dying" or "refusing to take action." Perhaps the repetition means that Beloved's is not a story to die, or that the story demands action from its readers. If it was unwise in the 1880s to remember Beloved, maybe it is wise, even essential, to do so in the 1980s and the following decades.

That thought returns us to the historicist principle that social factors influence the production of literary works. Despite many important changes, because too many social conditions of the 1980s echoed those of the nineteenth century, the genre of the slave narrative re-emerged. To deal with the crisis of the present, *Beloved* invokes the heroic ordinary lives of the past. Its hopeful picture shows both individual people and the community overcoming divisions caused by slavery and its legacy. Real change in *Beloved* begins, not with denying the past, but with ac-knowledging it and moving forward to find new forms of unity. The agents of change here—Stamp Paid, Paul D, and Denver—come from representatives of the African American groups most maligned by the popular press of the 1980s, men and young women.

As Stamp Paid and Denver draw courage from Baby Suggs, the spir-itual ancestor, so Morrison drew inspiration for *Beloved* from Margaret Garner, a real woman who killed her child rather than return it to slavery. In revising the slave narrative of the nineteenth century, Toni Morrison has created a free story for the twentieth. Whether it liberates the twenty-first century from the slavery of the past depends upon readers' decisions: Will we pass on it, or will we pass it on?

Jazz
(1992)

Jazz is the second novel of Morrison's trilogy responding to the three works of Dante's *The Divine Comedy: Inferno, Purgatorio*, and *Paradisio*. *Beloved* depicts the hell of slavery and its immediate aftermath. Paralleling purgatory rather than hell, *Jazz* depicts much suffering but with a more positive and certain ending. Its title draws attention, first, to the world-renowned music created by African Americans in the 1920s, and second, to the book's jazz-like narrative structure and themes. *Beloved*, the first in the trilogy, takes place in the 1880s, with references to earlier events. *Jazz* begins where *Beloved* leaves off. Its two main characters, Joe and Violet Trace, are born in the 1870s, and the main action occurs in the 1920s. As in *Beloved*, crucial earlier events are related indirectly to the reader, by way of the narrator or the characters' memories.

SOCIAL AND LITERARY CONTEXT

Jazz resembles *Beloved* by being grounded in historical events. The initiating event, the murder of a young girl who refuses to name her killer, is based on a story explaining a photograph in James Van der Zee's 1978 *The Harlem Book of the Dead*. Two other real events figure importantly in the characters' development: the St. Louis race riot of 1917 and the resulting NAACP protest march in New York City. ("NAACP" is an acronym for the National Association for the Advancement of Colored People, which was founded in 1909.)

The characters of *Jazz* participate in several of the major historical events affecting African Americans from 1880 through 1926. In the novel, Joe and Violet Trace move from small country towns in Virginia to New York City in 1906. In real life during the late nineteenth and early twentieth century, so many African Americans from the rural South settled in the urban North that historians call the movement the Great Migration. This migration was driven by several factors. Most African Americans in the South had been forced into sharecropping, a system that was in practice little different from slavery. Even aside from the resulting poverty, the social conditions of segregation were harsh. And racist organizations such as the Ku Klux Klan grew increasingly powerful, not only murdering individuals but sometimes burning whole towns.

Although their economic opportunities improved in the North, many black immigrants were disappointed in their hopes for peace and social equality. Racist violence began to escalate in southern states at the end of the Reconstruction period (about 1878). Forty years later this violence characterized northern race relations as well. (Joe Trace is living in the North when he is beaten with a pipe.) A wave of riots and lynchings during 1919 gave rise to the term "the red summer." These events stemmed not merely from random, individual criminal acts, but from organized groups intent on large-scale violence.

Since the late 1960s, race riots in the United States have been understood as explosions of violence within black communities in the impoverished inner cities. The resulting deaths, injuries, and property damage have been almost entirely inflicted by and limited to the black inner-city residents. In the early part of the twentieth century, "race riot" described an entirely different phenomenon. Then, armed gangs of whites invaded and warred on African American communities, which were mostly shut out from police protection or legal recourse.

Jazz uses one of these violent episodes, the East St. Louis riot of 1917, as an off-stage event affecting two major characters, Alice Manfred and her niece Dorcas. Dorcas's parents are killed in the riot, her father dragged from a streetcar and beaten to death, her mother burned to death when their house is torched. Alice takes in the orphaned child. These plot developments are not literary exaggeration, as a Pulitzer-prize winning historian's account of the riot shows:

> The City exploded the next morning [July 2]. More than six thousand men, women, and children were made homeless

and many fled the City in the first hours or would return under the protection of the National Guard to root for their few belongings before departing forever. Two policemen died and two square blocks of black shanties went up in flames. All day long on the third, white people roamed the downtown area, exchanging souvenirs from the rampage, ghoulishly touring the morgues, and cheering whenever an increase in the black body count was announced. Mangled black corpses ("horribly mutilated floaters") bobbed to the surface of the Mississippi. By July 5, almost $400,000 worth of property had been destroyed and thirty-nine black and eight white people were dead. (Lewis 537)

This devastation called forth the first major protest march in the history of the United States.

The march testified to the increasing strength of the NAACP, a civil rights organization founded seven years earlier. Thousands of people dressed in white clothing marched silently through the streets accompanied by the muffled drumbeats of unspoken resistance. It was the first large, organized public display of African American protest against racist violence. Witnessing this march in *Jazz*, Alice loses the fear that racial violence has instilled. Two sounds echo in Alice's consciousness throughout the novel. The first is the drums that pace the march; the second, a more pervasive sound of New York in the 1920s, the music known as jazz.

Jazz developed as part of the Harlem Renaissance, a creative flowering of African American culture made possible, in part, by the new concentrations of black population in Northern cities. The Renaissance lasted roughly from 1910 until the beginning of the Depression in 1930. During these two decades, black writers like Claude McKay, Langston Hughes, Jessie Fauset, Nella Larsen, and Zora Neale Hurston published novels and poetry centered on African American experience. Alain Locke compiled *The New Negro*, an anthology devoted to new African American political and artistic self-definitions.

The Harlem Renaissance's best known artistic creation, however, is jazz. Jazz is reckoned throughout the world as one of America's most significant cultural contributions, and it originated with African American artists. Jazz evolved from the blues and retains several blues qualities, such as "call and response, repetition, and, most importantly, signifying: thoughtful revision and repetition of another's work" (Andrews 395). In addition, jazz relies on syncopation and improvisation. Syncopation affects the rhythm of a musical piece by moving the strong beat off the even counts of the "time." (Thus, jazz in 4/4 time might have strong beats on 1 ½ and 3 ½ rather than on 2 and 4.) In improvising, musicians use a set melody or recognized tune but vary it, responding to the makeup of their combo during a particular performance, or to their audience. No two performances of a jazz piece, even by the same musicians, will be identical. Jazz makes change, originality, and unpredictability within a recognized structure into central parts of musical process. For this reason, it provides an apt metaphor for social change. Jazz developed in the honkytonks of the red light districts and the speakeasies that flouted Probihition. (The eighteenth amendment to the Constitution, adopted in 1919, prohibited the sale of alcohol). Associated with danger and illicit sexuality, jazz provided the soundtrack for the Roaring Twenties.

Although *Jazz* and *Beloved* both concern actual historical events, they develop differently. Much of *Beloved* presents African American experience common in its time setting, and social forces such as the Fugitive Slave Law certainly affect the plot. (The Fugitive Slave Law allowed slavemasters to reclaim slaves who had fled to the so-called free states where slavery was illegal.) However, *Beloved* focuses on individual psyches. The reader does not, for example, watch the debate over passing the Fugitive Slave Law. In addition, the originating historical incident of Margaret Garner's arrest for murdering her child remains unique. By contrast, *Jazz* broadens the focus to deal directly with large, public events such as the Great Migration, the East St. Louis riot, and the subsequent NAACP protest march. The difference in focus may be clearest in *Jazz*'s presentation of its urban setting. A collective force in itself, the city energizes, terrifies, and inspires the individual characters.

PLOT DEVELOPMENT

Jazz has ten sections, many more than Morrison's earlier novels. The sections are often subdivided, with extra blank spaces providing a visual gap between parts of the text. Completely blank pages separate the larger sections. This typography accents the large number of sections and subsections to create a sense of disconnection between the novel's segments. Overall, the novel tells the story of Joe and Violet Trace over more than fifty years. Both are born in rural Vesper County, Virginia, and orphaned young. Joe's mother abandons him to a neighboring family. Violet's father must be absent because his political activities are so dangerous. Unable to cope alone with the financial and emotional difficulties of her young family, Violet's mother, Rose Dear, goes mad. Joe and Violet marry young. When the nearby town of Vienna is burned by vengeful whites, they leave the Virginia countryside for New York City. (New York is presented as the City throughout the novel to designate it as an active character.)

They enjoy the City, their financial status improves, and all appears well until, in late middle age, Violet begins to long for a child. When she withdraws emotionally, Joe feels abandoned again. Joe chooses a sixteen-year-old girl, Dorcas, as his lover. After some months, she prefers a boy of her own age to Joe. Joe follows Dorcas to a party and shoots her while she is dancing to jazz. Refusing to go to a hospital or to reveal Joe's identity, Dorcas bleeds to death from a shoulder wound. Violet causes a scene in the funeral home by stabbing Dorcas's corpse.

As Joe, Violet, and Dorcas's aunt Alice try to figure out the meanings of these events, the reader learns piecemeal about much of their past experience. Violet establishes relationships with Alice and with one of Dorcas's friends, Felicity. Felicity frequently visits Joe and Violet, who re-establish their emotional intimacy.

Section One opens with the narrator gossiping about a woman named Violet, who has disrupted the funeral of a young girl by knifng the corpse. Later we learn her husband's name, Joe Trace, and the girl's name, Dorcas. The attack is only Violet's first vengeful act. Later, she takes a silly revenge on Joe by conducting a brief, meaningless affair in their home.

The narrator suggests that Violet's actions stem from the long-ago suicide of her mother, Rose Dear. Although Violet's grandmother, True Belle, arrived to rescue her daughter from destitution and loneliness, Rose Dear did not recover from her emotional paralysis. Mentioning that True Belle tells Violet and her sisters stories about a boy named Golden Gray, the narrator hints that he will be important to our later understanding of the Traces.

Finally, the narrator notes some of Violet's oddities. Wanting a child so much, she half-consciously kidnaps a baby and, when caught immediately, indignantly denies it—and believes herself to be telling the truth. Violet becomes increasingly inward-focused and less aware of the external world. Once she simply sits in the street to rest, and she often makes mistakes in choosing words.

By the end of the first section, the narrator has communicated the outlines of Violet's history, which are fleshed out in Sections Four and Six. Joe's story is largely delayed until Sections Five and Seven.

Section Two shows Joe and Dorcas exchanging information about their lost mothers. Joe bonds emotionally with Dorcas, unaware that she remains aloof. To facilitate their love trysts, Joe rents a room from a neighbor, Malvonne.

Section Three introduces a new character, Alice Manfred, who is watching the July 1917 march protesting the East St. Louis riot that has killed both parents of her seven-year-old niece Dorcas. Alice emerges as a repressed woman who fears the energies of the new music, jazz. In rearing Dorcas, Alice passes on her parents' fear of sexuality. After Dorcas's death, Alice ponders womanhood and analyzes why particular women become victims. This section includes Joe's first, accidental meeting with Dorcas and Violet's initial visit to Alice after the girl's death. In Violet's presence, Alice remembers for the first time in many years her own violent potential when she was faced with her husband's infidelity.

Section Four opens with Violet meditating on herself, feeling split off from the woman who stabbed Dorcas's corpse. To make sense of her experience, she considers her past. Choosing Joe as a husband, she realizes, had something to do with her grandmother's stories of Golden Gray. Naturally she drifts into thinking about what brought her grandmother, True Belle, into her childhood home. Hearing that Violet's mother, Rose Dear, has been left destitute with five children, True Belle arrives with financial and emotional support. She is too late for Rose Dear, who commits suicide by jumping in a well. Two weeks after her death, her husband returns. Only at this point does the reader learn the reason for his long absence: his work for civil rights has made it too dangerous for him to live openly in Virginia. The teen-aged Violet cannot figure out what made her mother's life unbearable and decides not to have children.

Violet's memories continue with a humorous account of her first meeting with Joe, who falls out of a tree next to her. They marry, and because neither wants children, Violet does not mourn her three miscarriages.

In the novel's present, Violet and Alice discuss Violet's options. At one point, an angry Alice forgets to be proper—and to move her hot iron, which burns through the blouse that she is finishing. When Alice swears, she and Violet laugh heartily at her lapse in propriety, and Violet is reminded of True Belle's laugh. When True Belle first entered Rose

Dear's cabin to survey a room empty except for a mother and five hungry children, she unexpectedly laughs hard. With that memory, Violet gains sufficient objectivity to laugh at her irrational attempt to cut the already-dead Dorcas.

Section Five devotes its opening to a description of the City in spring. Joe then sketches his life, noting that he has recreated himself seven times. He remembers his early life as the Williamses' informally adopted child, then his training in woodcraft with a man so expert that he is called Hunters Hunter. Joe's recollections follow major social events such as the 1893 burning of his Virginia hometown, his move to the City with Violet in 1906, the riots and protest march of 1917, and their personal disaster of 1925, when Violet begins to sleep with a doll. Joe is proud of choosing Dorcas as his lover, feeling that this is his first choice because Violet chose him for a partner.

In Section Six, the narrator mentions True Belle's attempt to rescue Rose Dear, then segues into True Belle's earlier life in Baltimore. There Rose Dear lived with the white woman who originally owned her, Vera Louise, and Vera Louise's child, Golden Gray. The narrator imagines and then reimagines eighteen-year-old Golden Gray's life after Vera Louise reveals that he is not wholly white (as he has always assumed) but of mixed race. In the narrator's scenario, Golden Gray sets out to find and perhaps kill his black father. Unsure even of his father's name, he is looking for "Henry LesTroy." (The man is really named Henry Lestory, and he has the nickname Hunters Hunter.) On the way Golden sees a pregnant, naked young black woman who knocks herself unconscious fleeing from him. Carrying her in his buggy, he arrives at the empty cabin belonging to his father.

Section Seven continues the narrator's construction of Golden Gray's experiences. Henry Lestory returns to his cabin to discover for the first time that he has a son. Both men are distracted by the presence of the unconscious girl, whom Henry christens "Wild." Wild's baby is born, but she has no motherly instincts or training. Although the novel never explicitly states who the baby is, the reader assumes that it is Joe.

The narrative then turns to thirteen-year-old Joe, who is looking for his mother amid the chaos of Vienna's burning. He makes two more searches for her in later years, the last after he and Violet have married. This search leads him to an underground lair that has clearly been inhabited because it contains the remains of a cooking fire—and clothing that probably belonged to Golden Gray. The story of Joe's last search for

Wild is interrupted by a section from Joe's consciousness more than twenty years later, when he is tracking Dorcas to the party where he shoots her.

Considerably the shortest piece, Section Eight consists of Dorcas's thoughts at the party. She is very satisfied with her new boyfriend Acton. When Joe shoots her, she feels no pain, just weakness and a growing distance from the world around her.

Section Nine depicts the growth of friendship between Felicity (one of Dorcas's friends), Violet, and Joe. Felicity makes her first visit in search of a ring that Dorcas had borrowed and may have been buried with. Felicity particularly wants the ring because her mother stole it for her after a jeweler in Tiffany's treated them disrespectfully. Felicity describes her life with her grandmother, who cares for her. Her parents, who are servants, are allowed to be with her for only two and a half days of every three weeks.

On her second visit, Felicity tells Joe and Violet how Dorcas died. Felicity is angry that Dorcas did not fight dying, that she did not allow anyone to call an ambulance. Then Felicity reveals Dorcas's last words, which connect to an earlier conversation between Joe and Dorcas.

After crying for the first time over her friend's death, Felicity decides that the ring she came looking for is, after all, unimportant—somehow like Violet's memory of Golden Gray. Violet invites Felicity to come for another visit. When Joe observes that their home needs birds, Felicity suggests that they also get a record player.

Section Ten opens with the narrator examining her limitations as a storyteller and supplying information on the continuing development of the major characters. Alice Manfred moves from the City. Felicity maintains her attractive independence. Joe and Violet re-form their lives, with new jobs and renewed emotional intimacy. Lying peacefully in bed with Violet, Joe sees the image of a wounded shoulder metamorphosing into a red-winged black bird, the bird associated with Wild.

The novel ends with the narrator speaking directly to the reader: "... make me, remake me. ... Look where your hands are. Now" (229). The reader's hands are presumably holding the book, so that the narrator's words are an invitation to make and remake interpretations.

CHARACTER DEVELOPMENT

Jazz presents five generations of traditional, human characters, and two nontraditional characters—the City and the narrator of the novel. The City and the narrator provide the context for the other characters and the action in the novel's present, 1926. The oldest group of characters—adults during slavery (before 1863)—are two generations older than the main characters, Joe and Violet Trace. This grandparent generation includes Vera Louise Gray, Henry Lestory (Hunters Hunter), and True Belle. The second generation takes in the son of Vera Louise and Henry, Golden Gray, True Belle's daughter Rose Dear, and Wild.

Joe, Violet, and Alice Manfred belong to the third generation, born in the 1870s. Violet's mother is Rose Dear; her father's name is not specified, though he lives with his family until racist violence drives him away. Joe's parentage is uncertain, but Wild may be his birth mother. Rhoda and Frank Williams parent Joe.

The expected next generation, the fourth, is largely absent. Joe and Violet have no children. Alice's younger sister and brother-in-law are killed in a riot, leaving her to care for their child, Dorcas. Dorcas's friend Felicity has living parents, but they are present only in her report to Joe and Violet. Dorcas and Felicity belong to the fifth and youngest generation, born about 1909.

Vera Louise Gray, the daughter of a well-to-do white family, becomes pregnant without being married. She does not name the father of her child. When her angry parents give her money and instructions to leave, she goes to Baltimore with a slave, True Belle. The move separates True Belle from her own family. In Baltimore, Vera Louise gives birth to a baby whom she names Golden Gray, after his complexion. Vera Louise does not lie to Golden, but simply allows him to grow up thinking that he is completely white. When he is eighteen, she tells him the truth, that he is both black and white. (Legally, of course, this makes him black.)

Finding that he is of mixed race, Golden Gray journeys to the Virginia countryside to find his father, Henry LesTroy. On the way he frightens a naked, very pregnant young woman, who knocks herself unconscious while running away. The narrator changes the description of Golden's feelings several times. In some versions, he is more concerned with his clothing than with the young woman. In others, he is preoccupied with anger and confusion over his identity. In all, however, he carries the girl with him to Henry's empty cottage. When Henry returns, Golden Gray confronts him with resentment and sarcasm. Violence might have ensued if the young woman had not started to give birth. Golden continues to resent Henry's no-nonsense insistence on respect, not as a father, but as a man, but his urge to violence becomes less intense.

Years later, Joe Trace discovers the cave that the young woman, whom Henry has christened "Wild," lives in. There he finds a shirt that belongs to Golden Gray. Golden has apparently turned his back not only on Vera Louise's Baltimore but on Henry's rural society as well.

Wild gives birth to a son, probably but not certainly Joe Trace, in Henry Lestory's cabin. After that, she is never seen again, though Joe feels her presence many times. Wild is completely unsocialized, with no conventional clothing or even speech. She lives around Vienna, but no one knows exactly where. A force of nature as opposed to society, she is associated with red-winged blackbirds.

Henry Lestory, sometimes called Henry LesTroy or Hunters Hunter, is Golden Gray's father. Because he remains in the Virginia countryside when Vera Louise goes to Baltimore, he does not know of Golden's existence until Golden appears and claims kinship. He accepts Golden Gray as his son immediately, provided that Golden offers him no backtalk. Their confrontation might have become violent had they not been distracted by Wild. As his name implies, Hunters Hunter has traditional knowledge of woodcraft. He teaches the fatherless Joe Trace the skills of tracking and hunting, and the ethics of country life.

Overcome by racism and poverty, Violet's mother, Rose Dear, commits suicide. Her husband, whose name is not mentioned, lives with his family until his political activities make that impossible. He visits infrequently, and at irregular intervals. Unable to support their five children alone, Rose Dear sinks into a depression so deep that she sits silently on the dirt floor of their empty cabin.

True Belle, Violet's grandmother, leaves Baltimore in 1888 on hearing that her daughter, Rose Dear, is unable to care for her family. True Belle is enormously capable. When she finds the family sitting in their cabin without food, furniture, heat, or hope, she laughs loudly. Her laugh testifies to her blues humor, laughing to keep from crying. She communicates to Rose Dear's children her sense that the world will continue and may even be comic. True Belle rescues Rose Dear's family but is unable to save Rose Dear, who four years later jumps down a well. Rose Dear's death leaves Violet psychically wounded. Later Violet realizes that, however well-intentioned, True Belle's nurturance was tainted by internalized racism. True Belle brings up Violet and her siblings on stories of the perfection of Golden Gray, the perfect little white boy. The children thus absorb whiteness as an ideal.

Violet is aware that she cannot know exactly why her mother, Rose Dear, committed suicide. She thinks the death is intimately linked, however, to Rose's responsibility for five children. Violet decides to avoid Rose's fate by never having children herself. She therefore does not mind at the time when, after marrying Joe Trace, she has several miscarriages. In late middle age, however, she wants a child badly. Violet's self-awareness is sufficiently clouded that she does not always know her own motivations or expect her own actions. Preoccupied, she often says or does socially inappropriate things.

When the book opens, Violet has surprised herself by causing a scene in a funeral parlor, where she knifes the corpse of her husband Joe's teenaged lover, Dorcas. She and others call this half-familiar self "Violent." Violet tries out some standard reactions to her husband's affair—the knife attack, an attempt to re-acquire her youthful, voluptuous hips, and a brief affair. She recovers some sense of stability and joy through her relationships with two women, Alice Manfred and Felicity. She seeks out Alice, who is Dorcas's aunt, and the two speak frankly about love and women's roles. These conversations enable Violet to become clearer about her needs and motivations. In Felicity, who was Dorcas's friend, Violet finds a surrogate granddaughter. Because they address her own needs, these relationships help Violet reconcile with Joe.

Joe Trace meets Violet in rural Virginia when they are both field workers. Later he feels that she chose him, and while he does not dislike their marriage or Violet, he wants to choose a lover himself. This need to exercise choice may be related to Joe's earlier experience. He selects his last name, "Trace," as a reference to his parents' disappearance "without a trace." He likes the couple who care for him, Frank and Rhoda Williams, but they chose him. Joe considers that he has changed identities seven times. Most of these changes are forced on him, such as the move from Vienna when racists burn it, or his injury during a riot. Even pleasant events, like being the chosen student of Hunters Hunter, do not satisfy Joe's need for self-determination. Joe may take Dorcas as a lover as much for pleasure in self-assertion as for the pleasure of sex.

When Dorcas asserts herself and wants to end their relationship, however, Joe falls into the same half-conscious, unself-aware state that Violet lives in. Without ever admitting what he is doing, he tracks Dorcas to a party and shoots her. In the aftermath of her death and Violet's attack on Dorcas's corpse, he sits and cries, too dispirited to attempt a ninth self. Finally he responds to Felicity and a reinvigorated Violet. The end of the novel shows Joe and Violet choosing, over and over, to renew their intimacy.

Alice Manfred's contact with Joe and Violet at first seems unlikely to renew her, but it leads to a fresh start. Alice cares for her orphaned niece Dorcas, trying to raise her to be moral and proper in the midst of what she sees as the wicked city's temptations during the Jazz Age. When Joe first seduces Dorcas, then shoots her, and Violet causes a scandal at the wake, Alice loses her niece, and in a particularly disgraceful way. No wonder that she does not wish to talk to Violet.

When Violet insists on visiting, the fifty-eight-year-old Alice finds herself remembering many repressed experiences and rethinking her attitudes. She abandons her self-righteousness and remembers hating her long-dead husband's lover, for example. Alice also feels unhappy that she tried to control her niece's sexuality in the same way that her parents controlled her. Understanding herself better, Alice recovers her own sexuality. She moves to a smaller city, the better to find a suitable companion.

Dorcas shares several traits with Rose Dear, though they are not related by blood. She is, first, the victim of racial violence that deprives her of her parents as it deprived Rose of her husband. Like Rose, she eventually lacks the will to live. Joe's shot would not have killed Dorcas if she had allowed anyone to call an ambulance or take her to a hospital. Instead, she insists on being left alone and simply bleeds to death.

Dorcas apparently wants to participate in the life around her, the vibrant sexuality of jazz and the City. Her interest in Joe is shallow, however, and the reader feels that she responds to him mostly because it would horrify her aunt Alice. Her interest in Acton, a boy close to her own age of sixteen, seems more genuine, but her motivations are horrifying. Dorcas likes Acton because he tells her what to do and what to be. She has no sense of identity other than a revolt against her aunt. Dorcas is willing to build an imitation self from Acton's detailed blueprints, but she has no deep commitment even to that. Her death is a kind of passive suicide.

As her name implies, Felicity holds the vigor and promise of youth that have been destroyed in Dorcas. She becomes a catalyst for Joe and Violet's emotional growth. In turn, their conversations allow Felicity to explore her own grief and anger over Dorcas's willing abandonment of life. When she hears Violet's tale about the unhealthy influence of True Belle's Golden Gray stories, Felicity is able to identify and resist a similar influence in her own life. She thus develops a stronger sense of self than any of the older characters. In return, she brings music back into the Traces' home, and the jazz records orchestrate their return to enjoyable lives.

This rebirth occurs in the City. Several sections open with descriptions of the City at particular times of year. The importance of the City extends beyond that of an ordinary setting (as the capitalization suggests). The City exists as a powerful force, capable of motivating characters as well as establishing their moods. Joe and Violet respond to the City's energy immediately; from the moment their railway car arrives at the City limits, they are "train-dancing" in the aisle. The City and jazz are inseparable. At different times, Alice fears and Dorcas yearns for the City's sexuality, as expressed in its music. The narrator too links the City and the new music. Describing a faithful husband in late middle age, the narrator comments that the City "pulls him like a needle through the groove of a Bluebird [studio] record. . . . the City spins you. Makes you do what it wants" (120). Because all the characters respond to the City, the narrator's statement of its importance may be believed. The reader should be skeptical, however, of the narrator's statement that the City controls the characters absolutely, because the narrator herself is a character with a viewpoint, as the next section discusses.

NARRATIVE TECHNIQUE

In *Jazz*, Toni Morrison uses an unusual narrator to explore the relationship of African American literature and European literature. With this narrator, Morrison plays with and extends the conventions of European printed storytelling.

Traditional narrators fall into three categories: (1) the omniscient, anonymous third-person narrator, who can take the reader into all the characters' minds; (2) the third-person limited narrator, who stands outside the story's action but can take the reader into one character's mind; (3) the first-person narrator, who tells his or her own story. Narrators from the second two groups are understood to be occasionally unreliable. That is, the reader can believe that the plot events happen—otherwise there is no story at all—but understands that the narrators' judgments about the meanings of those events may be limited or even wrong. Much of the alert reader's interpretation of fiction using third-person limited or first-person narration depends upon locating the viewpoints and biases of these narrators. Toni Morrison, however, has fused aspects of the traditional omniscient narrator with the unreliable element of more limited narrators.

Like the rest of the characters, then, the narrator of *Jazz* develops. Hissing a "Sth," like a gossip getting a listener's attention, the narrator confidently escorts the reader into the minds of several different characters. She is supremely confident—why not, if you're omniscient?—of her descriptions of other characters. In Morrison's conception, however, fictional characters have a being and an integrity of their own. The author is not free simply to create and manipulate characters. Instead, the writer beckons characters, who appear and must be interacted with just like actual people. In short, just as Morrison believes in continued interaction between the living and the dead, so she sees true relationships between fictional characters and living writers.

The narrator of *Jazz*, however, does not initially understand the limits of her own power. Her confidence in her own power and omniscience lasts until the section in which Golden Gray sets out to find his father. Then, she discovers that she has done a violence to the character by oversimplifying him, stereotyping him. She has at first thought that Golden Gray set out to find Henry Lestroy with a comparatively simple emotional mixture of hatred and vengeance—and told the story that way. Later, she sees her mistake: "How could I have imagined him so poorly? . . . I have been careless and stupid and it infuriates me to discover (again) how unreliable I am" (160). In this last phrase, Morrison's narrator—who is also a fictional character—pokes fun at the conventions of narration.

The plot of *Jazz* draws attention to the narrator's fallibility. The narrator expects the Felicity-Joe-Violet triangle to repeat the violent experiences of the Dorcas-Joe-Violet triangle. Instead, Felicity, Joe, and Violet help one another to happier and more productive lives. This unexpected outcome arises from two factors. First, Violet and Joe, even in their mid-fifties, have more capacity for self-knowledge and change than the narrator allows for. Second, the narrator errs in thinking of Felicity and Dorcas as identical or interchangeable figures. The narrator's surprised increased understanding points to Morrison's divergence from traditional European modes: If so-called omniscience is fallible and even biased, then an objective view is impossible, and reality becomes merely a continually developing understanding of events rather than the truth.

Whereas traditional European omniscient narration slowly unfolds a plot that has already happened to the characters, *Jazz* makes storytelling an ongoing development. The narrator of *Jazz* revises her own under-standing, cooperates with characters in making the plot, and in the final pages invites the reader to participate in making the story.

THEMATIC ISSUES

Jazz uses its unusual narration to portray the developing black com-munity through five successive generations. The novel emphasizes the need to invent new ways of understanding experience, and new forms of art to imagine the understanding. The development of the individual characters is intertwined with the development of the community's ar-tistic expression. This connection is clearest in the events that surprise the narrator, such as the characters' refusal to recreate the fatal triangle of Dorcas-Joe-Violet.

To prevent another disaster, the characters must change their self-images from static, destructive blues roles to dynamic jazz roles. The characters begin by remembering that they can change. In the first tri-angle, the three orphans—Violet, Joe, and Dorcas—all have empty places inside. To fill this place, each adopts a rigid, conventional role that pre-cipitates the tragedy. To do better, Violet and Joe have to understand what caused the initial catastrophe and then change so they can behave differently rather than sing another, repetitive verse of the blues.

Whereas blues lyrics concentrate on a few roles for both men and women, the improvisational nature of jazz implies continual redefinition of any role. In traditional blues lyrics, the woman is generally lamenting the loss of her man and either despairing or plotting vengeance. The music of Violet's youth offered her this role, which reiterates the story of her mother's abandonment, despair, and suicide. Faced with Joe's in-fidelity, Violet tries to enact the vengeful woman. She finds her brief affair as unsatisfying as her attack on Dorcas's corpse, however, and realizes that she needs another approach.

Through her talks with Alice Manfred, Violet finds an alternative self-definition. At first, Violet believes that only violent defense of her right to her man will preserve her self-respect. Alice replies, ''Fight what, who? Some mishandled child who saw her parents burn up? . . . No-body's asking you to take it. I'm sayin make it, make it!'' (123). Alice's last words here use ''make it'' in a double sense. The phrase means making love, not in the simplistic sense of merely having sex, but in the more complex sense of creating love. ''Make it'' also means to survive, to make a self that is capable of surviving. In Alice's apartment, Violet learns to laugh at her earlier self, *"that* Violet" with her knife, trying to do "something bluesy" (114, emphasis in original).

Like Violet—and from her—Felicity learns to use experience to grow into new roles. Violet passes on to Felicity the idea developed in her conversations with Alice, that one must create her own world: "What's the world for if you can't make it up the way you want it?" (208). Skeptical, Felicity notes that she can't change the world. Violet replies that either you change the world, or it changes you. She acknowledges her own mistake in letting the world shape her life into something she didn't want. Her chief error, she says, was allowing her grandmother's stories of Golden Gray to create a false self-image. When Felicity asks how Violet recovered from the mistake of becoming Violent, Violet highlights the continuing process of making self:

> "Killed her. Then I killed the me that killed her."
>
> "Who's left?"
>
> "Me." (209)

Being exposed to a genuine "me" that is Violet allows Felicity to identify her own genuine feelings. The first is grief for Dorcas. The second, self-respect, leads her to re-evaluate an earlier incident. When a jeweler in Tiffany's was rude to them, Felicity's mother stole a ring for her. Felicity now sees that loving the ring would duplicate Violet's mistake of adopting white values from True Belle's stories of Golden Gray. Instead, Felicity decides to love her mother's attempt to compensate for Tiffany's disrespect. Rather than loving the material object, she loves familial connection. In a similar way, Violet's honesty makes it possible for Felicity to recognize her mixed feelings about Dorcas. Felicity is curious about why Violet attacked Dorcas's corpse. Violet's truthful response not only admits a mistake but counsels that moving forward is simply a matter of decision:

> "Lost the lady," [Violet] said. "Put her down someplace and forgot where."
>
> "How did you find her?"
>
> "Looked." (211)

Once she sees that irrational anger isn't irrevocable, Felicity can admit that she is angry with Dorcas for having let herself die—and for thinking about Joe rather than her best friend Felicity. In expressing this anger, she tells Joe what Dorcas's last words were and thus gives him the impetus to move on, too.

Like Violet, Joe has to move from a blues self-conception to a jazz image. Rather than developing a completely new definition of himself, however, Joe can simply return to his earlier ideas, which have always been more flexible than Violet's. Joe tells the reader that by the time he met Dorcas, he had recreated himself seven times (123), and his eighth change—loving her—was one too many. While he is stalking Dorcas to her party, Joe passes a bluesman playing his guitar, a suggestion that he has frozen his self-image in a blues conception. Romantic abandonment shatters Joe because he connects it with his mother's abandonment. Unlike Violet, Joe accomplishes real damage by acting on his blues. Having lost Dorcas, having *killed* her, he has difficulty imagining any future. Blues offer no help because their essence is expression of feeling, not reforming experience. Joe sinks into depression.

By giving him a way of not losing Dorcas, Felicity moves Joe from the static blues to the dynamic constructions of jazz. Earlier, when Joe risks someone's seeing him with Dorcas, he muses, "no point in picking the apple if you don't want to see how it taste" (40). Dorcas's last words, Felicity tells him, were "There's only one apple. . . . Tell Joe" (213). If there's only one apple (if everything partakes of the same essence), that apple is the City (New York City, nicknamed "the big Apple"). Joe knows that Dorcas remains somehow in the City, and that her last human thoughts were of him. His blues sense of abandonment dissipates, and he moves on to a renewed relationship with Violet. Lying in bed with her, he sees outside their window a bloody shoulder that becomes a red-winged blackbird. His last image of Dorcas thus merges with his image of his mother. Significantly, he can see them; they are emotionally available to him.

Each major character's development leaves him or her happier and more stable, though, ironically, each is now committed to change. The importance of the characters' development is not limited to themselves, however. So long as children are orphans, the outcome for the African American community will be that of the first triangle—black-on-black violence, generational destruction, and tragedy. When people undertake the honest exchanges that help to educate orphans emotionally, the outcome changes to black-on-black nurturance, generational instruction, and laughter at the human comedy. People are "comic," Joe insists (214). Divinely comic, Dante might concur.

As the second work of a trilogy, *Jazz* naturally comments on and develops the themes of the first, *Beloved*. *Beloved* ends its characters' stories with all the questions of what makes up the self implied by Paul D's statement that Sethe is her own best thing and her answering question, "Me?" The narrator then leaves the characters to consider the nature and purposes of storytelling. These questions about self and storytelling merge in *Jazz*, where stories construct the self, where the self-in-process is always constructing the story of its ever-changing life.

The concept of self in *Jazz* differs from that of *Beloved*, in part because the works are set in different time periods that require different modes for survival. In the immediate aftermath of slavery, Sethe must identify what in herself is continuous, what lived through slavery. Farther from slavery, the characters of *Jazz* must discover how to let their selves evolve, what will facilitate the continual redefinition necessary to survival—and to enjoyment. This process belongs to a conception sometimes called postmodernism. Postmodernists do not accept the belief that each of us has an unchanging core of traits that constitutes our unchanging individual self. Instead, postmodernists think of the self as malleable, continually subject to change even in its basic elements.

A postmodernist self is a construction, then, something that an individual decides upon—or is forced into. The postmodernist self is not necessarily discontinuous, however; each successive self develops a story of its prior experience. Thus, Joe might say either that he killed Dorcas, or that he shot her and she let herself die, depending on his definition of himself. In a like manner, Violet's blues self understands her violent actions as the only ones possible, while her jazz self understands them as the result of mislaying the Lady. These selves do not successively obliterate each other; they continue to coexist. Violet will always carry within her the self the community has christened Violent, just as she will always carry the child who saw her mother's spirit break. As Joe's nine changes imply, the postmodernist self is always in process, never finished.

Contextual elements—the social, physical, and cultural settings of experience—greatly affect the self's transformations. Much of the social influence on African American self-construction consists of violence. Dorcas's violent death, for example, necessitates new selves for Alice, Felicity, Joe, and Violet. This black-on-black violence does not result merely from individual pathology, however. (That is, Joe's action is not entirely motivated by the purely personal loss of his mother.) The larger social context has set the stage for this act. The disintegration of Violet's family, the murder of Dorcas's parents, and Joe's beating with a pipe—all the result of racist whites—contribute heavily to forming the selves that later interact violently.

The physical setting too exercises an influence. The City's power and energy invigorate Joe and Violet, and it offers economic opportunities that the Virginia countryside never could. Further, the sheer size of the African American population in the City makes possible new strategies of resistance to racism. The protest marchers in the City number several thousand, many more than the entire population of Vesper County, Virginia.

Historically, this large concentration of African Americans produced changes not only in politics but in the art, literature, and music that became the Harlem Renaissance. This novel, of course, concentrates on the new music, on jazz. Jazz both makes the City what it is and owes its creation to the City. To various listeners, jazz expresses sexuality, anger, a threat, or self-assertion. This variety of interpretations comes not only from the diverse temperaments of the listeners but from the nature of jazz. Jazz musicians might at different times improvise on the same melody to convey all of these. As much as the City is home to the characters, so is jazz the constantly shifting center of the home. The rhythms of jazz are the processes of reconstituting families and redefining selves within them. The postmodernist self is a jazz performance, endlessly improvising on the combined melodies of our changing physical bodies and sociocultural contexts.

AN ECLECTIC AFRO-MODERNIST READING

In literary criticism, "eclectic" simply means using parts of several different critical approaches (such as mythic, feminist, and so on). An Afro-modernist reading is based on elements of African American culture that produce, surround, and are an integral part of a literary text. Most observers agree that African American culture is distinguishable from other American cultures by its emphasis on music. This attention to music has produced two original forms, blues and jazz, and has developed distinctive traditions of others like gospel. An Afro-modernist reading might be based on any of these forms, depending on the text's references.

Jazz is an extraordinarily challenging novel. A successful interpretation must address (1) the novel's technique of using a self-conscious narrator aware of her flaws (see Narrative Technique); (2) the nature of the self portrayed through the characterization; and (3) the pervasive theme of jazz. In fact, the third area subsumes the first two, because jazz provides technique, subject, and theme for the novel.

The Social and Literary Context section of this chapter gives a working definition of jazz, but the writer Ralph Ellison's less technical definition of jazz performance in his 1964 *Shadow and Act* provides better grounding for literary interpretation: "True jazz is an art of individual assertion within and against the group. Each true jazz moment . . . springs from a contest in which each artist challenges all the rest; each solo flight, or improvisation, represents (like the successive canvases of a painter) a definition of his identity; as individual, as member of the collectivity and as a link in the chain of tradition" (Ellison 234). Ellison's definition highlights two issues, the relationship of the individual to the collectivity (or group) and tradition. Because *Jazz*'s attitude toward tradition underlies its presentation of the individual's relationship to the group, we will consider tradition first.

As a link in a chain of tradition, a jazz performance improvises variations on earlier musical themes. The novel *Jazz* forms an analogous link in three different ways: (1) it shows its characters as part of a continuous spiritual community; (2) it consciously participates in the large-scale history of literature in English; and (3) it acknowledges its place in small-scale literary history—Toni Morrison's development as a writer.

The most important of the characters' initial problems stems from feeling outside of, or separated from, nurturing traditions. In this novel, isolation means death. In the last chapter, Joe and Violet's new bird pines; to cure it, they take it to their apartment roof, where it can hear street musicians. Connection with other music-makers rescues the bird, which needs the same kind of connection as human beings. Earlier, Joe and Violet are in the bird's position. Literally orphans, they are symbolically separated from tradition. Joe's choice of his name, for example, is essentially negative. If his mother left "without a trace" and she left without him, he decides that he must be "Joe Trace."

Developing jazz selves, however (see Thematic Issues), allows Joe and Violet to re-link themselves with ancestral tradition. Lying in bed, they use the materials of everyday life to envision connection. Through the window, Joe sees the night become "a shoulder with a thin line of blood.

Slowly, slowly, it forms itself into a bird with a blade of red on the wing" (225). Simultaneously, Violet's fingers caress Joe's body "as though it were the sunlit rim of a well and down there somebody is gathering gifts . . . to distribute . . ." (225). The imagery here connects Joe with both Dorcas and Wild. At the same time, Violet is connected with the well in which her mother drowned—but the well contains, not Rose Dear's dead body, but her live spirit blessing her children with gifts.

Analogously, *Jazz* acknowledges the past on the meta-level of literary history. The novel constantly refers to earlier writers' works. Hunters Hunter, for example, strongly resembles a character in William Faulkner's *Go Down, Moses*, and Golden Gray revisits Charles Bon in another of Faulkner's works, *Absalom, Absalom!* Violet frees her birds as Miss Flite does in Charles Dickens's *Bleak House*; Violet's parrot echoes the bird in the opening scene of Kate Chopin's *The Awakening*. These examples could be multiplied indefinitely. A reader knowledgeable about the tradition of literature in English meets an ancestral presence in virtually every section of the novel; being *Jazz*, of course, it doesn't simply reproduce these presences but redefines them in the context of its own stories.

Likewise, *Jazz* acknowledges its place in Morrison's literary productions, and particularly its place as the second of a trilogy. Morrison constructs parallels in setting, character, and image to underscore the continuity of *Beloved* and *Jazz*; further, several passages of *Jazz* echo the phrasings of the earlier novel. Both books are set after a diaspora of the black population. In *Beloved*, slavery has disrupted systems of family and kinship; in *Jazz*, racist violence and economics remain disruptive, finally fueling the Great Migration to the urban North.

The situations of the main female characters resemble each other too. Sethe mourns the daughter she killed, Beloved, while after Dorcas's death, Violet wonders if the girl might not, somehow, have been one of the children whom Violet had miscarried (108–9). The character Beloved, last seen hugely pregnant and naked, reappears in *Jazz* as the girl who Henry Lestory calls Wild. Beloved's memories include images of slave ships; when *Jazz*'s Alice leaves a hot iron on her blouse, the burn leaves the print of a black ship. These parallels prepare the reader for the explicit echoes, which are loudest in the sections dealing with female identity and development. Violet and Denver both "mislay the Lady" and must find her again to regain their sanity. For Denver, the Lady is a real person, her teacher Lady Jones, who can help her become an adult. For Violet, the Lady is a part of herself that she has forgotten and must reclaim. In another echo, Violet makes Sethe's hesitant final recognition, "Me?," into a triumphant self-assertion during her conversation with Felicity:

> "Who's left?"
> "Me." (209)

Just as Violet's statement revises Sethe's question, so does the ending of *Jazz* revoice the finale of *Beloved*. In both, the narrators muse on story-telling. *Beloved* considers the story itself, however, whereas *Jazz* focuses on the storyteller, the narrator.

The narrator is central to *Jazz*'s exploration of the relationship between the individual and the collective. To use Ellison's terms, each solo-ing individual is continually improvising a self-definition within and against the group. These definitions can be injurious to the individual and harm-ful, even deadly, to the group. To take the simplest example on the level of the characters, Joe shoots Dorcas, and Dorcas's death grieves not only him but Alice and Felicity as well. The development of the narrator's character operates on the meta-level of investigating how stories are cre-ated and understood. The jazz metaphor indicates that literary creation and understanding are never purely individual matters. Instead, they are a collaborative process within and against the group of writers and read-ers, past and present. As mentioned in Narrative Technique, the narrator realizes her mistakes, analyzes her own deficiencies: ". . . loving the City . . . distracted me . . . I missed the people altogether. . . . They knew how little I could be counted on; how poorly, how shabbily my know-it-all self covered helplessness" (221). The omniscient narrator of literary con-vention has become a mistaken know-it-all. The formerly all-powerful storyteller, in having misunderstood the characters, has mis-anticipated the plot too: "I was sure one would kill the other" (220). The characters assert themselves to contradict the narrator's initial stereotypes. The nar-rator must give up her false ideas about the characters and trust them. When the narrator accepts the characters, even those most foreign to her, she is enlightened. Hugged by Wild, who now seems playful rather than only feral, she can finish narrating the book because she now knows the characters. She can tell how they behaved after their latest transforma-tions in the same way that the reader knows how his or her friends will behave. Plot has become collaborative.

Morrison did not originate such collaboration, which began appearing in a genre called metafiction in the 1970s. Like a few other metafictionists, Morrison extends collaboration from author-character to the narrator-reader relationship. At the end of *Jazz*, the narrator talks directly to the reader, confessing that she envies Joe and Violet, longing to speak "out loud what they have no need to say . . . *That I have loved only you . . . That I want you to love me back and show it to me. That I love the way you hold me*" (229, emphasis in original). If she could speak aloud, the narrator would "[s]ay make me, remake me. You are free to do it and I am free to let you because look, look. Look where your hands are. Now" (229). The reader's hands are holding the book, thus holding the narrator. The narrator's last words are a confidence, an intimate communication. Writing a story and interpreting it become intimate, shared activities. Even in her first novel (*The Bluest Eye*), Morrison demands an active reader. Now, in a vision of intermingling creative, interpretive, and sexual energies, she invites the reader to be a partner.

Paradise
(1998)

This novel implicitly comments on and extends both European and African American literary traditions. The title echoes the last of Dante's works in his *Divine Comedy, Paradisio*. (Morrison's earlier novel *Beloved* corresponds to *Inferno; Jazz*, to *Purgatorio*.) The religious imagery adopts a few Dantean touches, such as intercession by divine female figures. The religious sensibility, however, differs drastically. Dante's paradise transcends earth, whereas Morrison's shows earth and the spiritual world as inextricably mixed. Morrison's earlier novels have shown the persistence of spirits after human characters die, but *Paradise* shows these spirits as far more active in human life—a traditional African view. For the first time in a Morrison novel, spirits continue to grow and age after their human deaths. Further, certain human beings may be incarnations of eternal, divine energies. Whereas the *Divine Comedy* poetically expresses Catholic cosmology, *Paradise* conveys an Africanist, feminist religious sensibility.

Paradise re-examines the ideal of a self-governing, all-black society that recurs in a considerable body of African American writing. The novel suggests that earlier works such as Zora Neale Hurston's *Their Eyes Were Watching God* have romanticized the rural black town. So long as the idea of "paradise" rests on excluding those who are unworthy, human-created utopias will fail because all human beings have the capacity for sin and violence. Paradoxically, only by accepting evil in ourselves and others can we enjoy a true haven.

PLOT DEVELOPMENT

The novel's first sentences—"They shoot the white girl first. With the rest they can take their time" (3)—immediately draw the reader into shocking action. In this opening scene, nine armed men are storming an unlocked building referred to as "the Convent" and attacking the group of five women who live there. The men come from the all-black town of Ruby, Oklahoma, and the women have drifted one at a time to the Convent. The attack occurs in 1976, and the present of *Paradise* remains the 1970s. Before returning to the opening scene, Morrison develops a dizzying variety of subplots. The novel explores the histories and memories of numerous characters to show how these men and women came to battle.

Even more complicated than the other Morrison novels, *Paradise* has no continually building plot sequences. Instead, the reader must constantly connect bits of information. Hints and half-stories tantalize the reader but frequently turn out to be dead ends, unconnected to the main action. With much information either fragmentary or of dubious validity, no definitive story emerges.

Paradise presents, first, an account of the attack on the Convent. From there, the reader can build histories of the warring communities—the black community of Ruby and the women's community at the Convent— from their foundings until the 1970s. *Paradise* supplies us with life stories for the six women who are living in the Convent when it is attacked, and significant episodes from the lives of three of the attackers. Finally, smaller narratives show the relationships between individual men and women from Ruby and individual women from the Convent.

The attack on the Convent is not simply a battle between all of Ruby and the women. A group of men incite one another to attack the Convent at an outdoor gathering place and symbol of the community, the Oven. They are overheard by an older woman, Lone DuPres, a founder of Ruby, who attempts to warn the Convent. The women there, however, are joyfully dancing in the rain, one of them with her newborn baby, and they ignore her. Lone returns the seventeen miles to Ruby and alerts the DuPres household, which she can count on to oppose the impending violence. The DuPres family in turn notifies the Beauchamp, Sands, and Poole families.

Meanwhile, nine men—Steward and Deacon Morgan, their nephew

K. D. Smith, Sergeant Person, Wisdom Poole, Harper and Menus Jury, Arnold and Jeff Fleetwood—gather at Sergeant's house to eat and organize equipment. Arriving at the Convent at dawn, they attack. Steward shoots the unlocked door, then a white woman in the hall. (The identity of this woman is never directly specified; the reader is left to infer which of the women is white.) Seeing objects that they do not understand—a baby crib in a house without children, paintings on the cellar floor—the men misinterpret these as ritual objects for child-sacrifice and devil worship.

The women vigorously defend themselves with picture frames and a kitchen knife, injuring Menus, Harper, Arnold, and Jeff. In a passage combining the imagery of hunting, track, and religion, three men shoot at the women who have fled outside into the fields. They fall. When the last woman, Consolata, comes into the hall, Steward shoots her in the head, though Deacon tries to stop him. The wounded Consolata sees a vision over the heads of the men.

The restraining forces summoned by Lone arrive, but too late. The attackers offer rationalizations that are condemned by the Beauchamps. Soane and Dovey Morgan (the wives of Deacon and Steward) pronounce Consolata dead. Lone stays at the Convent until Roger Best, the undertaker, arrives. He searches but finds no bodies, not even Consolata's. The absence of bodies relieves the town of Ruby of one great fear, that white lawmen would have to be notified and involved. Although the two dominant versions excuse the men, the community creates multiple stories to explain the attack.

This multiplicity of perspective recurs in Morrison's treatment of Ruby's history. Ruby is the second all-black community founded by different generations of the same families; the first was Haven. The reader gets two somewhat different versions of Haven's founding. The first consists of Steward Morgan's memories of stories he heard as a child, presented in the chapter titled "Seneca." The second is the attempt by the town researcher, Patricia Best Cato, to synthesize and organize town lore into a coherent history.

The community's history can be traced to the collapse of Reconstruction. As the white South revoked African Americans' civil rights in the 1870s and 1880s, talented black men in Mississippi and Louisiana were thrown permanently out of work. In 1890, the families of Zechariah Morgan, Drum Blackhorse, Brood Poole, Jupe Cato, Able Flood, a Beauchamp, and two DuPres moved westward. Their hopes of joining one of the western all-black towns were dashed by an event referred to as "The Disallowing." Moving west, the group reached the established town of Fairly, Oklahoma. Although the citizens of Fairly offer food, they refuse the migrants not only the right to settle there but even shelter for the night—because of their dark skin.

Zechariah performed a spiritual ritual to entreat help for the outcasts. In response, a supernatural force embodied in a small man with a satchel appeared. The group followed him, and on the twenty-ninth day, began to build Haven on the spot where the guide had vanished. The townspeople construct a communal oven, the practical and symbolic center of Haven. The Oven bears an inscription including the phrase "the Furrow of His Brow." The community strives for self-sufficiency, with its own farming and banking enterprises. Until World War II, Haven prospers.

When veterans return from the war, they find Haven gone to seed. Observing the nationally hostile atmosphere toward black veterans, fourteen families seek greater separation from mainstream society by moving farther west to create Ruby in 1950. Patricia Best Cato believes that both Haven and Ruby are founded on the largely unspoken premise that only dark-skinned people are acceptable. (Although Pat's father Roger Best was among Ruby's founders, Pat is convinced that the other men never accepted her mother, who was by Haven standards both light-skinned and foreign—from Tennessee.) The founders immediately reassemble the Oven brought from Haven. The town's birth is celebrated with a horse race won by a boy henceforth known as K. D. (Kentucky Derby) Smith, the nephew of Steward and Deacon Morgan. A few years later, the town is named Ruby for K. D.'s deceased mother, Ruby Morgan.

The town of Ruby prizes tradition. Steward Morgan, as representative of the founders, strives to be worthy of his grandfather Zechariah's legacy. Every year, the children's Christmas pageant melds the story of the Disallowing with that of Christ's birth in a manger. By the 1970s, however, the young people of Ruby have become dissatisfied with the elders' traditions. For instance, the Oven's inscription has gradually worn away, and though many remember it as "Beware the Furrow of His Brow," the younger generations insist on "Be the Furrow of His Brow." When someone paints a red fist reminiscent of the Black Power emblem on the Oven, the older generation of men feels that the community is falling into evil ways. They see disrespectful children, inappropriate sexual goings-on, and a general loss of moral social order.

There are other, perhaps more objective signs of decline as well. With only one newcomer over several generations, the Haven/Ruby blood-lines are seriously inbred. All four of the Fleetwoods' children are dying of a congenital disease. Looking for the cause of these woes, many of the town fathers decide that the Convent is to blame.

The Convent never functioned as a convent. Built by an embezzler as his hideout, the mansion displayed sensual statues, pictures, and even bathroom fixtures. After the embezzler's arrest, Mary Magna, the mother superior of a very small group of nuns, reorganizes the house as a Catholic-run school for American Indian girls. With them is Connie, whom Mary Magna rescued from the streets of a South American city. The nuns do their best to obliterate the embezzler's art because it strikes them as obscene and sinful. When the government stops sending them children, the nuns disperse.

For some years, Mary Magna and Connie live alone in the mansion. They support themselves by selling produce and baked goods to Ruby. Connie discovers a talent for mystic healing, and she keeps Mary Magna alive into advanced old age. Just before Mary Magna's death, they are joined by Mavis Albright, the first of a series of women who drift into the Convent. Gradually, the community expands to include Gigi (Grace), Seneca, and Pallas Truelove. The women have different personalities but similar experiences of men's indifference or brutality. To help them, Connie metamorphoses into Consolata Sosa, the healer. Together, the women paint representations of themselves on the Con-vent's cellar floor and participate in "loud dreaming" (264) as therapy. Meanwhile, Consolata provides them with a vision of a beautiful fe-male divine force, Piedade. The women have largely healed from their horrific experiences—their rain dance is a celebration—when they are attacked.

The narratives of Ruby and the Convent frame many smaller, inter-active stories of particular individuals. The stories of the Convent women's lives tend to be concentrated in the chapters bearing their names while the stories of Ruby-dwellers are dispersed throughout the novel.

Like the other Convent women, Mavis Albright arrives after a tragedy. When Mavis left her infant twins, Pearle and Merle, in a car on a hot day they suffocated while she ran a brief errand. Mavis's husband Frank is clearly a batterer, and Mavis fears that he and their other children are planning to kill her. She flees westward, picking up hitchhikers for company, until her car breaks down near the Convent. Alone in its kitchen, Mavis feels her twins' presence and stays.

When she and her lover, Mikey Rood, are arrested and he is jailed, Gigi sets out on the journey that brings her to the Convent. Gigi is looking for a huge rock formation that Mikey described as a natural expression of a couple having sex. Eventually Gigi concludes that the formation does not exist, but she finds a new destination in another man's story of a lake with two twined trees, near the Convent. Going there is supposed to bring sexual ecstacy and make one irresistible. Walking through Ruby, Gigi attracts the attention of K. D. Smith, who becomes her lover.

Whereas Gigi has a healthy sensuality, Seneca's sexuality has been twisted. When her very young mother, Jean, abandons her, five-year-old Seneca decides that it is her fault. An abused foster child, she begins her habit of self-mutilation as punishment for attracting men's attention. When her boyfriend Eddie Turtle is jailed, Seneca finds herself stranded, financially and emotionally, at a bus stop. Seneca accepts a chauffeur's suggestion that she join his employer, Norma Keene Fox. While Fox's husband is away, Seneca is a well-kept prostitute. Ostensibly free to leave, she remains because of her financial and emotional circumstances. When Norma's husband returns, Seneca is unceremoniously dumped. While hitchhiking through Oklahoma, Seneca sees a distraught woman from Ruby, Sweetie Fleetwood, walking unprotected into a growing blizzard. Seneca leaves her ride to steer Sweetie to the nearest shelter, the Convent.

Pallas, the last of the Convent women to arrive, is sixteen when she leaves her father's home and an exclusive school to rejoin her mother. She travels with her lover, Carlos, an artist and the school's maintenance man. When Carlos and her mother become sexual partners, the doubly betrayed Pallas hits the road by herself. After some never-specified terrible event—probably sexual violation in or near a pond—she is picked up by a group of American Indians. They take her to a clinic where a young Ruby woman, Billie Delia Cato, works. Having once taken refuge there herself, Billie Delia delivers the shell-shocked Pallas to the Convent. Somewhat restored, Pallas tries to return to her earlier life. Her legalistic father, however, is more interested in suing the school than in nurturing her, and she comes back to the Convent. She gives birth to a baby son shortly before the attack.

Consolata's individual story cannot be extricated from the narratives of the Convent's founding and the attack. Having been rescued by Mary

Magna, Consolata accepts the mother superior's religious view of the world, with its condemnation of physical pleasure. Then, at thirty, she sees Deacon during the celebration of Ruby's founding. Their passionate affair—Deacon is already married to Soane—takes place by the lake and the twined fig trees. Deacon ends the affair when he is repelled by Connie's biting his lip during love-play and then licking the blood. Pursuing him, Connie begins the seventeen-mile walk to Ruby. She accepts a ride back to the Convent from a man she at first thinks is Deacon but who is his identical twin Steward. Soane visits Connie, pretending to want drugs to abort a pregnancy. Soane really desires to make Connie face the reality of Deacon's marriage with her. The abandoned and penitent Connie tries to return to her earlier religious views. Her situation is complicated by an undeniable talent that does not fit within these conventional views.

A midwife, Lone intuits Connie's ability to enter mystically into sick people's bodies to heal them. When Deacon and Soane's son Scout is killed in a car accident, Connie is able to bring him back from the dead. Connie resists using this power, which she considers sinful, but it helps her to keep the elderly Mary Magna alive. Soane makes another trip to the Convent to thank Connie for saving her son, and the two women become friends.

By 1975, several years after Mary Magna's death, the bereaved Connie has become alcoholic. Awakening from a stupor, she is suddenly disgusted by the immaturity and triviality of the Convent women's lives. All of the women have had terrible experiences, and consequently developed self-destructive attitudes and behavior. Exasperated by the girls' lying and their fixation on romantic love, Connie rouses herself to become Consolata. Through elaborate rituals, each woman's story of her past, and descriptions of a heavenly vision, Consolata heals the women. In her vision, a divine female force named Piedade sings a marvelous wordless song.

When the men attack, Consolata enters the hallway to try to help the wounded white woman. She looks over the heads of the men and says, "You're back" (301). Steward shoots her in the head. Soane and Dovey carry the dying Consolata into the Convent kitchen.

The characters of the Ruby men who attack the Convent are powerfully drawn, but aside from the climactic action, they have little part in the plot. Steward Morgan leads the attack, for example, but we know him primarily through having eavesdropped on his thoughts and perceived him through other characters' views. Except for Lone, the women of Ruby have little part in the action, though their opinions are a constant critique of the men's approaches to success, to the younger generation, and to the Convent. Of the attackers, only Deacon Morgan and K. D. Smith have a substantial role in the rest of the plot, and they contribute mostly to subplots involving the Convent.

Although Steward is first through the Convent door and first to shoot, Deacon "gives the orders" (286). He tries to stop Steward from shooting Consolata, but is ineffectual. And Deacon, unlike Steward, repents. In broad daylight Deacon walks barefoot through town to the Reverend Misner's house, where he discusses his understanding of the event.

Deacon acknowledges having sinned through self-righteous violence toward the defenseless. He presents his relationship with Steward in the context of another relationship of brothers, that between the founder Zechariah and his twin. These ancestors, once close enough to be called Coffee and Tea, became alienated when their reactions to white oppression differed. Ordered by white men to dance, Tea danced; Coffee took a bullet in his foot instead, and lived out his life half-crippled. When Coffee became Zechariah and moved west, he did not invite Tea. Deacon does not want to recreate this alienation in his own generation. He sees Steward's sin in killing Consolata as something shared, a part of himself.

Still other plot lines wind in and out of *Paradise* to develop themes and characters. The subplot involving K. D. Smith, Arnette Fleetwood, and Gigi intersects both of the other main plot lines. K. D. and Arnette are always problematic for the powers of Ruby. Respectively the nephew of the Morgans and the granddaughter of the founding Fleetwood, they do not conform to the founders' ideas of morality or even decorum. Gigi's arrival precipitates a crisis. Arnette has just announced that she is pregnant by K. D. when Gigi strolls across his line of sight exuding sexuality. Dismissing the pregnancy as Arnette's problem, K. D. openly lusts after Gigi. Miffed, Arnette insults him, and he slaps her. To prevent a scandal, the Morgan and Fleetwood families meet with the Reverend Misner to decide on restitution for the slap.

The elders remain ignorant of Arnette's pregnancy. Desperate, she appears at the Convent one night pretending to have been raped. The women allow her to stay, unaware that she is abusing her body to induce a miscarriage. When the child is born three months premature, Arnette completely ignores him. The Convent women name him Che and care for him, but he lives only three days. Meanwhile, K. D. comes to the Convent frequently because he and Gigi have become lovers. K. D. wants more control than Gigi will allow, however. When he threatens to hurt her, Mavis, Seneca, and Gigi throw him out.

Some years later, K. D. and Arnette marry, an event that the townspeople hope will put to rest the quarrel between the Morgans and the Fleetwoods. Instead, the wedding ceremony is an ideological tug-of-war between Ruby's two ministers. The Reverend Senior Pulliam, an insider, preaches hellfire and brimstone; Reverend Richard Misner, a newcomer, is interested in youth and the civil rights movement. When Pulliam's sermon reopens the Morgan-Fleetwood family feud, Misner's rebuttal is silent and ineffectual: he holds the church's heavy cross in front of the congregation. Violence might erupt at the wedding reception, except that the arrival of the Convent women provides a distraction.

That very night, Arnette asks the Convent women for her baby. Later, K. D. relays to the other men what he says are Arnette's statements: that the Convent women told her the child was stillborn and then stole it. He also volunteers that the women assaulted Arnette when she confronted them; in reality, he has beaten her. K. D.'s desire for vengeance and Arnette's desire for respectability combine in deceptions that help form the rationale for the attack.

If there were any doubt that killing the Convent women could not end Ruby's troubles, K. D.'s behavior would be conclusive proof. When the second contingent of Ruby men question the attackers, K. D. not only tries to throw the blame on the women but publicly names his uncle Steward as a killer. (Without eyewitnesses, it would be hard for anyone to establish legally which of the men had killed.) To shut him up, Steward slaps him. Later, K. D., Arnette, and their child move into a house on Steward's land. Worthy or not, they are the heirs of Ruby's founders.

The end of *Paradise* returns the focus to the women of the Convent. The final chapter, "Save-Marie," includes the reappearances of Mavis, Gigi, Seneca, and Pallas, as well as the narrator's vision of Piedade, the divine force of Consolata's stories.

In one way, the Convent women's stories "break" the narrative of the two scenes detailing the attack. After they have been shot, the women's bodies simply disappear. Their stories continue, however. Only Consolata is not shown after the attack. Except for her, each of the women is depicted interacting with her family. After the attack, Mavis cheerfully reconciles with one of her older children, Sally, over breakfast in a New Jersey diner. Gigi visits her imprisoned father. Seneca meets Jean, the woman who abandoned her, in a parking lot. Jean suspects Seneca's identity, but Seneca denies that they know one another. Pallas and her baby appear to her mother, Divine Truelove, but Pallas refuses to speak. These scenes do not suggest that the women escape death. As in most Morrison novels, spirits persist and interact with embodied human beings.

Visually separated from the rest of the narrative, the final three paragraphs of *Paradise* depict a mystical scene. On a beach sit a black woman, Piedade, and a younger woman with ruined hands. (Save-Marie also has damaged hands.). Piedade sings as they watch for a ship bringing more work for them to do "down here in Paradise" (318).

CHARACTER DEVELOPMENT

Character development in *Paradise* proceeds generally by the reader's inferences about plot development, rarely by seeing directly into a character's consciousness or being offered an interpretation by the narrator. *Paradise* sketches many more characters than Morrison's earlier novels. Those novels primarily explore individual growth, with the surrounding community's sentiments supplied by the narrator or, at most, one or two representative characters. Here, Morrison presents individuals' parts in a collective, the entire town of Ruby. *Paradise* contains two large groups of characters associated either with the Convent or Ruby. By perspective and experience, the Ruby group is subdivided by gender and age.

Six women are associated with the Convent. Mary Magna (Mother), the mother superior of a small band of nuns, rescues nine-year-old Consolata (Connie) from the streets of a Brazilian city, where the abandoned child had been sexually abused. Mary Magna's religious beliefs, those of traditional Western Christianity, set body and soul in opposition, with the body's desires as sinful barriers to achieving heaven. In the United States, Mary Magna runs a school for native (American Indian) girls; these schools were organized to separate Indian children from their native languages, cultures, and families to assimilate them into European American norms.

Loyal and loving, Connie/Consolata lives by Mother's code until she is thirty and meets Deacon. When Deacon ends their passionate affair, she repents, condemning her own sexuality. Through Lone, Connie discovers that she has extraordinary healing powers. (Though blinded by daylight, she has true "insight," the ability to move into another person and see what is wrong.) She claims that Lone tricks her into bringing Deacon and Soane's son Scout back to life. Scout's recovery initiates a friendship between Connie and Soane, who formerly competed for Deacon. After the school closes, Consolata supports herself and Mother by cooking and cultivating a rare hot pepper to sell to Ruby.

Devastated by Mother's death, Connie becomes an alcoholic. Finally the desperate state of the women who have drifted into the Convent rouses her to become Consolata Sosa, the healer. During this period she is described as wearing blue and white, colors traditionally associated with Mary, the mother of Christ. Through rituals of painting their bodies, permitting them to share their traumatic experiences, preaching that body and soul are inseparable, and describing her own experience of a divine female force named Piedade, Consolata is steadily improving their health and happiness when the Convent is attacked. As Consolata attempts to help the wounded white girl, Steward shoots her in the head. Her last words, just before the shot, are "You're back" (301). These words may refer to Deacon (though he does not believe so), to Mother, to Piedade, or to someone else entirely. Because Consolata is the only one of the Convent women who does not reappear after the attack, and because in the last pages of the novel the narrator describes a vision of Piedade similar to Connie's, it seems likely that Connie/Consolata is an incarnation of Piedade.

The first of the drifters to come to the Convent is Mavis Albright, a battered woman who is confused and frightened enough to leave her infant twins Pearl and Merle in a hot car, where they suffocate. Fearing that her husband and other children will try to kill her, she drives first to her mother (Birdie Goodroe), and then aimlessly westward. At the Convent, she hears her twins and stays. At least once she returns east to check on her other children. A rather conventional woman, she disapproves of Gigi's open sexuality and jealously competes with her for Consolata's attention. She demonstrates continuing love for her children when, after the attack, she reconciles with her daughter.

Gigi/Grace arrives next. An intensely sexual woman, she looks for two representations of human love-making. One, which might be mythical, is a large sandstone statue; the other is a natural growth near the Convent, entwined fig trees. Gigi and K. D. make love often at the Convent until he threatens her; then she, Mavis, and Seneca drive him away. Gigi and Seneca become lovers as well. Occasionally selfish, Gigi finds some financial certificates (the Convent was originally built by an embezzler) and plans to keep them for herself, but they turn out to be worthless. After the attack, Gigi has a companionable visit with her father, who is working on a chain gang.

Seneca has great compassion for everyone but herself. When Seneca's very young mother Jean abandons her, five year-old Seneca decides that it is her fault. An abused foster child, she mutilates herself as punishment for attracting men's attention. Later she responds to all violence as though she were responsible. To somehow make up for the political assassinations of Kennedy and King, for example, she slashes herself with razors. Seneca wears long-sleeved shirts and trousers to keep her scarred flesh hidden. Her vulnerability is graphically imaged in her sadomasochistic prostitution to Norma Keene Fox. Seneca saves Sweetie Fleetwood from freezing in a blizzard despite Sweetie's voiced opinion that Seneca is a demon. Seneca is particularly kind to Pallas. After the attack, Jean half recognizes her in a parking lot, but Seneca denies that they have met before.

More economically privileged than the other women, Pallas also is betrayed by her family. Pallas runs away when her mother, Divine Truelove (Dee Dee), and her lover, Carlos, themselves become lovers. Unprotected and alone, she undergoes some kind of violation near a pond. Pallas is haunted by nightmare images from her real experience—a crazy woman saying "Here's pussy. Want some pussy, pussy" (164) and memories of the pond. She tends to withdraw and to deny reality, for example ignoring Connie's insistence that she's pregnant. Pallas gives birth to her son the night before the attack. After the attack, Dee Dee sees and tries to speak with her, but Pallas, with her son strapped to her, silently reclaims some sandals and leaves.

The Ruby contingent of women includes Soane Morgan, Dovey Morgan, Patricia Best Cato, Billie Delia Cato, and Lone DuPres. Soane and Dovey are sisters who marry the Morgan twins. Less conventional and more open to emotional and spiritual growth, Soane shows great honesty and courage in accepting the consequences of her own errors in judgment. She might have remained jealous and hostile over Connie's affair with Deacon, but instead recognizes that Connie has saved her son, Scout. The two women become improbable friends.

Though the Ruby men believe themselves to be repositories of the original founders' values, Soane and some of the other women seem closer to the historical ideal. Soane Morgan provides the Ruby women's perspective on many of the issues that Steward has considered, such as the Oven, as well as introducing some new ones. Soane ponders, for instance, why Ruby has difficulties when whites neither live there nor control it. She focuses as much on shifts in the town's financing (run by the bankers Steward and Deacon) as on the generational divide that concerns the men. Considering some of the town members' recent financial disasters, she recalls when monetary aid would have been automatically forthcoming. Soane needs to believe that Deacon is, if not innocent, at least incapable of deliberately killing Consolata, who had been his lover. She insists on Steward's responsibility as primary.

Like her husband Steward, Dovey has limited flexibility. Able to see that her husband is losing emotionally and spiritually while he gains financially, she cannot imagine alternatives. Her considerable alienation from Steward is imaged by her desire to remain in town, alone in a house, rather than return to their farm. In the Ruby house, she entertains someone she calls her Friend, possibly a supernatural being who takes the form of a man. The Friend's visits provide an escape, but she does not have the independence to preserve it. When the Morgans sell the town house, Friend never comes again. Soane and Dovey are originally quite close, but grow apart because Dovey does not want to face the full truth of her husband's character. Despite the evidence, Dovey wants to believe that Deacon and Steward are equally culpable in killing Consolata.

Lone DuPres represents the life-force of Ruby. An orphan picked up by Fairy Dupres on the trek to Haven, Lone is elderly in the 1970s. Both Fairy's name and Lone's foundling status give her development a fairy-tale air. Fairy trains Lone as a midwife, and over decades, Lone never loses a mother. In old age, however, she has no professional function in Ruby because the women now prefer to give birth in hospitals. Lone intuitively identifies others with mystical, healing gifts, such as Consolata. She tries to prevent the attack on the Convent, first by warning the Convent women and then alerting those who are Ruby's moral conscience.

Soane and Dovey belong to the first generation of Ruby's powerful founding families, and Lone, though an outsider, is an adopted member of the Haven group. A generation younger, Patricia Best Cato occupies a different kind of outsider's position. Her father, Roger Best, married the only light-skinned outsider ever to enter Ruby's population. The embittered Pat believes that Ruby men let her mother die in childbirth out of sheer indifference. Pat considers her relationship with her own daughter, Billie Delia, in the context of the genealogical research she has carried on for years. Because only nine families founded Haven in 1890, and

Pat's mother was the only addition, the bloodlines are incredibly tangled. The town's focus on purity of blood, she realizes, puts incredible sexual pressure on its women. Further, she understands that she has treated Billie Delia badly in an unconscious attempt to measure up to Ruby's exclusive standards. Disgusted by the conformity that has made her unjust to her daughter and uncivil to Richard Misner, Patricia burns the research papers.

Billie Delia Cato, Patricia's daughter, endures considerable social disapproval. Her reputation in Ruby is determined when she is still a small child. As a toddler, she rides on a horse with founder Nathan DuPres, who is unaware that the ride is sexually stimulating to her. At three, when she publicly asks for a ride and drops her underpants in preparation, her reputation as a loose woman is made. In fact, as a teenager she remains a virgin while her friend Arnette Fleetwood acquires sexual experience. Billie Delia loves two young men, however, the brothers Brood and Apollo Poole, both of whom love her. When one of the brothers shoots at the other, Patricia and Billie Delia quarrel over her behavior, and Patricia badly mauls her daughter. The Convent women heal Billie Delia, sealing her reputation—and their own. After the attack on the Convent, Billie Delia is never forced to choose between the brothers. Instead, the three coexist peacefully. Billie Delia mourns the Convent women and hopes that they will return to destroy what she sees as Ruby's historically sexist and violent social order.

Billie Delia is a bridesmaid when, in 1974, Arnette Fleetwood realizes her life's ambition to marry K. D. Smith. Extending Dovey's and Pallas's tendency to deny reality, Arnette lies. She hides her abandonment of her child, for example, by saying that the Convent women stole him. Arnette remains obsessed with K. D. despite his refusal to take any responsibility for her pre-marital pregnancy and his physical abuse of her. At the end of *Paradise*, Arnette and K. D. have a toddler son who will inherit the Morgan wealth.

Save-Marie Fleetwood and Piedade are divine female energies that take on temporary human identities to work within the social world. Save-Marie takes form as the youngest of the Fleetwoods' terminally ill children and the first to die. Eulogizing her, Richard Misner emphasizes that she lived in love and that she was saved. Piedade appears only in Consolata's stories and as a black woman in the narrator's final vision. Some characters, particularly Consolata, share her aspects of caretaker, artist, and so on. Her name suggests the *Pièta* (a statue representing a seated, grieving Mary holding the crucified Christ). So does her pose in the vision: sitting on a beach, she cradles a woman with crippled hands. Piedade, like Consolata, is associated with the Catholic version of Mary, Christ's mother.

All of the major male characters belong to Ruby. Of the two ministers, Senior Pulliam was a resident by the time of Ruby Morgan Smith's death, whereas Richard Misner is a newcomer. Pulliam preaches a traditional message of human sinfulness and divine retribution. Clearly a divisive force, he destroys any potential unity at the Fleetwood-Morgan nuptials. Lone thinks that Pulliam covertly incited the attack on the Convent.

Misner is interested in the town's youth, the civil rights movement, and in working through social problems. Unlike Pulliam, he works for social unity, as when he facilitates a meeting between the angry Fleetwood and Morgan elders. At the novel's beginning, he is unable to combat Pulliam's message effectively and uncertain whether he will stay in this unfriendly town. At the end, engaged to marry a Ruby woman (Anna Poole), he is committed to the town. His spiritual capacity is underlined by the vision that he and Anna share. Although they decide not to climb through it, the open window of the abandoned Convent invites them into another world.

Aside from Lone, Nathan DuPres is the only living member of the Ruby community who participated in the founding of Haven. At ninety-one, he has only one official function, a speech before the school children's annual Christmas pageant. His pointless, wandering talk suggests the loss of traditional guides for Ruby.

The men who try to prevent the attack on the Convent—Pious DuPres, Aaron Poole, Ben and Luther Beauchamp—are barely mentioned outside the scene in which they confront the others. Especially articulate and direct, Luther verbally exposes the obvious falsity of K. D.'s rationale that the women had threatened them.

Nine men attack the Convent: Sergeant Person, Wisdom Poole, Harper and Menus Jury, Arnold and Jeff Fleetwood, Steward and Deacon Morgan, and their nephew K. D. Smith. To determine the motivation of Sergeant and Wisdom, the reader has only Lone's speculations that Sergeant wants the Convent land and Wisdom needs a scapegoat for his inability to control his brothers, Apollo and Brood.

Before the attack, Menus's behavior identifies him as an oddity in Ruby. His alcoholism is officially explained by his Vietnam War experiences, but Lone considers it the result of his giving in to pressure to abandon the light-skinned woman he loved. (Some pressure may have been financial because the Morgan bank forecloses on Menus's house.)

Because Menus has lived with the Convent women and enjoyed their nursing during an attempt at sobriety, his part in the attack is particularly reprehensible. Perhaps the women are avenged: Although several of the men receive serious wounds, only Menus is permanently disabled.

Arnold and Jeff Fleetwood are the father and son patriarchs of a literally dying family line. The Fleetwood resources—space in the house, money, emotional energies—are consumed by caring for Jeff and Sweetie's four ill children. Further, in their necessity to deny Arnette's scandalous behavior, the Fleetwoods must quarrel with the Morgans. The attack on the Convent serves simultaneously as a vent for frustration and a means of reuniting with the Morgans. Afterward, Arnold retires to his room, his vitality sapped.

K. D. Smith receives his nickname when the settlers celebrate the founding of their as-yet-unnamed town. Still a boy, he wins the festive horse race and becomes "Kentucky Derby" Smith. Because the race was not really competitive, K. D.'s name suggests his position as an undeserving heir. K. D. has sex with Arnette but considers the resulting pregnancy her problem because she pursued him. He drops the pregnant Arnette for Gigi, whom he visits at the Convent. When K. D. reacts violently to her independence and assaults her, Mavis and Seneca help Gigi drive him away. K. D. beats Arnette on their wedding night but blames the bruises on her visit to the Convent. Not a trustworthy ally for anyone, he breaks the attackers' solidarity by publicly identifying his uncle Steward as a killer. He and Arnette have a four-month-old daughter when the Convent is attacked, and a sixteen-month-old son when they build a house on Morgan land.

Identical twins, Steward and Deacon Morgan are two of the founding fathers of Ruby. Ironically, neither has living children. Bankers, the Morgans ostensibly manage a system in which everyone in the community has shares. Steward sees the Reverend Misner's ideas about a nonprofit credit union as a threat to the bank, however. Above all else, Steward wants to be worthy of his courageous, upright ancestors. He is morally rigid, judgmental, and unforgiving. Feeling that he knows the truth, he is unsympathetic to the young and completely uninterested in the world outside Ruby. The reader finds him most sympathetic in his deep, continuing love for his wife Dovey. Steward sees Deacon's affair as a powerful threat to social order, and makes his judgment with the bullet to Consolata's head. He leads the attack on the Convent.

Deacon resembles Steward emotionally and morally as well as physically. Whereas Dovey sees Steward as losing over the years, however, Deacon develops. As guilty as Steward, Deacon participates in the attack despite—or perhaps because of—his knowledge that it will kill his ex-lover Connie. He publicly repents this action, however, in the traditional form of walking barefoot to confession. Having told the Reverend Misner of his actions, Deacon thinks of himself as having become "what the Old Fathers cursed: the kind of man who set himself up to judge, rout, and even destroy the needy, the defenseless, the different" (302). Although Deacon values the Old Fathers, he understands them as men who could make important, even critical mistakes.

Deacon is anxious not to let his penitence recreate Zechariah's self-righteous separation from his brother. Knowing that Steward does not regret the attack, Deacon nevertheless claims his brother, and in doing so acknowledges his own capacity for evil action.

Deacon's greater capacity for growth may result from his spiritual wellspring. His image of the sacred differs significantly from Steward's veneration of Zechariah and Rector Morgan. First, it comes directly from his own boyhood experience, rather than from stories of historical experience. Second, it focuses on women rather than men—the group of nineteen elegant women that he and Steward see during their tour of all-black towns in 1932.

THEMATIC ISSUES

In its critique of Ruby, *Paradise* confronts one of African American culture's most sacred cows, the myth of unity and perfection in black society relieved of white oppression. The myth is based on real, historical all-black (or largely black controlled) institutions and art forms. The all-black towns established by Exodusters (blacks moving west in the 1880s) and black churches, for example, showed African Americans governing themselves. Black art forms—blues, gospel, folktales—were recognized as African American contributions to world culture.

Intransigent racism produced both numerous pop culture versions of a romanticized Africa and, in the political realm, various separatist movements such as Marcus Garvey's back-to-Africa program. The novelist Zora Neale Hurston depicted the most widely known romantic vision of an all-black town in *Their Eyes Were Watching God*. (In fact, though many readers remember Hurston's Eatonville as Utopian, the literary presentation is actually more nuanced.) Of course, no real place could live up to the cultural myth, which nevertheless continues to have enormous emotional power.

Morrison critiques the myth by showing bitterly opposed forces within a black community not controlled by whites. In response to exclusion, Ruby is established as a separatist, specifically dark black community. Yet it generates its own patterns of exclusion. Most obviously, men and women are divided, and the attack on the Convent makes the battle of the sexes literal. Black men are warring on black women. (Only one of the five female victims is white.) The men of Ruby are also divided among themselves. While some attack, others try to restrain them. *Paradise* investigates the divergence between the social realities of a separatist establishment and an all-black Utopia.

The novel treats the origins of separatism sympathetically, but depicts it as ultimately destructive of the community that it is designed to protect. The novel locates the impetus for separatism in the experience of social exclusion, and not simply the exclusion of blacks by whites: Fairly, Oklahoma, an all-black town, will not accept Ruby's forefathers and mothers because their skin is too dark. In self-protection, this excluded group defines its own nature, goals, and values. But its processes of definition inevitably involve the creation of an "other"—"them" as opposed to "us." Naturally, good qualities appear in us; evil qualities in them. The world is defined in absolute terms, with no middle ground, only binary opposites.

Ruby's most powerful men, Steward and Deacon Morgan, see the world through these oppositions: good versus bad, themselves versus the young hooligans, good young girls like Arnette versus bad ones like Billie Delia, Ruby versus the Convent. The problem here lies not just in the occasional misidentification—Arnette rather than Billie Delia is sexually active—nor even in the value itself (should sexual inexperience be a virtue). Instead, *Paradise* shows that opposed, mutually exclusive categories can never be maintained because they deny social complexity.

Ruby's separatism sets up the most important oppositions: Ruby versus the evil of the outside world, and Ruby versus the Convent. But in fact, Ruby participates in the structures of the larger world, both for good and for ill. While in South America, Mary Magna adopts an abandoned child, Consolata; on the trek to found Haven, Fairy DuPres insists that her group absorb the orphaned Lone. In New Jersey, Mavis's husband Frank beats her; in Ruby, K. D. beats his wife Arnette. Mavis loses her brothers and Soane loses two sons to the Vietnam War. Though the characters may not be aware of these similarities, the reader sees that the commonalities contradict separatist ideas.

All the characters must know, on the other hand, that Ruby and the Convent are connected on a daily basis. Ruby folk buy produce and baked goods from the Convent. Lone and Soane visit Connie as friends. Some meetings must remain hidden, however. Deacon, K. D., Menus, Arnette, and Billie Delia go for reasons that cannot be publicly acknowledged—and all involve sexuality in some way. The Convent women accept those who come as lovers and generally try to help those in trouble. Precisely because Ruby must be perfect, the results of all imperfect behavior are siphoned to the Convent.

Demonizing the Convent women allows Ruby to ignore its home-grown sources of conflict. At the Fleetwood-Morgan marriage celebration, for example, families on the verge of renewing their quarrel instead agree on a substitute target—the Convent women's dress and behavior at the reception. Anna Poole recognizes that "the Convent women had saved the day. Nothing like other folks' sin for distraction" (159). In a foreshadowing of the attack, Steward leads the group that orders the Convent women to leave. Listening to the men plan their attack, Lone later thinks, "So . . . the fangs and the tail are somewhere else. . . . [I]n a house full of . . . women who chose themselves for company . . . not a convent but a coven" (276). The bi-polar opposition of good versus evil, identified as Ruby versus the Convent, leads directly to violence.

Once begun, there's no end to such false oppositions. To maintain the opposition, individuals try to prove their own goodness by separating themselves from all who are evil or even questionable. This process splits families and even psyches. For example, when their approach to white oppression differs, the patriarch Zechariah disowns his twin, whose name is blotted out of the family Bible. In another instance, Patricia's need to prove that she is good enough for Ruby makes her mistreat her own daughter, Billie Delia. Sweetie Fleetwood accepts Deacon Morgan, who ignores her to open the bank, and rejects Seneca, who keeps her from freezing to death—clearly insane standards necessary to maintain the Ruby/Convent divide.

Even Sweetie does not approach Arnette Fleetwood Smith's self-delusion and psychic breakdown. Unable to admit that she tried to abort her pregnancy and abandoned her son, she says—and probably believes—that the Convent women forced an abortion on her. Separatism's necessary mechanism, bi-polar opposition, fragments society and leads to madness.

Haven's patriarchs did not invent bi-polar opposition, of course. The racism that ousted Zechariah from his position in government and the racism that barred his group from Fairly also rest on a bi-polar opposition: white = good; black = evil. Importantly, then, the Haven/Ruby patriarchs have not invented a new way of thinking. By exalting blackness, they have only inverted the values of the old way.

Paradise repeatedly demonstrates the falsity of separatism's oppositions. Consolata specifically denies the body/soul opposition central to Mary Magna's Catholicism. Recognizing the Virgin Mary and Eve as symbols of womanhood, divided into good and evil, Consolata rejoins them: "Never break them in two. Never put one over the other. Eve is Mary's mother. Mary is the daughter of Eve" (263).

The separation of Ruby from outsiders is supposed to keep its blood pure. Whatever this illusory purity is supposed to consist of, it cannot really be purely African. One of Haven's founders had an American Indian name, Drum Blackhorse. Straight hair appears in Soane and Dovey, then in Soane's twins. Further, the South America-born Consolata immediately connects Ruby's founders with her early companions: "And although they were living here in a hamlet, not in a loud city full of glittering black people, Consolata knew she knew them" (226). The artificial oppositions of separatism can never hold because reality is composed of mixtures, analogues, and connections. Ruby belongs to the world and the world to it.

A FORMALIST READING

Many types of literary criticism such as historicism and cultural studies explore texts in relation to the societies that produce them. Concentrating instead on the text itself, formalism—once called New Criticism—seeks to understand the work's artistic integrity and unity. The dominant theme of the work, formalists believe, must be expressed in its structure and technique. Formalism focuses on structural forms and patterns of repeated or clearly connected imagery. For a formalist, a novel's form consists of its genre and the design of its organizing sections.

Although *Paradise* uses aspects of several genres, epic characteristics of theme and narrative technique dominate. The novel explores subjects characteristic of classic epics. Like Homer's *Iliad* and Virgil's *Aeneid*, this novel depicts the founding and downfall of civilizations. Signifying on

Dante's *The Divine Comedy* and John Milton's *Paradise Lost, Paradise* depicts humanity's place in the cosmos.

Morrison's narrative technique adapts two epic conventions. First, classical epics often include long lists of ships or warriors called "catalogs." *Paradise*'s catalog appears in Patricia Best's research, the roll-call of the ancestors. Second, classical epics such as the *Iliad* begin *in medias res*, that is, "in the middle" of a large-scale action. The novel begins midway through the attack on the Convent. Then, like other epics about war, it depicts past events to explain the battle's origins, later returning to the battle's outcomes and consequences.

Having established genre, a formalist analysis proceeds to the relationships of a work's sections to one another and to the whole plot. *Paradise* creates a different kind of unity from the self-enclosed artistic integrity that the New Critics generally looked for. In fact, the formal coherence of *Paradise* depends on each section's revisions of the "facts" in the others. Its major theme is the impossibility of generating a single description that adequately represents human experience. Each of the ten sections casts doubt on the information of the others. In "Patricia," for example, Pat's surmise that Zechariah's original name of "Coffee" is a corruption of the African "Kofi" seems quite reasonable, especially given her methodical research. In the later chapter "Save-Marie," however, Deacon reveals that the strong original bond between Zechariah and his twin brother led to their nicknames, Coffee and Tea. Because it gives the reader information that individual characters lack, this narrative structure supports and creates one of *Paradise*'s major themes. Aware that almost any apparent fact may be undercut, the reader rejects the two absolutist premises on which Ruby's social structure is built: first, that eternal truth can be known, and second, that the founders of Ruby know it.

With its several competing versions of reality, *Paradise* maintains coherence with patterns of imagery. It would be possible to explore numerous chains of imagery, but three are particularly important: community, symbolized by the Oven; oral/written culture; and art as sacred expression. These chains are cross-linked, of course. Through telling stories and singing hymns, Ruby makes sacred expression the cornerstone on which its symbol of community, the Oven, sits.

Emerging as a major focus for open generational and hidden gender strife in the chapter "Seneca," the Oven recurs in crucial scenes. By way of Dovey's memory, "Seneca" recounts a town meeting over the Oven's partially obscured inscription. The powerful men remember the legend as "Beware the Furrow of His Brow." When teenagers with an interest in the Black Power movement insist it must be "Be the Furrow of His Brow," violence nearly breaks out. The male elders approach the Oven as fundamentalists approach the Bible. From their point of view, the unchanging and unchangeable original is inscribed in their memories, and it requires no interpretation. Their attitude violates a central process of African American culture, call-and-response. In call-and-response, a leader issues a call, group members respond, and the leader then issues a new call modified or directed by the responses. The teens are respond-ing to the ancestor's call, as recorded on the Oven. The male elders have stopped issuing calls, much less listening to responses. Steward expresses their fundamentalism in particularly chilling terms: "If you . . . ignore, change, take away, or add to the words in the mouth of that Oven, I will blow your head off . . ." (87). Despite Steward's threat, by the end of *Paradise*, the young are reading the inscription as "We Are the Furrow of His Brow" (298).

The men seem unaware that, although they consider all their attitudes as protective of women, Ruby women do not accept their fundamental-ism. Even the conservative Dovey sees no need to restore the first word to the inscription. Nor does she favor a single interpretation: "Specifying it, particularizing it, nailing its meaning down, was futile. The only nail-ing needing to be done had already taken place. On the Cross" (93). Dovey sees the attempt to dictate meaning as blasphemous, part of the force that crucified Christ. In a similar way, Soane diverges from Dea-con's position. At the town meeting, Deacon proudly retells the story of dismantling the Oven that had been central to Haven, transporting it, and reassembling it as the center of Ruby. Soane and other women, how-ever, resented the space that the Oven took up during their migration. Once in Ruby, they resented the reassembly time, which had to be taken from other tasks.

Part of the community still gathers regularly at the Oven, as in Haven days. However, the gatherings consist of those working to change its meaning, and their presence disgusts the elders. Even the older women dislike the Oven's role as a place for sexual assignation. The teens' gath-erings have no evil effects beyond upsetting the elders, however. Ironi-cally, the elders gather there to plot their attack on the Convent.

The Oven's physical condition suggests the town's decay. The partial loss of its inscription might indicate lost ideals. The Oven was, in Haven, central to feeding the community physically as well as spiritually. Now that it has no real function, its cold bricks suggest Ruby's dormant spirituality. When the rain on the night of the attack soaks its supporting ground, the Oven shifts, tilts. No longer level, it symbolizes the community's lack of solid foundation

The generational divide that has killed all but the semblance of community in Ruby centers on the Oven's inscription. Given the historic struggle to validate the orality of African and African American cultures in writing-oriented European authority systems, a reader might expect *Paradise* to take orality as its premise. One of Morrison's earlier novels, *Song of Solomon* shows orality as essential to African American identity. *Paradise* affirms neither written nor oral culture, however, showing instead the inherent unreliability of all human communication.

Paradise plays up the flaws of even a vital oral tradition: important information can be lost. The greatest devotée of the past, Steward Morgan, doesn't know Zechariah's surname—it might have been Moyne or Lemoyne. Patricia Best Cato has collected the oral scraps of information, only to find that they do not make a complete story. She wonders in particular about the lives of women now known in town lore only by their first names. The absence of women's perspectives in oral history persists in the present—Deacon tells the story of the Oven from a male perspective; Soane's memory of the women's different experiences remains unspoken.

The novel shows that Ruby has lost the call-and-response development central to orality. The older generation was trained and nourished by stories. The annual pageant's conflation of their ancestral migration and the Christian Christmas story assures them of their sanctity. As Richard Misner points out, though, Ruby has created no stories beyond the founding of Haven, no stories about itself and present generations (161). More oral history will be lost because the younger generation ruthlessly derides orality. Not invited to participate in call-and-response, forced to listen silently, the young will not retell the stories that imprison them. Like the Oven, oral tradition no longer unites the community.

Written culture offers no useful alternative, however, because the novel shows it to be equally faulty. If oral memory is porous, so is written memory, which fails both society at large and the individual. The Oven's commandment is written, if not in stone, at least in iron—and it does not endure whole. In a similar way, Jean's lipstick letter written to explain her abandonment to Seneca rapidly becomes illegible. In the circumstances imaged by *Paradise*, the word—whether spoken or written—cannot offer salvation.

Because interpretations of the word remain frozen with the male elders, and because the word itself is unstable, other forms of aesthetic expression must grace humanity. *Paradise* connects both painting and song to spiritual healing. Much painting is spiritually useless, of course. The Convent's portrait of the martyred St. Catherine of Siena is mostly useful to the women for its heavy frame—it cracks Jeff Fleetwood's head during the attack. For graphic art to heal, the sufferer must create. Painting images of themselves under Consolata's guidance is a crucial part of the Convent women's healing process, for example. In a similar way, the red fist painted on the side of the Oven portrays the painter's self-concept as a revolutionary. Both the women's paintings and the fist convince Ruby fundamentalists that deviltry is among them. Artistic self-expression is risky business in *Paradise*. Like words, art is susceptible to uncongenial interpretation by those with the guns.

If painting can help heal humanity, music connects it to divinity. Contaminated by habitual, set words, music becomes trivial—the psalms sung at the Fleetwood-Morgan wedding, the carols sung by children in the Christmas play. In contrast, music without words or with original, felt words can carry all human experience. To receive divine guidance, Zechariah prays for hours with wordless, humming sounds. Piedade's song for Save-Marie "evoke[s] memories neither one has ever had" (318), memories of growing old with a loved one, of conversation and food that nourish, the delight of returning to a cherished home. Song is the way home, the way to Haven, and the only paradise we'll ever know.

Bibliography

Note: Page numbers referred to in the text are to the paperback editions of *The Bluest Eye, Sula*, and *Song of Solomon*. For *Tar Baby, Beloved, Jazz*, and *Paradise*, the page references are to the hardcover editions.

WORKS BY TONI MORRISON

Novels

The Bluest Eye. New York: Knopf, 1970. Rpt. New York: Simon and Schuster, 1972.
Sula. New York: Knopf, 1973. Rpt. New York: Penguin, 1982.
Song of Solomon. New York: Knopf, 1977. Rpt. New York: Penguin, 1987.
Tar Baby. New York: Knopf, 1981.
Beloved. New York: Knopf, 1987.
Jazz. New York: Knopf, 1992.
Paradise. New York: Knopf, 1998.

Other Works

"City Limits, Village Values: Concepts of the Neighborhood in Black Fiction." In *Literature and the Urban Experience: Essays on the City and Literature*, edited by Michael C. Jaye and Ann Chalmers Watts. New Brunswick, New Jersey: Rutgers University Press, 1981.

Dreaming Emmett (unpublished play).

Honey and Rue. Lyrics set to music by André Previn. 1992.

"Introduction." In *Race-ing Justice, Engendering Power: Essays on Anita Hill, Clarence Thomas, and the Construction of Social Reality,* edited by Toni Morrison. New York: Pantheon, 1992. vii–xxx.

"Life in His Language." In *James Baldwin: The Legacy,* edited by Quincy Trope. New York: Simon and Schuster, 1989. 75–78.

"Memory, Creation, and Writing." *Thought* 59 (December 1984): 385–90.

"Nobel Lecture, 7 December 1993." *Georgia Review* 49.1 (Spring 1995): 318–23.

"The Official Story: Dead Man Golfing." In *Birth of a Nation'hood,* edited by Toni Morrison and Claudia Brodsky Lacour. New York: Random House, 1997. vii–xxviii.

Playing in the Dark: Whiteness and the Literary Imagination. Cambridge, Massachusetts: Harvard University Press, 1992.

"Recitatif." In *Confirmation: An Anthology of African American Women Writers,* edited by Amiri Baraka and Amina Baraka. New York: Quill, 1983. 243–61.

"Rediscovering Black History." *The New York Times Magazine* (August 11, 1974): 14–24.

"Rootedness: The Ancestor as Foundation." In *Black Women Writers, 1950–1980: A Critical Evaluation,* edited by Mari Evans. Garden City, New York: Anchor Press, 1984. 339–45.

"The Site of Memory." In *Inventing the Truth: The Art and Craft of Memoir,* edited by William Zissner. Boston: Houghton Mifflin, 1987. 101–24.

"A Slow Walk of Trees (as Grandmother Would Say), Hopeless (as Grandfather Would Say)." *The New York Times Magazine* (July 4, 1976): 104, 150, 152, 156, 160, 164.

"Unspeakable Things, Unspoken: The Afro-American Presence in American Literature." *Michigan Quarterly Review* 28 (Winter 1989): 1–34.

INTERVIEWS

Bellinelli, Matteo. "A Conversation with Toni Morrison." *In Black and White.* Part 3. San Francisco: California Newsreel, 1992. 25 minutes.

Brown, Cecil. "Interview with Toni Morrison." *Massachusetts Review* 36.3 (Autumn 1995): 455–73.

Byatt, A. S. "Toni Morrison with A. S. Byatt." *Writers in Conversation.* London: ICA Video; Northbrook, IL: Roland Collection of Films on Art, 1989.

Carabi, Angels. "Toni Morrison." *Belles Lettres* 9.1 (Spring 1994): 38–39, 86–90.

Dreifus, Claudia. *Interview.* New York: Seven Stories Press, 1997. 267–77.

"The Nobel Laureates of Literature: An Olympic Gathering. Panel Discussion I." *Georgia Review* 49.4 (Winter 1995): 832–60.

Richardson, Robert. "A Bench by the Road." *The World: Journal of the Unitarian Universalist Association* 3 (January/February 1989): 4–5, 37–41.

Verdelle, A. J. *Essence* (February 1998): 78–80.

Schappell, Elissa, with Claudia Brodskey Lacour. "Toni Morrison: The Art of Fiction CXXXV." *Paris Review* 35.128 (Fall 1993): 82–125.

Taylor-Guthrie, Danille, ed. *Conversations with Toni Morrison*. Jackson: University Press of Mississippi, 1994.

BIOGRAPHICAL INFORMATION

Blake, Susan. "Toni Morrison." In *Afro-American Fiction Writers After 1955*, edited by Thadious M. Davis and Trudier Harris. *Dictionary of Literary Biography*, vol. 33. Detroit: Bruccoli Clark, 1984.

Clark Hine, Darlene, ed. *Black Women in White America: An Historical Encyclopedia*. Brooklyn, New York: Carlson, 1993.

Denard, Carolyn. "Toni Morrison." In *Modern American Women Writers*, edited by Elaine Showalter. New York: Scribner's, 1991. 317–38.

Dowling, Colette. "The Song of Toni Morrison." *The New York Times Magazine* (May 20, 1979): 40–42, 48–58.

Harris, Trudier. "Morrison, Toni." In *The Oxford Companion to Women's Writing in the United States*, edited by Cathy N. Davidson and Linda Wagner-Martin. Oxford: Oxford University Press, 1995. 578–80.

Lubianao, Wahneema. "Toni Morrison." *African American Writers*, edited by Valerie Smith. New York: Scribner's, 1991. 321–33.

Mobley, Marilyn Sanders. "Toni Morrison." In *The Oxford Companion to African American Literature*, edited by William L. Andrews, Frances Smith Foster, and Trudier Harris. New York: Oxford University Press, 1997. 508–10.

"Toni Morrison." *Norton Anthology of African American Literature*, edited by Henry Louis Gates, Jr. and Nellie McKay. New York: Norton, 1997. 2094–98.

REVIEWS AND CRITICISM

The Bluest Eye

CLA Journal, December 1971: 253.
Newsweek, 30 November 1970: 95.
The New York Times, 13 November 1970: 35.
The New York Times Book Review, 1 November 1970: 46.
The New Yorker, 23 January 1971: 92.
Times Literary Supplement, 24 November 1978: 1359.

Sula

Black World, June 1974: 53.
Hudson Review 27.2 (1974): 283.

Ms., December 1974: 34.
The Nation, 6 July 1974: 23.
The New Republic, 9 March 1974: 31.
Newsweek, 7 January 1974: 63.
The New York Times Book Review, 30 December 1973: 3; 1 December 1974: 70; 2
    June 1974: 6.
Times Literary Supplement, 4 October 1974: 1062.
The Village Voice, 7 March 1974: 21.
The Washington Post Book World, 3 February 1974: 529.

Song of Solomon

Callaloo, October 1978: 170.
Christian Science Monitor, 20 October 1977: 25.
CLA Journal, March 1978: 446.
Harper's, October 1977: 94.
The Nation, 19 November 1977: 536.
The New Republic, 3 December 1977: 33.
Newsweek, 12 September 1977: 93.
The New York Review of Books, 10 November 1977: 6.
The New York Times, 6 September 1977: 43.
The New York Times Book Review, 11 September 1977: 1.
The New Yorker, 7 November 1977: 217.
Saturday Review, 17 September 1977: 41.
Time, 12 September 1977: 76.
Times Literary Supplement, 24 November 1978: 1359.
Voice Literary Supplement, 29 August 1977: 41.
The Washington Post Book World, 4 September 1977: 1.

Tar Baby

Atlantic, April 1981: 119.
Callaloo, February–October 1981: 193.
Christian Science Monitor, 13 April 1981: B3.
The Nation, 2 May 1981: 529.
National Review, 26 June 1981: 730.
New Republic, 21 March 1981: 29.
New York Review of Books, 30 April 1981: 24.
New York Times Book Review, 29 March 1981: 1.
New Yorker, 15 June 1981: 147.
Time, 16 March 1981: 90.
Times Literary Supplement, 30 October 1981: 1260.

The Village Voice, 1 July 1981: 40.
Washington Post Book World, 22 March 1981: 1.

Beloved

Callaloo, Spring 1988, 387.
Chicago Tribune Books, 2 August 1987: 3; 30 August 1987: 1.
Christian Science Monitor, 5 October 1987: 20.
CLA Journal, December 1987: 256.
Los Angeles Times Book Review, 30 August 1987: 1.
The Nation, October 1987: 418.
The New Republic, October 1987: 38.
Newsweek, 28 September 1987: 74.
The New York Review of Books, 5 November 1987: 18.
The New York Times, 2 September 1987: C24
The New York Times Book Review, 13 September 1987: 1.
The New Yorker, 2 November 1987: 175.
Time, 21 September 1987: 75.
Times Literary Supplement, 16 October 1987: 1135.
Voice Literary Supplement, September 1987: 25.
The Washington Post, 5 October 1987.
The Women's Review of Books, March 1988: 4.

Jazz

Atlanta Journal and Constitution, 12 April 1992: N10.
Boston Globe, 12 April 1992: B41.
Christian Science Monitor, 17 April 1992: 13.
Guardian Features, 30 April 1992: 56.
Houston Chronicle Zest, 26 April 1992: 23.
London Review of Books, 14 May 1992: 12.
Los Angeles Times Book Review, 19 April 1992: 3; 24 May 1992: 2.
Minneapolis Star Tribune, 17 May 1992: F10.
The Nation, 25 May 1992: 706.
National Review, 8 June 1992: 57.
The New Republic, 18 May 1992: 43.
Newsweek, 27 April 1992: 66.
The New York Times, 2 April 1992: C21.
The New York Times Book Review, 5 April 1992: 1; 31 May 1992: 78.
Orlando Sentinel-Tribune, 19 April 1992: F8.
Saint Louis Post Dispatch Everyday Magazine, 3 May 1992: C5.
San Diego Union-Tribune Books, 12 April 1992: 1.
Seattle Times Books, 19 April 1992: L2.

Southern Review, Summer 1993: 614.

Time, 27 April 1992: 70.

Times Literary Supplement, 8 May 1992: 21.

Tribune Books, 19 April 1992: 1; 6 December 1992: 13.

Voice Literary Supplement, May 1992: 25.

The Washington Post Book World, 19 April 1992: xi.

The Women's Review of Books, June 1992: 1.

Paradise

The Atlanta Journal and Constitution, 12 January 1998: D2.

The Atlanta Journal and Constitution, 18 January 1998: K7

The Boston Globe, 11 January 1998: F1.

The Boston Herald, 18 January 1998: 75.

The Buffalo News, 18 January 1998: F6.

Chicago Sun-Times, 11 January 1998: Sec. 7, 6.

Hartford Courant, 11 January 1998: G3.

The Houston Chronicle, 18 January 1998: 26.

Los Angeles Times, 11 January 1998: 2.

The New York Times, 6 January 1998: E8.

The New York Times, 8 January 1998: E1.

The New York Times Book Review, 11 January 1998: Sec. 7, 6.

New Yorker, 12 January 1998: 78.

New York Newsday, 19 January 1998: B6.

Newsweek, 12 January 1998: 62.

The Orlando Sentinel, 18 January 1998: F6.

The Plain Dealer, 11 January 1998: 101.

The Rocky Mountain News, 18 January 1998: Edition F, E1.

Sacramento Bee, 18 January 1998: EN3.

St. Louis Post-Dispatch, 11 January 1998: D5.

The San Diego Union-Tribune, 18 January 1998: Books, 1.

The Seattle Times, 18 January 1998: M2.

Time, 19 January 1998: 62.

Star Tribune [Minneapolis], 18 January 1998: F16.

The Sun [Baltimore], 11 January 1998: L5.

Sun-Sentinel, 11 January 1998: D8.

Time, 19 January 1998: 62.

The Times-Picayune, 11 January 1998: D7.

USA Today, 8 January 1998: D7.

US News and World Report, 19 January 1998: 71.

The Washington Post, 6 January 1998: B1. [combination interview and review]

The Washington Post Book World, 11 January 1998: X01.

MORE REVIEWS AND CRITICISM

"Beloved." *Contemporary Literary Criticism*, vol. 87, edited by Sharon Gunton and Jean Stine. Detroit: Gale Research, 1995. 261–311.

Bjork, Patrick Bryce. *The Novels of Toni Morrison: the Search for Self and Place within the Community*. American University Studies, vol. 31. New York: Peter Lang, 1992.

Bloom, Harold, ed. *Toni Morrison*. Modern Critical Views. New York: Chelsea House, 1990.

Christian, Barbara. *Black Women Novelists*. Westport, Connecticut: Greenwood, 1980.

Duvall, John. *Descent in "The House of Chloe": Race, Rape, and Identity in Toni Morrison's* Tar Baby. *Contemporary Literature* 38.2 (1997): 325–49.

Furman, Jan. *Toni Morrison's Fiction*. Columbia: University of South Carolina Press, 1996.

Gates, Henry Louis, Jr., and Anthony Appiah, eds. *Toni Morrison: Critical Perspectives, Past and Present*. New York: Amistad, 1991.

Harris, Trudier. *Fiction and Folklore: The Novels of Toni Morrison*. Knoxville: University of Tennessee Press, 1993.

Kolmerton, Carol A., and Stephen M. Ross, eds. *Unflinching Gaze: Morrison and Faulkner Re-envisioned*. Jackson: University Press of Mississippi, 1997.

McKay, Nellie Y., ed. *Critical Essays on Toni Morrison*. Boston: G. K. Hall, 1988.

Middleton, David L. *Toni Morrison: An Annotated Bibliography*. New York: Garland, 1987.

Otten, Terry. *The Crime of Innocence in the Fiction of Toni Morrison*. Literary Frontiers Edition, no. 33. Columbia: University of Missouri Press, 1989.

Peach, Linden. *Toni Morrison*. New York: St. Martin's Press, 1995.

Rigney, Barbara Hill. *The Voices of Toni Morrison*. Columbus: Ohio State University Press, 1991.

Samuels, Wilfred D., and Clenora Hudson-Weems. *Toni Morrison*. New York: Twayne, 1990.

Smith, Valerie, ed. *New Essays on* Song of Solomon. New York: Cambridge University Press, 1995.

Strouse, Jean. "Toni Morrison's Black Magic." *Newsweek* 97 (March 30, 1981): 52–57.

"Toni Morrison." *Black Literature Criticism*, vol. 3, edited by James Draper. Detroit: Gale Research, 1993. 1422–45.

"Toni Morrison." *Contemporary Authors*. New Revision Series, vol. 42, edited by Susan M. Trotsky. Detroit: Gale Research, 1994. 319–28.

"Toni Morrison." *Contemporary Literary Criticism*, vol. 22, edited by Sharon Gunton and Jean Stine. Detroit: Gale Research, 1982. 314–23.

Werner, Craig H. *Black American Women Novelists*. Pasadena, California: Salem Press, 1989.

WORKS OF GENERAL INTEREST

Andrews, William, Frances Smith Foster, and Trudier Harris, eds. *The Oxford Companion to African American Literature*. New York: Oxford University Press, 1997.

Butler, Octavia. *Kindred*. Garden City, New York: Doubleday, 1979.

Byerman, Keith. *Fingering the Jagged Grain: Tradition and Form in Recent Black Fiction*. Athens: University of Georgia Press, 1985.

Callahan, John. *In the African-American Grain*. Urbana: University of Illinois Press, 1988.

Campbell, Joseph. *The Hero with a Thousand Faces*. 1949. Bollingen Series XVII. Princeton, New Jersey: Princeton University Press, 1968.

Carby, Hazel. *Reconstructing Womanhood*. New York: Oxford University Press, 1987.

Chopin, Kate. *The Awakening: An Authoritative Text*, edited by Margo Culley. New York: Norton, 1994.

Christian, Barbara. *Black Women Novelists: The Development of a Tradition, 1892–1976*. Westport, Connecticut: Greenwood, 1980.

Dante Alighieri. *The Divine Comedy*. New York: Random House, 1986.

Denis, Denise. *Black History for Beginners*. New York: Writers and Readers Publishing, 1984.

Dickens, Charles. *Bleak House*. New York: Norton, 1977.

Douglass, Frederick. *Narrative of the Life of Frederick Douglass*. 1845. New York: Signet, 1997.

DuBois, W. E. B. *The Souls of Black Folk*. 1903. New York: Penguin, 1996.

Eliot, T. S. *The Waste Land and Other Poems*. New York: Harcourt Brace, 1955.

Ellison, Ralph. *Shadow and Act*. 1964. New York: Vintage, 1972.

Equiano, Olaudah. *The Interesting Narrative and Other Writings*, edited by Vincent Carretta. New York: Penguin, 1995.

Faulkner, William. *Absalom, Absalom!* 1936. New York: Vintage, 1990.

———. *As I Lay Dying*. 1930. New York: Vintage, 1990.

———. *Go Down, Moses*. 1942. New York: Vintage, 1973.

Frazer, Sir James. *The Golden Bough: A Study in Magic and Religion*. 1890. New York: Penguin, 1998.

Gaines, Ernest. *The Autobiography of Miss Jane Pittman*. 1971. New York: Bantam, 1982.

Gates, Henry Louis, Jr., and Nellie McKay, eds. *The Norton Anthology of African American Literature*. New York: Norton, 1997.

Haley, Alex. *Roots*. 1976. New York: Dell Books, 1980.

Harris, Joel Chandler. *Uncle Remus: His Songs and Sayings*. 1880. New York: Penguin, 1982.

Harris, Middleton et al., eds. *The Black Book*. New York: Random House, 1974.

Homer. *The Iliad*, translated by Robert Fagles. New York: Viking, 1990.

————. *The Odyssey*, translated by Robert Fagles. New York: Penguin, 1997.

Hughes, Langston. *The Weary Blues*. New York: Knopf, 1926.

Hurston, Zora Neale. *Mules and Men*. 1935. New York: HarperCollins, 1990.

————. *Their Eyes Were Watching God*. 1937. New York: HarperCollins, 1990.

Jacobs, Harriet. *Incidents in the Life of a Slave Girl*. 1861. Cambridge, Massachusetts: Harvard University Press, 1987.

Jones, Gayl. *Corregidora*. 1975. Boston: Beacon Press, 1986.

Joyce, James. *Ulysses*. 1922. New York: Knopf, 1997.

Karenga, Maulana, "Black Art: Mute Matter Given Force and Function." In *The Norton Anthology of African American Literature*, edited by Henry Louis Gates, Jr., and Nellie McKay. New York: Norton, 1997. 1973–77.

Kelley, Edith Summers. *Weeds*. 1923. New York: Feminist Press, 1996.

Kubitschek, Missy Dehn. *Claiming the Heritage: African-American Women Novelists and History*. Jackson: University Press of Mississippi, 1991.

Lewis, David Levering. *W. E. B. DuBois: Biography of a Race*. New York: Holt, 1993.

Locke, Alain. *The New Negro*. 1925. New York: Atheneum, 1968.

Milton, John. *Paradise Lost: An Authoritative Text*, edited by Scott Elledge. New York: Norton, 1996.

Mitchell, Margaret. *Gone with the Wind*. 1936. New York: Warner, 1994.

Prince, Mary. *The History of Mary Prince, a West African Slave, Related by Herself*, edited by Moira Ferguson. Ann Arbor: University of Michigan Press, 1993.

Sobel, Mechal. *Trabelin' On: Journey to an Afro-Baptist Faith*. Princeton, New Jersey: Princeton University Press, 1979.

Stepto, Robert B. *From Behind the Veil: A Study of Afro-American Narrative*. Urbana: University of Illinois Press, 1979.

Tate, Greg. *Flyboy in the Buttermilk: Essays on Contemporary America*. New York: Simon and Schuster, 1992.

Thompson, Robert Farris. *Flash of the Spirit: African and Afro-American Art and Philosophy*. New York: Random House, 1983.

Van der Zee, James. *The Harlem Book of the Dead*. New York: Morgan and Morgan, 1978.

Walker, Alice. *The Color Purple*. 1982. New York: Washington Square Press, 1998.

————. "Everyday Use." In *In Love and Trouble: Stories of Black Women*. New York: Harcourt Brace, 1973.

Werner, Craig. *Playing the Changes: From Afro-Modernism to the Jazz Impulse*. Urbana: University of Illinois Press, 1994.

Williams, Sherley Anne. *Dessa Rose*. New York: Morrow, 1986.

Woolf, Virginia. "Professions for Women." In *The Death of the Moth and Other Essays*. New York: Harcourt Brace, 1942.

Index

About the Author

MISSY DEHN KUBITSCHEK is Professor of English, African American Studies, and Women's Studies at Indiana University–Purdue, Indianapolis. She is the author of *Claiming the Heritage: African-American Women Novelists and History* (1991).